Illusions, Patterns and Pictures

ACADEMIC PRESS
SERIES IN COGNITION AND PERCEPTION

SERIES EDITORS:

Edward C. Carterette
Morton P. Friedman

Department of Psychology
University of California, Los Angeles
Los Angeles, California

Stephen K. Reed: *Psychological Processes in Pattern Recognition*

Earl B. Hunt: *Artificial Intelligence*

James P. Egan: *Signal Detection Theory and ROC Analysis*

Martin F. Kaplan and Steven Schwartz (Eds.): *Human Judgment and Decision Processes*

Myron L. Braunstein: *Depth Perception Through Motion*

R. Plomp: *Aspects of Tone Sensation*

Martin F. Kaplan and Steven Schwartz (Eds.): *Human Judgment and Decision Processes in Applied Settings*

Bikkar S. Randhawa and William E. Coffman: *Visual Learning, Thinking, and Communication*

Robert B. Welch: *Perceptual Modification: Adapting to Altered Sensory Environments*

Lawrence E. Marks: *The Unity of the Senses: Interrelations among the Modalities*

Michele A. Wittig and Anne C. Petersen (Eds.): *Sex-Related Differences in Cognitive Functioning: Developmental Issues*

Douglas Vickers: *Decision Processes in Visual Perception*

J. B. Deręgowski: *Illusions, Patterns and Pictures: A Cross-Cultural Perspective*

Illusions, Patterns and Pictures:

A Cross-Cultural Perspective

J. B. DERĘGOWSKI

*Department of Psychology,
King's College
University of Aberdeen, UK*

1980

ACADEMIC PRESS

A Subsidiary of Harcourt Brace Jovanovich, Publishers
London · New York · Toronto · Sydney · San Francisco

ACADEMIC PRESS INC. (LONDON) LTD.
24/28 Oval Road,
London NW1

United States Edition published by
ACADEMIC PRESS INC.
111 Fifth Avenue
New York, New York 10003

Copyright © 1980 by
ACADEMIC PRESS INC. (LONDON) LTD.

British Library Cataloguing in Publication Data

Deręgowski, J B
    Illusions, patterns and pictures. —(Academic
    Press series in cognition and perception).
    1. Visual perception 2. Pattern perception
    I. Title.
    152.1'423   BF241   80-40890
    ISBN 0-12-210750-0

    Printed by W. & G. Baird Ltd. at the Greystone Press, Antrim.

Preface

The idea for this book arose in the course of preparation of a review chapter for the "Handbook of Cross-Cultural Psychology". The survey of cross-cultural studies on perception which that work entailed suggested that cross-cultural data on visual perception could profitably be examined and speculated upon more freely than the confines of a work of reference permitted; especially the data on perception of patterns, whether meaningful or otherwise, presented on plane surfaces. The interest which pattern perception aroused outside cross-cultural psychology seemed to ensure that such examination and speculation would not be conducted *in vacuo* and would not merely interest that motley assembly of psychologists who term themselves "cross-cultural".

The two aims, of relating cross-cultural studies to "Western" studies and of presenting cross-cultural studies to non-cross-cultural psychologists are somewhat difficult to reconcile. The difficulties are caused by the sheer number of such studies, their extent and history. A comprehensive presentation of both "Western" and cross-cultural studies on pattern perception and allied topics would not only result in an enormous volume which few would be tempted to open but the comparison which resulted would be one between a Western dog and an inter-cultural flea which although born and bred on this very dog had chanced to spend some of its time on other animals. In short the cross-cultural element would be almost completely submerged, and that, in my view, would be grossly unfair.

The only way in which such imbalance could be redressed seemed to be to juxtapose a number of Western studies and a number of studies done either partly or wholly in other cultures, which appeared to be particularly relevant to the issues in question.

But even among the cross-cultural studies a selection had to be made. In this the guiding precept was relevant to the central theme of the book; i.e. the nature of the perceptual process. It was accordingly decided to exclude studies which are, as it were, once removed from this theme, which analyse the phenomena in question using responses of large samples of subjects tested on standard tests or their close derivatives.

Discussion of such studies, although informative, would extend the framework of the book unduly. Some phenomena which have for a long time fascinated students of cross-cultural variation, but which hitherto have yielded only ambiguous data, are also omitted. Outstanding among these is the problem of eidetic imagery to which one of the pioneers of cross-cultural studies, L. W. Doob, has devoted some of his efforts.

The mutual relevance of "Western" and cross-cultural studies need not imply agreement of conclusions reached. Agreements although pleasant and gratifying are rather uninformative and probably yield fewer seminal ideas than disagreements or even apparently unrelated observations, a certain common conceptual ground is however necessary for any evaluation. Since the concern here is with visual processes the assumption was made that the purpose of inter-cultural comparisons is to elucidate the psychological nature of those processes using the opportunities which various populations differing both in culture and genetic endowment offer. This interest in the process *per se* made the task easier since the need for a distinction between genetic and cultural effects in the studies considered was thereby obviated. This gain, on the other hand, had to be paid for by accepting the compounding of genetic and cultural differences which characterizes most of the studies, and makes it impossible to attribute any particular mode of perception to either one of these two vectors.

Those visual processes which are here described as pattern perception traditionally fall into three categories and are often thought of as almost unrelated, although in fact have much in common. The traditional categories are: (i) perception of visual illusions, (ii) perception of non-illusory patterns and (iii) perception of meaningful pictures. One of the aims of this book is to examine the relationship between these traditional categories in the light of cross-cultural data, and to sketch out their mutual relationships. It is hoped that this may help to foster understanding of the psychological processes involved. It is also hoped that the book may prove of interest to anthropologists who must occasionally wonder what psychologists are doing in *their* backyard, and to people interested in pictures as means of communication.

The inter-cultural approach in psychology is gaining popularity. Several books have been published in the last decade and various others are in preparation. This is due, one suspects, not only to the fascination with "them" which seems to affect some students but also to the greater ease of conducting such studies. It is now easy to travel and facilities in some field stations at last are not merely bearable but pleasant; one is seldom more than three days away from a place where a bath and beer are to be had.

Academic acceptance and understanding of cross-cultural psychology has also increased greatly. Admittedly now and then obscurants are encountered who believe that the psychologist's place is in a "proper" laboratory or even in an armchair from whence he can pontificate *ad lib*; that he should not intrude into what they conceive to be the domain of anthropology. Such vessels, preserving a belief in strict interdisciplinary divisions, should be cherished for their quaintness and antiquity but not taken seriously.

The spread of the very facilities which make cross-cultural work pleasant reflects too a decrease in cultural differences, not so much in social rituals which are very often kept alive for both commercial and political reasons; but more subtly in changes in training and upbringing, in kinds of food consumed, in kinds of entertainment indulged in and in the language spoken. The steady and relentless Western advance erodes gradually the most basic cultural contrasts, and creates a monotonous plain. It is in the interest of Psychology to exploit these contrasts whilst they are still available, and it is hoped that this book will encourage some psychologists to do so.

May 1980   J. B. Deręgowski
The 485th year of King's College   *King's College*
                                             Aberdeen

Acknowledgements

Several of my colleagues and some of my friends helped and encouraged me at various stages in preparation of this volume. They are therefore at least in part responsible for its content. For sharing this responsibility I gratefully list their names. Professor E. Salzen and Drs N. E. Wetherick and H. D. Ellis and J. W. Shepherd, all of the University of Aberdeen; Professor G. Jahoda of the University of Strathclyde; and further afield Professors W. Lonner (University of Western Washington, USA) and J. Berry (Queen's University, Ontario, Canada).

In addition when conducting some of the experiments reported I have ruthlessly exploited the hospitality of Mr A. Bentley (then of Harambee School, Kimilili, Kenya, now of University of Swaziland), Dr P. Dasen (then of Ivory Coast, now of University of Geneva), Professor D. Munro (University of Rhodesia) and Dr R. N. Serpell (University of Zambia).

I have of course relied greatly on the help of a variety of research assistants and am especially grateful to M. M. Kurdelebele for his companionship on some of the journeys.

Several public bodies have sustained me generously at various times in this work. These were, The University of Rhodesia whose fellowship enabled me to carry out one term's fieldwork in that country, the Carnegie, Nuffield and Hayter funds and the British Ministry of Overseas Development who assisted in paying for various field trips. I am grateful to them.

Several authors and publishing houses gave permission for reproduction of figures published by them. These were: Dr Crawford-Nutt and The National Institute for Personnel Research, Johannesburg for Fig. 3.4; The African Medical and Research Foundation of London, for Figs. 4.8a, b; Unesco, Paris for Fig. 4.8c; Dr W. Hudson and the National Institute for Personnel Research of Johannesburg, for Fig. 4.9; Professor G. Jahoda and Dr H. McGurk for Fig. 4.15; Arkady Publishing House, Warsaw for Mr K. Jabloński's photograph of the Rybenko stove, Fig. 5.7. I am grateful to them too.

Contents

xii   *Contents*

1. Introduction

Cross-cultural studies in psychology are more appropriately regarded as one of the many approaches to the subject than as its sub-division because the problems with which they deal are identical with those of psychology in general; only the populations which they study and in consequence the methods which they employ differ from those of the mainstream of psychology. Therefore such studies are seldom innovative as far as the broad processes are concerned. They act generally as verifiers which test the universality of findings and when such universality is not found attempt both to define and to explain why this should be so. These attempts lead to purification of general psychological concepts both by circumscribing the extent to which psychological phenomena are subject to cultural and ecological influences, and by encouraging the study of the phenomena which might be overlooked if populations are not found wherein they are so abundant that they are rescued from condemnation as mere random or freak effects.

Both historically and epistemologically one can think of cross-cultural psychologists as asking two questions.

The basic question is:

"Does it also happen to 'them'?"

This question embodies all that is needed for the preliminary, heuristic stages of work.

It is an appropriate question when a research worker encounters a population of which he knows practically nothing when no specific hypothesis is called for or indeed possible. This has been the approach of many pioneers in the field.

A more refined approach can be used when a psychologist has an hypothesis that a particular process is subject to cultural, ecological or genetic influences: he may then scan the entire human species for populations which could be used to test it. It may also determine his experiments on populations derived from other cultures, living in environments which are different from his own.

The question which is now asked is a variant of the question asked during so many psychological experiments.

"Given an hypothesis that a process X is influenced by a variable Y, will there be an expected difference in the process between the two populations differing on the variable Y?"

This is currently the most common approach. It has almost entirely replaced the approach epitomized in the first question, just as the rapidly increasing cross-cultural contacts and therefore decreasing number of exotic populations and naïve psychologists would lead one to expect.

An obvious extension of this procedure relies on ranking groups on a variable Y and observing the correlation of these rankings with those on the variable X.

A somewhat different approach which we have already mentioned, derived from the consideration of similarity rather than of contrast, is that of seeking the population in which a particular psychological process is particularly easy to observe, and hence easy to study. The population in question is of no special interest but the process is, and it is assumed that whatever can be learned about the process from the population studied is *mutatis mutandis* applicable to other populations. The analogies of this approach to those used by natural scientists such as biologists are obvious. Genetic observations of the fruit fly and neurological studies of the visual cortex of cats are not initiated primarily from the inherent interest in these species but because their physiology is convenient for studying genetics and vision, respectively, and from the belief that such studies can contribute to general understanding in these disciplines.

In this volume I shall not endeavour to examine every psychological phenomenon that has been explored cross-culturally but concentrate on those which have been studied in enough detail to make an impression on pyschology in general. I shall not therefore follow Doob's (1966) will-o'-the-wisp down the enticing alley of eidetic imagery nor examine isolated studies of such issues as olfactory aesthetics; not because they are thought to be of lesser importance than the studies considered here but simply because conclusions which can be drawn from them are at the moment too weak and diffuse.

The topic which we have chosen for the present review is that of pattern perception.

The notion of pattern as used in this paper extends somewhat beyond that generally used by psychologists. Conventions sustained by convenience rather than rational premise dictate that the term pattern should be limited to regular or irregular geometric figures or assemblies of dots, and extend perhaps to the recognition of letters, the latter being considered as very familiar geometric patterns rather than as linguistic symbols. Studies of illusions, which are often evoked by simple geometric stimuli and also of pictures (which can be thought of as representational patterns) are often not taken into consideration.

It seems to me that it might be profitable to broaden the usage so as to include both of the excluded groups of stimuli. After all, simple patterns are responsible for optical illusions, and optical illusions because of their very nature are often incorporated in "meaningful" pictures. Thus the three phenomena are closely related and, as will be seen, this relationship is not free of cultural influence.

Indeed so close is this relationship that in the discussion I shall not endeavour to deal with them separately but juxtapose them so as to show their mutual relationships in an attempt to elucidate the nature of the perceptual processes involved.

The Cambridge expedition to Torres Straits (Rivers 1901) was historically one of the earliest cross-cultural endeavours. It set out to gather data systematically from a non-Western culture and to compare them with the existing data on a variety of topics which have never been matched for sheer breadth in cross-cultural psychology. Other more recent studies have involved larger samples and more intense investigations of one particular aspect, but none of them has concerned itself with the visual acuity, colour vision, perception of space, as well as with various non-visual aspects of perception. The expedition included workers whose names were later to become the common currency of psychological discussions: W. H. R. Rivers, C. S. Meyers, W. McDougall and C. G. Seligmann.

Both Rivers and Seligmann studied visual illusions. Their objectives were simple. They had no notion whether the illusions which were well known to occur in Western populations were also to be found in the natives of those remote parts of the world and if so what was their strength; and wanted to answer these questions. Two illusions were investigated especially thoroughly; the Horizontal-Vertical illusion in all its three variants, and the Muller-Lyer illusion. Several others were examined rather more superficially, the workers merely trying to confirm their universality and not to compare their magnitudes with those prevailing in Europe. The results yielded by the latter group will here be mentioned but briefly whilst those of the first two illusions will be treated in some detail since they are, as will become apparent, the most commonly investigated and have a very special place in the cross-cultural studies of perception.

Because the nomenclature of the illusions is somewhat confused we have decided to adopt that used by Robinson (1972) and in addition to provide drawings of appropriate figures to which we shall refer.

The illusions which were only rudimentarily investigated by the expedition were as follows:

(1) Zöllner, Hering and Wundt figures (Figs 1.1–1.3) all of which were found to yield the expected misperceptions.

(2) two Helmholtz squares, filled with parallel lines, vertical in one square, horizontal in another (Fig. 1.4); this and

(3) Fig. 1.5 appeared to have surprisingly little effect, in both cases the two of the figure elements being seen as equal,

(4) the irradiation illusions (Fig. 1.6): and illusion involving perspective (Fig. 1.7) which were not readily seen.

Fig. 1.1   Zöllner figure.

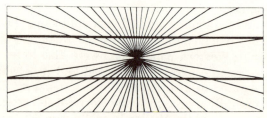

Fig. 1.2   Hering figure.

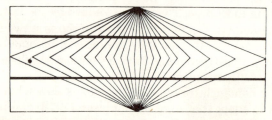

Fig. 1.3   Wundt figure. (Also known as Hering figure.)

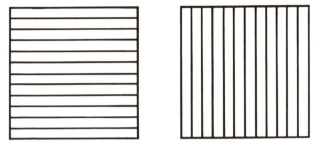

Fig. 1.4   Helmholtz squares.

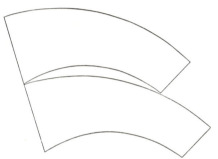

Fig. 1.5   Jastrow figure.

Fig. 1.6   Lipps irradiation illusion.

Fig. 1.7   Perspective illusion. (After Rivers 1901.)

Rivers attributes these weak effects to the lack of interest which these particular stimuli evoked in his observers: ". . . if I had a similar figure (to that shown in Fig. 1.7) representing two Murray Islanders, I have very little doubt that it would have been most popular and that the illusion would also probably have succeeded".

One of the thoroughly explored illusions, the *Horizontal–Vertical illusion* (Fig. 1.8) was investigated by requesting subjects to draw a line perpendicular and equal to a standard horizontal line. The line had to be drawn either from the middle point of the standard line, or from its end or through the middle point so as to form a cross. Three types of illusion figures were thus created; two of these have since been used by many other workers, whilst the cruciform type has (perhaps on account of the smallness of the effect which it yields) been largely neglected. The differences between these types are, as will be seen later, of import.

Perhaps the most striking of Rivers' findings was that of the considerable discrepancy between responses of his Murray Island samples of adults and children and those of his control groups of English students

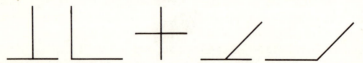

Fig. 1.8   Various versions of the "Horizontal–Vertical" illusions; *inverted T, L, cruciform,* **and two** *slanted* **figures.**

and of English school children. Consistently on the common types of stimulus (T and L) the Murray men were influenced by the illusion to the greatest extent. The English students, on the other hand showed, with the same consistency, least influence.

The differences between samples of children drawn from the same populations were not pronounced and were inconsistent, alternately the English and the Murray Island children being the more prone to illusion.

In the case of the cruciform illusion the results are less clear; the illusion is perceived by all groups of subjects but is small and the differences between the groups are probably not significant.

When considering the problem of illusions, Rivers makes several points which are discussed at length in his later psychological literature. He mentions, for example, the possibility of the shape of the field of vision affecting perception.

He comments on the possible effect of sophistication of his sample of English students, but thinks that the consistently greater illusory effects in the children and Murray Islanders indicate that "its source is sought in some physiological condition or if it is at present necessary to be content with psychological explanation it must be of simple and primitive nature".

The Muller-Lyer illusion was studied using a different method. The subjects were given a slide and had to adjust the length of the arrow with the inward pointing fins till it seemed to them to be equal to the arrow with the outward pointing fins.

On this task too differences were observed and again both groups, the Murray Islanders and their English controls, were found to be subject to the illusion, but unlike the case of the Horizontal–Vertical illusion, the Murray Islanders showed lesser proneness and there appeared to be no differences between children and adults in both ethnic samples. Furthermore an additional group of English adults who were not familiar with the illusion did not differ in their scores from the group of English students, who might have had some familiarity with the stimuli. In considering these results Rivers suggests that they may be due to the European subjects regarding the figure as a whole in making their responses whilst the Islanders attended more specifically to the task, thus postulating that attention may be an important factor. This suggestion has recently been revived and experimentally investigated.

Later Rivers (1905) extended his studies of the illusion to Todas who live in southern India. Using the same method as that used in Torres Straits he found that the magnitude of Toda proneness to the effects of inverted-T and L illustrations lay between that of the Murray Islanders and the English. On the cruciform, the least evocative of the stimuli, the results were different. English adults formed the intermediate group and Todas the least influenced group. An extension of the study using a new apparatus (which permitted investigation of the L form of the illusion only (Rivers and Darwin 1902)) yielded similar results, Todas being consistently more prone to illusion than English men, women and children. The conclusions derived from the Toda study are similar to those derived from the observations in Torres Straits which have already been discussed. "Physiological" conditions and the effect of experience in civilized life, such as experience derived for instance from study of geometry and drawings, are said to "diminish illusion". I shall have occasion to revert to these observations when discussing more recent data obtained in inter-cultural investigations of illusions.

As will be seen from our description of Rivers' work the problem of perception of illusions and more generallly the problems of pattern perception has been a theme of enduring interest in inter-cultural psychology from its very beginnings. The contrasting results obtained by Rivers from differing cultures clearly show that inter-cultural psychology can make a definite contribution to our understanding of these processes.

We shall now examine this contribution in greater detail and since, as has been shown, the study of illusions was the foundation stone of inter-cultural comparisons in studies of perception we shall begin by considering some recent studies of illusions.

2. Illusions

INTRODUCTION

Although there is a large number of illusory phenomena not all of these have been subject to equally intensive investigation or have been regarded as of equal interest. The following four illusions have, for theoretical reasons which we shall discuss, occupied cross-cultural researchers almost to the exclusion of all others:

(1) The Horizontal–Vertical illusion,

(2) The Muller-Lyer illusion,

(3) The Sander parallelogram,

(4) The Perspective illusion in various forms including the Ponzo illusion.

It will be recalled that both the Horizontal–Vertical and the Muller-Lyer illusions were major items in Rivers' research programme, and that he thought the effects which these figures evoke to be of different origins. This assumption of a difference between these two groups of illusions has persisted to the present day, although the hypothetical reasons for the difference have changed.

The hypotheses which have almost exclusively dominated recent cross-cultural studies of the illusions are those put forward by Segall *et al.* (1966), who have carried out the hitherto most extensive study of all the cross-cultural studies of illusions. The roots of the hypothesis can be traced to Brunswik's (1956) notion of ecological "cue validity" and the related concept that consistent encounters of certain cues direct the development of modes of perception. In consequence "The modes of operation are what they are because they are generally useful". The immediate cause which led to the investigation however is the opinion held by anthropologists (represented by Herskovits) that the basic character of human perception is affected by ecological and cultural variables and the contradictory opinion held by some psychologists that perceptual processes are essentially the same in all human beings.

These contrary views led to a "running debate" at Northwestern University. To resolve the debated issue an extensive research project was embarked upon.

Investigation of populations differing greatly in their cultures and living in different environments should enable one to clarify the issue. If no differences between such populations were observed then the claim for the impact of environment and culture would be weakened. It would not however be nullified because of the lack of control of genetic factors; a more complex and, *prima facie*, unlikely hypothesis that an egalitarian genetic mechanism redressed the imbalances introduced by the environments would still be sustainable. Lack of genetic control in such an investigation (and there are indications that susceptibility to illusions may be to some extent hereditary (Coren and Porac 1919)), restricts the interpretation of any finding of inter-group differences since these remain attributable to both genetic and environmental factors. Such restriction, although logically valid, does not in practice render the observations void. This is so because the evidence derived from a large number of environmentally disparate groups in which the genetic factors do not appear to form any definite pattern, can parsimoniously be said to support the environmental rather than the genetic interpretation of the formative influences.

If the environmental experience is such as to affect a particular type of percept, e.g. the length of a line or the size of an angle, one would expect such influence to affect all lines and angles, but with declining effect as the number of attributes which the stimuli share with the objects from which the relevant experiences were derived decreases. Hence the most efficacious manner in which one could test the effect of ecology upon perception would be to transfer people living in one ecology to another and observe their responses. A pigmy translated from the dense, closed environment of the jungle to open savannah or desert should make such errors as we would expect from a man whose experience did not provide him with opportunities of using normal distance cues. Indeed, such errors were made by Turnbull's (1961) companion, a pigmy, who on encountering cows on his first journey away from the native dense forest thought the animals to be ants; he did so although he was familiar with cows, but not with cows at a great distance.

This evidence suggests that such distance cues as there were, were not perceived correctly. The density gradients which must have stretched in front of the pigmy, the elevation in the field of view as well as other cues which might have been present did not affect his perception in the same manner as they did Turnbull's. One can try to refine this argument further and to postulate that the error was not so much due to the fault of the basic perceptual mechanism, but to the unusual (from the pigmy's point of view) conditions in which this mechanism had to work. Such unusual conditions may call for a different weighting of various perceptual cues than that normally used by the observer. Aerial perspective, for example, is likely to be of much lesser import when objects are near to the viewer than it is when they are far away; on the other hand the significance of such density gradients as are often provided by the surfaces of the objects may with the increasing distance be lost entirely, so that the only major perceptible characteristics are those of shape and colour. Such remnants of the normal perceptual cues would thus gain greatly in importance and compounded with the cue of the aerial perspective enable an experienced observer to say: "These cows at a distance *look* as small as ants". His failure of size-constancy does not lead him astray. He discounts it and arrives at a decision by other means.

THE ECOLOGICAL EFFECT AND THE HORIZONTAL–VERTICAL ILLUSION

Although pictures and geometrical figures cannot convey all the cues presented by objects in three-dimensional space they can convey some of them, but the cues so provided are always contradicted by the cues derived from the surface on which the figures are drawn. Consider a simple vertical line on a plain piece of paper. This approximates in its retinal projection to a line which could be projected by a long straight object placed at *any* angle in the subject's median plane; it could represent a sapling, a spear inclined against a hut, or a path stretching away into the far distance in front of the observer. Obviously the first of these objects is likely to be a common experience of the inhabitants of dense forests, whilst the last is likely to be a common experience of those who inhabit open plains. A simple vertical line could therefore be used to measure the impact of the environment upon perception. The judgement of the length of such a line requires a standard against which it can be assessed; and a line orthogonal to the judged line provides such a standard, if one accepts that the ecological effect responsible for the differences of the perception of the vertical line does not affect the horizontal line equally. This being so the Horizontal-Vertical illusion figure offers a suitable measuring instrument of the ecological impact.

The essence of the measured effect lies therefore in non-isotropy of the perceptual field. In a dweller of an extremely dense, enclosing environment, where the gross of the visual stimulation is derived from vertical planes which like stage props surround him, the panorama is essentially isotropic, i.e. it has the same properties in all directions and hence all the lines independently of their orientation are presumably subject to the same scaling effect.

The perceptual field of the dweller of open plains, on the other hand, is non-isotropic. The vertical dimensions are expanded relative to the horizontal dimensions. This is a result of extensive experience of an environment in which the notion of the "vertical" dimension is derived generally from projections of distances stretching away from the observer, whilst that of the horizontal dimension is derived from observation of features of the environment which lie in one of the observer's fronto-parallel planes. The resulting non-isotropy of the perceptual field is therefore an adaptive response of the organism to environmental press. Its effects can be detected either by transfer of an observer between environments differing in the characteristics of their pressure or by using test materials which create analogous effects.

Any material would serve the purpose and the use of illusion figures is not really necessary, although they may be thought of as being very convenient tools.

THE CARPENTERED WORLD EFFECT AND THE MULLER-LYER AND SANDER PARALLELOGRAM ILLUSIONS

The rationale for the Carpentered World effect is also derived from the consideration of individuals' experience. It rests, however, on the characteristic features of the man-made environment. It is an undisputed feature of man-made goods that they tend to display a greater regularity of form than do the natural objects encountered daily. The extent of such regularity is not, however, equal in the artefacts of all the cultures. It varies with the extent to which a particular culture imposes its own restrictions upon the vagaries of the natural phenomena; it is less in those populations whose technology is adaptive rather than transformative of the natural environment, than in those whose technology is primarily transformative rather than adaptive. A Zulu whose ploughing follows the contours of the land is, in this sense, less subject to the cultural determinants than a Chinese farmer planting rice in his rectangular paddy. The regularity of cultural artefacts increases with the sophistication of the technology and so does the number of such regular artefacts available. The reasons for this need not concern us here; what is important as far as the postulated effect is concerned is the fact that such cultural differences exist and therefore, if perception is affected by experience, they may lead to differences in perception among various populations.

One of the more striking aspects of the regularity is the presence of right angles in the artefacts. Hence in cultures where such angles are dominant one would expect subjects to interpret other angles as right angles whenever ambiguous angles are met. In the cultures where right angles are rare one would expect no such misperceptions. One would, therefore, expect to observe differences between such cultures as that of the traditional Zulu, the inhabitants of hemi-spherical huts, engaged in contour-agriculture and having practically no rectangular artefacts, and that of the Western urban man, who lives in a block of flats furnished with rectangular furniture.

Any geometric figure containing ambiguous representations of angles could be used for investigating the postulated effect and the well known Muller-Lyer and the Sander parallelogram illusion figures can therefore be used for the purpose.

The lengths of the "shafts" of the two parts of the figure are compared in the Muller-Lyer illusion but the interest of the comparison derives not from the perceived distortion of the shafts themselves but from perception of the depicted angles involving the shafts as well as the fins of the figure. The Carpentered World hypothesis is, as we have said above, not concerned with perception of length of lines but with perception of angles. A connexion between the perception of the angles and of the lengths needs therefore to be formulated. This has been done by Gregory thus: both the elements which are contrasted in the traditional illusion (see Fig. 2.1) can be said to show a corner of, say, a building, the

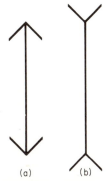

(a)   (b)

Fig. 2.1   Muller-Lyer figure. The right hand figure presents an arrangement of lines similar to that derivable from the intersections of a floor, walls and a ceiling inside a room. The left hand figure is similar to the arrangement obtainable to a viewer looking at a cuboidal building from outside.

14   Illusions, Patterns and Pictures

two fins being in both cases projections of right angled joints, but whilst one of the figures represents an exterior corner of a house, the other represents an internal corner of a room. The implications of this difference are taken into account by the perceptual mechanism. The angles are perceptually interpreted as right angles and the lines connecting them appropriately "shortened" or "lengthened". Gregory (1968, 1973) argues that such typical depth cues can trigger the constancy scaling mechanism without causing perception of depth. This type of misplaced constancy scaling is called by Gregory *primary* or *depth-cue* scaling to distinguish it from secondary scaling, which involves transformation of perceptual data. Secondary scaling commonly occurs in the processing of reversible figures and can be experienced, for example, by observing the changes in the perceived size of faces of a Necker cube as it reverses. Thus whilst *primary* scaling is *upwards* from data to hypotheses, *secondary* scaling is *downwards* from hypotheses to data. The simple illusion figures, such as those discussed here, are said to evoke *primary* scaling. In the specific case of the Muller-Lyer figure the lengths of the two shafts are scaled in accordance with the depth cues which they themselves and the fins provide.

An identical argument applies to the Sander parallelogram. The illusory effect evoked by this stimulus, like that evoked by the Muller-Lyer illusion, is a distortion of perceived lengths of straight lines. As is the case with the Muller-Lyer illusion, the effect can be thought of as resulting from misperception of angles. This is apparent from Fig. 2.2, where the standard Sander parallelogram is represented as if it were

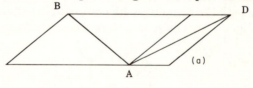

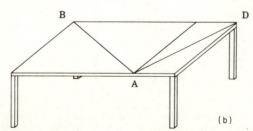

Fig. 2.2   Representation of the Sander parallelogram figure (a) on its own and (b) as if drawn on a table.

drawn on the top of a table. The drawing of the table is admittedly poor since there is no perspective convergence, but is none the less clearly recognizable. The corners are therefore perceived as right angled and line AD is perceived as being shorter than line AB.

The illusions affected by the carpenteredness are thus not dependent upon isotropy of the visual field but upon the tendency of the perceptual apparatus to treat all angles as if they were right angles.

PERSPECTIVE ILLUSIONS: THE PONZO ILLUSION

The experiential hypothesis which could be put forward to explain Perspective illusions, of which the Ponzo illusion is probably the best known example, is almost intuitively obvious. The two converging lines are thought to evoke to some extent the same percept as that evoked by a pair of parallel lines stretching away from the observer. Indeed they represent a configuration which would be obtained if such lines stretching away from an observer were projected upon a screen placed in the observer's fronto-parallel plane (provided that the focus of the projection lines were on the observer's side of the screen).

Two lines converging towards the top of a page are thus associated with the edges of a road stretching in front of the observer; two lines converging towards a side of a page with, say, top and bottom of a long wall. Under these circumstances in "real life" a stick placed at various distances along a road or along a wall would yield decreasing projections as its distance from the observer increased, and the constancy mechanism would try to compensate for this apparent shrinkage by taking account of cues indicating that the stick was at a distance, thus ensuring that the stick would be perceived as larger than it would be had the percept been based solely on its retinal projection.

The illusory effects on the figures such as that shown (Fig. 2.3) are therefore again a result of the perceptual analogy. The perceptual mechanism is tricked by the similarity of the stimuli and, notwithstanding certain contradictory cues (such as the surface of the paper) which indicate that all the elements of the figure are equidistant from the observer, indulges in constancy scaling, and the line which in the three-dimensional space would lie further away is seen as larger than the "nearer" line, in spite of being objectively equal to it.

One would expect, if the experimental factors are effective, the magnitudes of illusions evoked by the perspective figures to correlate positively with that of the Horizontal–Vertical illusion, since the postulated

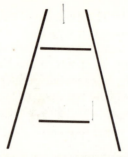

Fig. 2.3   Ponzo figure.

mechanisms responsible for both illusions embody an assumption that the effect is associated with perception of distances in the environment. One would also expect this illusion to yield results correlating positively with those of the Muller-Lyer illusion since the carperedness of the environment which is postulated to be responsible for the latter would ensure not only that the non-rectangular angles will be perceived as rectangular, but also that non-parallel and non-orthogonal lines will be perceived either as parallel or as orthogonal. It follows that the populations especially prone to the Perspective illusions would be those inhabiting open plains *and* living in a carpentered culture, whilst inhabitants of dense environment *and* coming from non-carpentered cultures should show relatively little proneness.

There is yet another reason why the probability of correlation between scores on these illusions would be expected. This does not involve a postulate of common determinants but rests upon the fact that a figure can be drawn which evokes an illusory effect, but is of such an appearance that it can with about equal degrees of arbitrariness be thought of as embodying elements of the Muller-Lyer figure, of the Ponzo figure, or of the Horizontal-Vertical illusion figure. Consider Figs 2.4a and 2.4b; in both of these the vertical lines are equal and are twice the length of the slanting segments. This figure evokes an illusion that the vertical on the right is longer than that on the left. This may be thought to be so because both the right and the left components consist each of a combination of two modified "Horizontal-Vertical" figures (Cormack and Cormack 1974); or it might be thought that each of the two figures is an incomplete Muller-Lyer stimulus, with a fin missing at both ends. Finally, it is possible to speculate that the fins are perceived as incomplete converging lines of the Ponzo figure.

The view that the three illusions are thus related was not shared by Segall *et al*. (1966, p. 89), who thought that the Perspective illusion reflected only that influence which affects both the Sander parallelog-

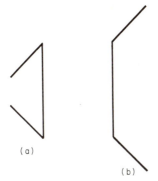

(a)

(b)

Fig. 2.4 Two figures which could be said to embody at least three of the generally recognized illusions.

ram and the Muller-Lyer figures but did so feebly; that it was influenced by the carpenteredness of the environment. They did not consider the possibility of the Horizontal–Vertical illusion and the Perspective illusion figures having a common determinant.

The Perspective illusions have not been found to discriminate clearly between different cultural groups. Rivers in his Torres Straits studies, it will be recalled, had obtained but weak effects which he attributed to subjects' lack of interest. Segall *et al*. (1966) also obtained rather unconvincing data from their samples (see p. 36).

SOME OBJECTIONS

Before examining some of the data obtained in investigations of the Ecological hypothesis and the Carpentered World hypothesis it is necessary to examine some of the objections to these hypotheses which are so fundamental that if correct they deprive these investigations of any *raison d'être* they might possess.

First there is a very general objection which is based, one suspects, on misunderstanding of the hypotheses put forward, and which maintains that an experimental demonstration of some other influence nullifies the value of such hypotheses.

This is not so. The hypotheses do not suggest that the particular environmental effects are the sole determinants of illusions, but merely that the illusory effects are influenced by the environment. This means that other influences, both environmental and non-environmental, may be present and hence that the effect may vary even when those environmental influences which are explicitly stated in the hypotheses remain constant. Therefore demonstration of other influences such as, say, pigmentation of the fundus oculi, does not deny the essence of the environmental hypotheses but merely shows that the extent of the effects put forward is moderated.

Other common objections are aimed not directly at the hypotheses but rather at the postulated involvement of the constancy scaling mechanisms in the phenomena. Some other mechanism could of course be postulated but it is difficult to conceive how such a mechanism could operate without affecting constancy scaling, or making the entire scheme grossly extravagant, unless the entire notion that illusion figures contain depth cues were dismissed. Suggestions of such dismissal have also been made. Several of these objections are examined in Robinson's (1972) book on illusions. We shall discuss here only those which are most pertinent to cross-cultural work.

Probably the most common of the objections uses the presence of related illusory phenomena in the "real" three-dimensional world as an argument against explanations involving notions of constancy scaling. This argument runs as follows:

> If the illusions are a result of misapplication of the perceptual mechanism because it treats a set of lines on a plane as representing a solid, then such misapplications cannot possibly occur in the case of solids because the perceptual conflict which is present in the case of figures between the depth cues and the surface on which the figures are drawn does not arise in the "real world". Therefore illusions cannot occur in the "real world". Furthermore misapplication of the scaling mechanism in the "real world" would be grossly maladaptive.

The evidence that illusions are not confined to drawings but occur in the "real world" has been provided by several experimenters working in a single culture (e.g. by Zanflorin 1967). Such evidence is however scarcely needed for application of illusions in architecture has a long and distinguished history. Pirenne (1970) provides two fully analysed examples of such application, an arcade by Borromini in the Palazzo Spada and Michelangelo's Piazza of the Capitol. Both these architects relied on the effect of convergence of buildings upon perceived distance. They introduced convergence where none would be expected by the viewer with the effect that his perceptual mechanism is tricked to regard it as a cue for distance and hence the buildings are perceived as distorted, which is exactly what the architects desired. A humbler but much more well known version of this phenomenon occurs in the Ames room (Ittleson 1952, Gregory 1973). Brislin and Keating's (1976) intercultural study also demonstrates this effect; it seems unlikely therefore that the argument could be faulted for lack of evidence.

There is a flaw in the argument however; it lies in the assumption that when a misapplication of perceptual mechanism occurs in the "real world", it is contrary to the postulated effect of misapplied scaling.

It seems reasonable to accept that the perceptual mechanism is triggered by certain cues and that the origin of these cues is unimportant but that their relationship to other cues is. Similar configurations of cues lead to similar percepts whatever their sources, whether illusion figures or "real world" configurations.

This point is elaborated upon in the following description of the application of the ecological hypotheses to perception of the Ponzo illusion:

All parallel edges encountered in the "real" world with the sole exception of those which are in the observer's fronto-parallel plane are projected as converging lines upon such a plane placed between the observer and the stimulus. In consequence, drawing of two converging lines evokes a scaling response appropriate in some measure to parallel lines and this leads to distortion of other elements of the figure. This distortion is the illusory effect which is measured in experimental investigation of illusion. But a retinal projection resulting from a drawing showing two converging lines is identical with retinal projections cast by two converging edges of a lamina which is placed at any inclination to the observer, with the exception of a unique position in which the inclination compensates for the convergence. Hence, if extensive experience of parallel edges leads to misperception of lines which cause projections of converging lines it is likely to do so for all such projections, whether they originate from a flat or from a three-dimensional stimulus, that is to say, illusory effects would be expected to occur in both circumstances.

Since additional visual cues, both mono and binocular, which are present in the "real world" are not found with equal intensity in stimuli used to investigate illusions, when such cues are in harmony, the illusory effect elicited by the latter is likely to be less. The inter-stimulus differences are therefore dependent on particular cues occurring and on their perceived intensity.

A reference to Fig. 2.5 will make this argument plain. In this figure density gradients are symbolically represented by circles which are of the same size when representing an invariant gradient, such as that provided by the surface of paper viewed normally, but differ in size when a variable gradient is symbolized.

All four figures show fronto-parallel projections. A shows the basic pattern and B the projection which such a pattern would yield if

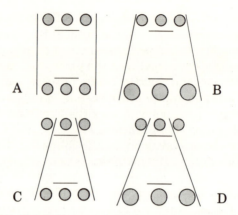

Fig. 2.5   **Symbolic representation of density gradients.**

presented on a plane sloping away from the observer and placed below his eye level. C shows a variant of the basic pattern in which the lines converge; it is, therefore, the common version of the Ponzo illusion, and D shows a projection of the same pattern placed on the plane receding away from the observer. Consider the organism which is concerned with determining whether the two lines are parallel. This can be done by assessing whether the information contained between the lines throughout their length remains constant as the eye moves along these lines. In our particular case this information has two components; size and number of the elements between the lines. Comparing their values at the two levels shown in each figure we obtain the following table:

	Figure	*Size*	*Number*
A	Drawing seen normally	same	same
B	A on a receding plane	different	same
C	Ponzo figure seen normally	same	different
D	C on a receding plane	different	different

It is well known that figures such as B evokes perceptual transformations such that the organism tends to regard the elements as equal provided that a sufficient number of elements is exposed (see p. 187). The implication of such a transformation is an apparent decrease in the convergence of the lines forming the figure. C is of course the common Ponzo figure and D, as the above table shows, combines the effects of B and C; and the distortions which these two figures evoke would, one expects, be compounded therein. D is also a representation of a projection derived from a "real world" array having converging members. One would accordingly expect such an intensification of effect to pertain to the "real world" stimuli.

If this argument is valid, then the presence of the "real world" illusions could not be thought of as damaging to the experiential hypotheses and one would expect cross-cultural differences in perception of the traditional illusion stimuli to be parallelled by similar effects in perception of the "real world". This indeed is the case, as the studies reported below show. The above reasoning can *mutatis mutandis* be applied to the other three illusions discussed in this section: Horizontal–Vertical, Muller-Lyer and Sander parallelogram, and indeed to any illusion figure the effect of which can be claimed to be determined by an environmental influence.

Apart from the fundamental issues just discussed, the constancy scaling approach has also evoked a number of rather specific criticisms. We shall discuss two of those involving the Muller-Lyer illusion, which are of especial relevance to the notion of depiction of the third dimension.

It has been argued that the Muller-Lyer figure when presented in the linear form (Fig. 2.6) contains a self-contradictory cue. This is embodied

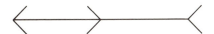

Fig. 2.6　A linear form of the Muller-Lyer illusion.

in the central arrowhead which has to be seen as portraying lines *receding* from the observer in order to frame the phenomenally nearer segment, and as inclined towards the observer in order to form the phenomenally further segment. The difficulties which interpretation of such a figure entails have been stressed by Fisher (1968). Whether these are really so fundamental is uncertain, for plane figures evoking contradictory perceptions of depth are widespread.

If they were not, then one would not be able to recognize drawings and pictures as depicting three-dimensional objects; for in all of these flatness of the surface on which the patterns appear is contradicted by the three-dimensionality of the objects which the very same patterns evoke, a point which has been made repeatedly by many (e.g. Gregory 1966, Gombrich 1962).

In the same paper Fisher put forward another objection to the theory of perceptual scaling. He showed that the figures such as 2.7a and 2.7b in which fins at both ends point in the same direction evoke illusion, albeit small, but in consistent direction; the shafts being over-

B

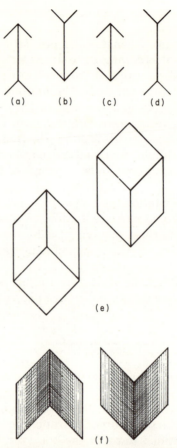

Fig. 2.7 Fisher's (1968) figures (a, b), and traditional Muller-Lyer figures (c, d). The former are reminiscent of projections of a cube (e) and Mach's book (f); and share with these figures the element of ambiguity which is common to pictorial stimuli capable of evocation of the percept of depth.

estimated. This he claims is contrary to the effect one would expect if scaling really took place, because in these figures "the perspective elements are as strongly defined" as in (c) and (d) and, furthermore, he implies that the distortions occurring should not be in the same direction. Why either of these views is held is not clear. Both (c) and (d) embody an element of convergence of the ipsilateral fins, an element which is missing in (a) and (b) whose fins, if extended, would form parallel lines. Hence it seems that the strength of perspective elements does in fact differ between the two pairs of figures. On the other hand, the difference between (a) and (b) which is alluded to by Fisher is by no means certain as both these figures can be said to represent the nearest vertical edge of a cube, or an open book as it would appear when looked at from above or from below, with the spine of the book either close to or far away from the observer.

The recurrent problem which the above remarks illustrate is that of obtaining pure and unambiguous forms of illusion figures which would enable one to associate responses evoked with a single variable. It is doubtful whether such stimuli are at all possible and whether there are perceptual mechanisms which can be triggered by only a narrow and precisely specifiable range of stimuli, when such complex processes as pattern perception are involved.

Our brief discussion is not intended to convey in detail the critique to which the inappropriate depth scaling theories and especially Gregory's theory have been exposed. A specialist study of these issues will be found in Robinson's (1972) book. The conclusion reached therein regarding the *status quo* of both Gregory's postulates and Day's (1972) extension of Gregory's ideas is that, on the whole, Gregory's theory has a great deal of appeal largely due to its sheer neatness. It is apparent that the inappropriate scaling cannot account equally adequately for all the illusory effects, but the unifying paradigms which it offers should not be dismissed lightly.

The significance of these paradigms to development of inter-cultural studies, although often unstated, was and is considerable. With this in mind we shall now proceed to examine some of the evidence from non-Western cultures, by considering the illusions in turn.

THE HORIZONTAL – VERTICAL ILLUSION

The largest body of cross-cultural data on this illusion is that obtained by Segall *et al.* (1966) in the study to which we have already referred. This study, included a comparison of adults drawn from 15 cultures and of children drawn from 13 cultures on the two versions of the Horizontal–Vertical illusion, namely the inverted-T version and the rotated-L version. It showed that illusion was experienced in all cultures but the extent to which it was experienced varied considerably among the cultures.

The inverted-T figure yielded illusion magnitudes ranging from 8% to 24% adults and from 11% to 23% for children. The rotated-L figure yielded, as one would expect from Rivers' (p. 6) studies, a lesser effect: 2% to 19% for adults and 1% to 21% for children. The scores of the two illusions correlated significantly but not at a very high level, thus suggesting that although the two stimuli evoke the same effect there are also other effects which are not shared. This in turn hints that the assumption that both stimuli are equally subject to ecological influence ought to be questioned. More so, because the observed age trends on the two illusion figures are not the same, higher scores being obtained for adults in seven of the 15 samples with the inverted-T figure but no such differences being observed with the rotated-L figure.

Although the results are not entirely consistent, a point which Segall *et al.* analysed thoroughly, the high illusion susceptibility of several African adult groups and the middling scores of the "Western" groups do offer support for the ecological hypothesis such that overall it emerges strengthened from the test.

It is appropriate to examine some of the observed discrepant effects in some detail. We shall begin with the disparities between responses to the two illusion figures and hence with the use of these figures as devices for measurement of the ecological influence.

The relationship between the particular aspect of the ecological press and the particular stimuli used in an experiment to evaluate the effect of such press upon perception should be relatively pure and uncontaminated by other factors. Ideally, a perfect correlation would prevail, but such ideals are not attainable and therefore one can merely hope to choose stimuli such that the obscuring effects are as unobtruding as possible. One can ask, bearing this in mind: "are the two Horizontal–Vertical stimuli used in Segall *et al.'s* study well chosen to measure the postulated effects?".

The data to hand suggest that the choice was more felicitous in the case of the L form of the illusion than in the case of the T form. There are important differences between these stimuli, the latter of which evokes illusion not simply owing to the orientation of its two component lines (as its name would erroneously suggest), but owing to at least one more factor. This was observed and investigated by Finger and Spelt (1947), who presented the two stimuli each in two orientations and noted that whilst the L-type stimulus, whether in the L or (Γ) orientation, always evoked the illusion that the vertical line was longer than it really was, rotation of the T stimulus from (⊥) to (⊢) orientation did not result in similar perception. The bisecting line of the figure continued to be seen as longer than the bisected line even though it was no longer vertical. This influence of bisection was further investigated by Kunnapas (1955). His investigation of the illusory effects by placing of the dividing line in several positions along the divided line shows that the Dichosection effect (as he called the phenomenon) remains essentially the same for all the four orientations of the figure investigated (i.e. T, inverted T and the two T-on-its-side settings) and varies systematically with placement of the disecting line, being maximum for the central placement and least for the placements at the ends of the intersected line (i.e. for "L" configurations). In addition to this effect there is the true Horizontal–Vertical illusion by which the vertical lines tend to be overestimated.

Since the L figures are free of the Dichosection effect they must evoke a purer form of the Horizontal–Vertical illusion and have closer correspondence to the ecological effects considered by Segall *et al.* than do the T figures.

A re-examination of Segall *et al.*'s data on the assumption that only the responses to the rotated-L figure are admissible does in fact strengthen the support for the ecological hypothesis. Two of the communities, both inhabitants of open savannah (Songe and Zulu), and therefore expected to score highly on the Horizontal–Vertical illusion, do score below the median on the inverted-T version of the figure, but not on the rotated-L version. Similar difference was not, however, observed in the case of children's responses to the corresponding illusion figures. If one follows Jahoda's advice and excludes Western societies, whose literacy might affect their responses and, in addition, whose ecological experience is difficult to classify, one can classify the remaining societies by their ecological experiences as follows:

(i) *social groups living in ecologically dense compressed environment*: Fang, Bété, Ijaw, Dahomey and Hanunoo,

(ii) *savannah and desert societies*: Senegal, Ankole, Toro, Suku, Songe, Zulu and Bushman,

(iii) *unclassified groups*: mine workers in South Africa.

One would expect, if the ecological hypothesis is valid, the observers from the second group to experience stronger illusory effects than the observers in group (i); this indeed is so in the case of adults' responses to the rotated-L figure and *not* to the inverted-T figure. Children's responses are again ambiguous.

The results thus suggest that in the case of T-type figures the dichosection effect is confounded with the postulated ecological influence which is measured by the L-type figures. Since Segall *et al.*'s scores on the Muller-Lyer illusion do not correlate significantly with their scores on either version of the Horizontal–Vertical illusion for the adult samples as well as for children's responses to the inverted-T configuration whilst for the rotated-L figure the children's correlation is negative, one has to accept that the two illusions: the Muller-Lyer and the Horizontal–Vertical, do probably differ essentially. It is possible, however, that the Dichosection effect on its own correlates with the

Muller-Lyer illusion, Sander parallelogram or even the Perspective figure. To check on these possibilities Segall *et al.'s* data were analysed as follows. The group scores obtained with the rotated-L figure was subtracted from the corresponding scores obtained with the inverted-T figure. The resultant scores which were taken to indicate the Dichosection effect were then correlated with the scores on each of the three illusions just listed. In no combination of variables did the resultant correlation differ significantly from nought. Hence if the Dichosection effect is culturally influenced, this influence probably cannot be explained by either of the two hypotheses which guided Segall *et al.'s* investigations. Since the differences between the adult group means on the two figures range from a small negative difference for the Zulu (the only negative difference obtained) to a 20 times as large positive difference for the Sene, such uninvestigated and hitherto unreported and unhypothesized inter-cultural differences may well be present.

An alternative way of isolating the Dichosection effect is to present subjects with the traditional T figure but at an inclination of 45° (see Fig. 2.8). In this setting both elements of the figure have equal horizontal and vertical components and hence the illusory effect produced can only be due to Dichosection. Use of such a figure with samples drawn from Scotland and Ghana showed no significant difference in susceptibility to the Dichosection illusion between these samples (Jahoda and Stacey 1970). Thus these results do not show the expected cultural difference.

The relationship between the Dichosection scores and Muller-Lyer scores in the Scottish and Ghanaian groups is contrary to that which the re-analysis of the Segall *et al.* data would lead one to expect. In both groups the scores correlate significantly and positively. Since not only the number of data points used to calculate Scottish and Ghanaian correlations is much higher than the number used in re-analysing Segall *et al.'s* findings, but also the samples providing these data are more homogeneous than their counterparts drawn from a variety of

Fig. 2.8   **A Horizontal–Vertical figure set at an inclination of 45°.**

cultures it seems likely that Jahoda and Stacey's data offer a finer picture of the relations between various illusions. The Dichosection scores also correlate positively, but at a lower level, both with the Sander parallelogram scores (in the Ghanaian sample only) and with the Horizontal–Vertical scores (in the Scottish sample only). The implication of those correlations is unclear. The correlations with the Muller-Lyer results do not share such ambiguity and raise an important question about the relationship between the Dichosection illusion and the Muller-Lyer illusion. There appears to be no *prima facie* reason to think that the Dichosection stimulus is similar to some characteristic of the carpentered world likely to trigger the constancy mechanism. If this is so then the dichosection and the Muller-Lyer stimuli share an element which, whilst evoking illusion, cannot be explained in terms of constancy and which therefore cannot be explained in terms of the Carpentered World hypothesis either.

Several other cross-cultural studies of the Horizontal–Vertical illusion were inspired by the ecological hypothesis. Of these, that by Gregor and McPherson (1965) who used the same stimuli as Segall *et al.* is of particular interest because their samples consist of Aborigines who live in the featureless and seemingly boundless terrain of central Australia. Such populations would be expected to score very highly indeed if the ecology has the effect attributed to it. This was found to be so. In the case of both versions of the illusion figure included in the test the Aborigines obtained the highest scores yet reported on the test.

An alternative method to measurement of illusions which seems intuitively compatible with the ecological hypothesis is provided by Gregory's Pandora's Box. This instrument, described in detail on p. 128, was used by Stacey (1969). Estimates of the distance of the two ends and the bend of the L figure were obtained both when the figure was presented on its own and when it was placed on a density gradient.

These very comforting findings are not confirmed in their entirety by an experiment (Gregory 1974) using a more sophisticated version of the same apparatus and three different stimuli: (i) an inverted-T figure, (ii) an L figure and (iii) two short vertical lines displaced horizontally and vertically relative to each other.

The illusion figures were found not to evoke a consistent perception of depth: either the tops of the figures or their bottoms were seen as closer to the observer, and in the case of the figure consisting of two lines either line was on occasions seen as closer to the observer. Correlations of the differences in depth (without taking account of whether the upper or the lower parts of the figure were perceived as being nearer to the observer) with the extent of illusion were significant both for the inverted-T figure and for the two line figure. In the former case the usual illusory effect occurred, in the latter the upper line was perceived as larger in 19 out of 20 subjects. (This effect is of particular import in the context of Jahoda's findings on reconstruction of simple pictorial arrays by young children; we shall refer to it again.) The L figure data yielded no analogous correlation. However, a comparison of the illusion scores obtained by Avery and Day (1969) by presenting an L figure in various orientations with the perceived difference in depth between two ends of a straight line presented in the same orientations yields a very high positive correlation (Gregory 1974). The conclusion put forward earlier by Stacey remains, therefore, largely unchallenged, although the perceptual mechanism appears to work in a more complex way than would appear from Stacey's observations.

It will be noted that an L figure was used in the investigations just discussed (with the exception of Avery and Day's work), whilst Segall *et al.'s* data were obtained using a rotated-L figure. In view of the complications which seem to arise whenever one attempts to investigate an apparently simple illusory effect, the implied equivalence of these two orientations of the figure ought to be questioned. The ecological hypothesis allows no prediction as to what differences in the illusory effect would be observed by comparing the responses to figures with the horizontal line at the top (such as Γ or ⊤) to those with the horizontal line at the bottom (such as L or ⅃). At one point in an attempt to clarify their hypothesis Segall *et al.* illustrate the illusion by referring to a pavement made of one yard squares. An eye looking along such a pavement would receive retinal images which would decrease with the squares' distance from the observer; but, and this is the important fact, the relative foreshortening of the sides parallel to the line of regard would be greater for the more distant squares than for the nearer squares. Further, in any particular square the foreshortening of the two edges normal to the observer's line of vision is not equal, the edge which is further away from the observer is foreshortened more drastically. A fronto-parallel projection of a square on the ground thus becomes a trapezium with the longer of its parallel sides (the base) at the bottom. A projection of a similar square drawn on a ceiling also becomes a trapezium but with its base at the top.

An explanatory illustration should not be taken to be the statement of the theory, a point which is occasionally overlooked. Segall *et al.* could, if they so wished, have chosen not a pavement, but a coffered ceiling of a cloister or some other receding horizontal surface to make their point. Furthermore, their illustration does not indicate whether when making comparisons between sides of the squares an observer uses as a standard the further or the nearer of the edges of the square. The former would of course yield an inverted-L figure and the latter an L-figure (or the corresponding enantiomorphs). These considerations force one to question Wober's (1972) interpretation of the ecological hypothesis as suggesting that the inverted-L forms of the stimulus should lead to a lesser illusory effect than the upright forms. His short experiment in which the sequence of presentation of various forms of stimuli was apparently left uncontrolled does not yield support to his interpretation of the hypothesis and provides but unconvincing data. The effect of orientation upon perception of the Horizontal–Vertical illusion merits more detailed examination, not in least because in other lengthier studies it has led to mutually contradictory conclusions. A sample of such studies will therefore be briefly examined.

Valentine (1912) observed that the inverted-L form of the illusion yielded greater effect than the L form. Consistent results were obtained by Finger and Spelt (1947) and by Avery and Day (1969). This harmony was, however, disturbed by Shiffman and Thompson (Thompson and Shiffman 1974, Shiffman and Thompson 1975), who report just the opposite and seem to be under a mistaken impression that both Finger and Spelt's and Avery and Day's results agree with their own, that the L figure yields greater illusion than the Γ figure. The latter type of stimulus, when presented tachistoscopically, they state, led to a reversal of the usual illusion, i.e. overestimation of the relation of the horizontal line to the vertical line. This reversal is particularly puzzling since the inverted-L form, it will be recalled, was used by Segall *et al.* in their study and they do not report any of their groups as consistently yielding such responses.

Given the assumptions about scaling implicit in the ecological hypothesis the following considerations apply to all the above results. The magnitude of the illusion depends in ecological terms on:

(i) whether the observer encodes the stimulus as reposing on a plane above his usual line of sight (say, on a ceiling) or below such a line (say, on the pavement or floor),

(ii) whether he encodes the horizontal line as nearer or further from him than the free end of the *vertical* line. The two factors yield four ways in which the stimulus can be encoded and hence suggest that four different percepts may result, and affect the magnitude of the illusory effect differently.

These considerations of the suitability of stimuli for the measurement of the ecological effects extend to other figures derivative from the traditional Horizontal–Vertical stimulus. Indeed, the Horizontal–

Vertical illusion may be thought of as just a particular instance of the more general class of illusion evoked by two straight and co-planar segments. Thus when the angle between the lines of the L-type figure is varied, with one of the lines remaining horizontal, the illusory effect (which can scarcely still be referred to as the Horizontal–Vertical effect, there being no vertical) is observed to vary and a continuum of systematic changes in its strength can be traced (Morinaga *et al.* 1962). Comparison of such continua derived from analogous transformations of the three traditional types of the Horizontal–Vertical stimulus, cruciform, L-type and T-type, have been made by Cormack and Cormack (1974). Figure 2.9 summarizes in a simplified form their results. The most striking discrepancy is that between the curves obtained for the inverted T and the cruciform versions and the curve for the L version. The two former are symmetrical, the latter is not. The increase in the illusory effect which occurs when the stimulus deviates from its "tradi-

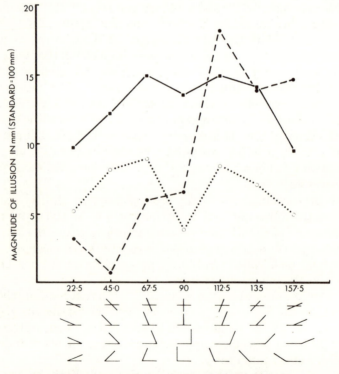

Fig. 2.9   Representation of the Cormack and Cormack (1974) results and of the stimuli used by them. Dotted line, cruciform stimuli; continuous line, inverted-T stimuli; dashed line, L stimuli.

tional" setting in the former two figures occurs whatever the sense of deviation, whereas in the case of the L figure such increase is only present when the deviation is such as to decrease the difference between the two angles formed by the arms of the figure, i.e. to open out the arms. When the arms are close together, the illusion tends to decrease, perhaps because when the free ends of the arms are near each other then the comparisons of length are very easy, as Cormack and Cormack suggest.

At the present juncture the asymmetry of the curve showing L responses is probably of less interest than the fact that all three types of stimuli yield higher illusions in one of the non-orthogonal settings of the line than in the traditional Horizontal–Vertical setting; and that in two of these settings the L curve (Fig. 2.9) shows higher illusion scores than the T curve.

Consider the influences hitherto discussed which have been said to affect the magnitude of illusion: (i) the effect of the verticality of one of the components, (ii) the section effect. Both these are at work and mutually augmentative in the inverted-T figure; only the verticality component is present in the other two figures because in the L figure intersection does not occur, and in the cruciform the two elements intersect each other and hence presumably this effect is nullified. When the vertical line is replaced by a line set at an angle, the verticality effect is *ex definitione* removed, but it is clearly replaced by some other effect since the illusion increases, or perhaps, and this appears to be more parsimonious, a strengthening takes place of the effect which was always present and which has been erroneously attributed to the verticality.

Would not more telling results have been obtained by Segall *et al.* had they used non-orthogonal stimuli?

This may well be the case. The open vistas of the hypothesis do not after all extend only directly in front of the observer, but also to the right and left of him. The orthogonal comparison is therefore unique and atypical. Yet, there may be an overriding argument for regarding Segall's *et al.'s* orthogonal stimuli as more satisfactory than the non-orthogonal figures, since the latter are likely to evoke responses correlating with responses to the Muller-Lyer stimuli to a larger extent. This may be so because the effect of the non-orthogonal stimuli may in part be due to the tendency of the perceptual mechanism to rectify the angles, the strength of such tendency being plausibly associated with the extent of exposure to the carpentered environment.

Cormack and Cormack have also studied the effect of nonorthogonality on dichosection. Comparison of their curves for L and inverted-T stimuli confirms that the dichosection effect was present when traditional orthogonal stimuli were used. Its presence does not, how-ever, ensure greater scores for all the inclinations of the bisecting line in the T figure. On the contrary, the increasing inclination of the "vertical" in the L figure leads to higher scores than those obtained with an equally inclined bisector of the T figure. Thus the opening up of the L figure enhances the illusion but the change of inclination of the bisector does not do so for the inverted-T figure. On the contrary, for the T figure a decrease in the illusory effect takes place at both large and small values of the angle of inclination. For the T figure presented on its side the effect of dichosection is such that it counteracts the effect of orienta-tion and the resulting illusion is either negative or positive but rela-tively small.

A characteristic which may be of relevance to these findings is sym-metry. Symmetry has been regarded by the *Gestalt* school as a factor contributing to figural goodness. Hochberg and Brooks (1960) have demonstrated that one of the factors which foster perception of pictorial depth is the asymmetry of patterns. Such patterns, evidence shows, tend to be seen as portraying three-dimensional objects more readily than symmetrical patterns. Asymmetrical Fig. 2.10a is, for example, more readily seen as a representation of a cube than symmetrical Fig. 2.10b.

Of the three classic "Horizontal–Vertical" figures the cruciform figure has four axes of symmetry, the T and the inverted-T versions have one axis lying in the observer's median plane and the L version one axis at 45° to the observer's median plane. One would therefore expect the perception of the third dimension and hence of illusion to increase in this order. This does not normally happen. The T figure normally evokes larger illusion than the L figure, but this, as has been pointed out above, is due to the effect of dichosection. On the other hand, given central intersection and a variable angle of inclination the illusion is larger for a certain range of angles than it is in the orthogonal setting. Such figures having a non-orthogonal bisector are, of course, asymmetrical.

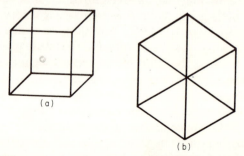

Fig. 2.10   **Symmetrical and asymmetrical representations of a cube.**

Similar increase in illusion evoked also occurs with the cruciform figures, in which inclination of the bisector reduced the number of the axes of symmetry from four to two.

These increases of illusion with the decrease of symmetry and hence with increased tendency to evoke perception of pictorial depth are entirely compatible both with the ecological hypothesis and with the observations of the *Gestalt* school. The absence of such increases towards the extremes of the continua of inclination which contradicts this observation does present a special problem. This irregularity can perhaps be said to be due to the increased ease of comparisons of the two lines forming the figures in question.

MULLER-LYER AND SANDER FIGURES

The data obtained by Segall *et al.* in response to the Muller-Lyer figures offer in their view "considerable support" for the Carpentered World hypothesis. Of the 15 groups of adults drawn from a variety of cultures those with the greater experience of carpentered environments were considerably more prone to the illusion than those with less experience. The Western samples were consistently at the top with percentage discrepancy scores between 13 and 19 and the other cultures' scores fell well below, down to about 1% for the Bushmen and the mineworkers.

Similar description applies to children's scores, which, whilst positively correlated with adult scores, were generally *higher* than the adult scores from the same cultural group. This finding is surprising since if the illusion susceptibility is in some measures a result of cultural exposure one would expect adults to be more susceptible than children, not vice versa. To account for this result Segall *et al.* propose an additional hypothesis that maturation brings about a more analytic approach to perception and thus modulates the effect of earlier learning. Older children, it is suggested, are better able to attend to the stimulus *per se* and to control their inferential processes. Thus the concept attention is, in some measure, restored to the explanatory role which it held in Rivers' theories.

Another aspect of the data which calls for elucidation is the detailed ranking of the societies tested on their susceptibility to illusion. This, Segall *et al.* acknowledge, cannot be explained entirely in terms of their hypothesis. However, such precise fit of data to the theory would only be possible if the carpenteredness were the only determinant of susceptibility to the illusion, but since, as the comparison between the adults' and the children's responses shows, it is not so, and since there may also be further influences, the lack of perfect concordance cannot be said to damage the hypothesis irreparably.

The Muller-Lyer results, for both adults and children, are reported to correlate positively with the Sander parallelogram results, which form essentially the same pattern, the only notable discrepancy being the absence of a pronounced difference between the responses of adults and children. These results, too, can therefore be said to support the Carpentered World hypothesis.

Replications and extensions of studies using these two stimuli are more frequent than those of the Horizontal-Vertical studies. Some of these experiments will be examined in some detail. Bonte's (1962) studies of the Muller-Lyer illusion were inspired by Segall's findings and question these findings most vehemently. The three cultural groups tested appear not to differ in susceptibility to the illusion, although drawn from cultures which differ greatly in their carpenteredness: European, Bashi and Ba-Mbuti. Both the Bashi and the Ba-Mbuti live in the Congo. The former are agricultural people settled on a lakeshore, the latter are hunters and gatherers. Of the two groups Ba-Mbuti are certainly less exposed to a carpentered environment. The apparatus which was used to obtain susceptibility to the illusion was similar to Rivers' original apparatus.

The method of measurement was therefore entirely different from that used by Segall *et al.* Such differences in apparatus ought not, however, in themselves destroy the relative differences between the three groups on a perceptual predisposition as well ingrained as the experience of the carpentered world is said to be. Only if the stimuli presented by the two types of apparatus differed radically would one expect such a difference between responses. Segall *et al.* who have examined photographs of the apparatus reproduced in Bonte's (1960) thesis, on which the published paper is based, maintain that the stimuli used in the two studies do indeed differ in several important ways.

The most serious query about Bonte's procedure is, however, probably that pertaining to instructions. Segall *et al.'s* procedure allows for a check on whether the instructions have been understood. There is no such check possible with Bonte's slide apparatus.

While it is impossible to attach definite weight to any of the points listed, their total effect is such as to endorse Segall *et al.'s* conclusion that Bonte's finding of *no* difference between the three samples ought perhaps to be set aside until confirmatory replications have been carried out.

Berry's (1968) study comparing the Temne and the Eskimo is important because it links the concept of susceptibility to illusions with the Witkinian concept of field-dependence, which has influenced most of cross-cultural work in recent years. A close examination of field-dependence lies beyond our scope and we merely refer an interested reader to those sources which have examined its significance for cross-cultural work (Witkin and Berry 1975) and confine ourselves to a very brief sketch of its relevance to the studies concerned with operation of perceptual mechanisms.

The essence of the concept lies in the differential ability of observers to disembed a stimulus figure from the surrounding field. This can be measured in several ways. The most apparently direct measure is that involving search for a figure concealed within a matrix of lines. A set of such stimuli differing in complexity and hence in difficulty forms the widely used Embedded Figures Test (EFT). Another measure is that involving construction of simple patterns using coloured wooden blocks. A series of such tasks forms the Kohs' Blocks test. Two further measures involve perception of verticality. In the Rod and Frame test the subjects, seated in a darkened room, adjust a luminous rod set within a luminous, square and tilted frame to the vertical. In the Body Adjustment test, subjects seated in a special chair within a tilted room similarly adjust the angle of their own bodies.

Berry (1968) postulated that the impact of a carpentered environment upon perception, which Segall *et al.* and others inspired by them (e.g. Heuse 1957, Morgan 1959, Bonte 1962, Mundy-Castle and Nelson 1962, Gregor and McPherson 1965, Jahoda 1966, Berry 1966, Deręgowski 1967, Jahoda and Stacey 1970, Richardson *et al.* 1971) sought to investigate, may be moderated by field dependence namely that increasing field-dependence will be associated with the decrease of the illusory effects. Now, since generally "African" subjects are more field-dependent and also belong to a less carpentered culture than their "European" counterparts the two opposing factors likely to influence the illusory effect are likely to affect the responses in both populations. It follows that failures to observe the expected differences between cultures may on occasion arise from the obscuring effects of field dependence. To check upon this, samples of Eskimos coming from highly carpentered and moderately carpentered environments were equated on their Kohs' Blocks scores as a measure of field dependence, and their susceptibility to the Muller-Lyer illusion compared. A significant difference in the predicted direction was observed, which was not detected when comparing unmatched Eskimo samples. Further, when the samples of the Temne drawn from similar, moderately carpentered environments were compared both the Kohs' Blocks scores and the Muller-Lyer scores were found to differ significantly, the higher illusion scores occurring in the group which was more field dependent. It is regrettable that these comparisons are intra-cultural, the Eskimos being compared with Eskimos and the Temne with the Temne. Such comparisons do, as Berry points out, complicate the picture and the reported data themselves and make it seem doubtful whether inter-cultural matching on Kohs' scores would have been equally convincing. This is so because the relationship between the illusion and the Kohs' scores may well be more complex than it would *prima facie* seem, as comparison of both Temne groups and one Eskimo group, all of which come from a moderately carpentered environment, shows. The Muller-Lyer illusion scores and Kohs' scores are as given in the brackets in this order:

(i) Rural/Traditional Eskimos (3·8; 89·8),
(ii) Urban/Transitional Temne (3·1; 15·6),
(iii) Rural/Traditional Temne (4·0; 6·6).

It is readily apparent that although the Eskimos' illusion scores lie between those of the two Temne samples their field independence is considerably greater than that of either of the two Temne samples. Matching of samples on only one of the variables clearly calls for additional care in interpretation of the results. Nonetheless the findings are interesting and deserve more attention than they have hitherto attracted.

PERSPECTIVE ILLUSIONS

The perspective illusion drawing used by Segall *et al.* yielded an effect which the workers themselves describe as weak; and this very small illusory effect has probably led to very few significant inter-sample differences.

In addition, the results obtained do not correlate with either of those obtained with the Horizontal–Vertical stimuli, the Sander Parallelogram and the Muller-Lyer figures.

It is probably safe to assume, especially in view of other evidence which we shall presently consider, that these results are due to the particular version of the stimulus which was used.

A set of stimuli which has been repeatedly used in a series of studies of the Ponzo effect was introduced by Leibowitz *et al.* (1969). It consists of four figures. The first figure is a traditional Ponzo figure in which two lines converge towards the top of the card and two short horizontal bars lie symmetrically on the imaginary bisector of the angle formed by the longer lines. The lower of the bars is entirely contained between the lines, but the ends of the upper bar overlap them slightly. This figure will be referred to as the *geometric* figure. The second figure, which will be called the *rail-track*, portrays a grassy rail track in such a manner that the rails form a pattern of two converging lines similar to that presented in the *geometric* figure. Two dark lines similar to the bars of the *geometric* figure and similarly placed are superimposed upon the photograph. The third figure is a photograph of a *sward* with two black bars superimposed thereon. The depth cue which this figure provides therefore embodies primarily a density gradient although it also shows some overgrown furrows which make a set of faint converging lines. Finally a *control* figure consisting simply of two parallel black bars on a plain background and looking rather like a fat equality sign. Leibowitz *et al.* (1969 and Brislin (1974)) used these stimuli to investigate the effects of culture upon perception. Their subjects came from Guam, a small island in the Pacific Ocean where such convergence cues as are associated with the Ponzo illusion are relatively seldom encountered because the terrain is hilly and overgrown and there are neither railways nor great lengths of straight road; and from Pennsylvania where such cues are plentiful and where indeed these photographs were taken. The results obtained (Fig. 2.11) show that although the illusion is perceived by the subjects from Guam, its magnitude is low and remains at about the same level for all three types of stimulus used, whereas the Pennsylvanian sample shows a steady increase in magnitude as the

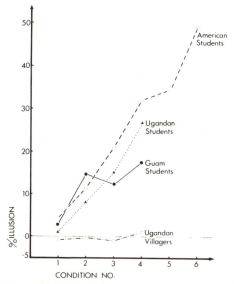

Fig. 2.11   Responses of American, Ugandan and Guam subjects to the Ponzo illusion configurations made under various conditions. The experimental conditions were: (1) control, two parallel lines above each other, (2) geometric figures, (3) photograph showing textured background, (4) photograph showing perspective convergence, (5) a monocular view of the scene, (6) a binocular view of the scene.

depth cues are increased step by step from the standard geometric figure through a photograph of the sward, a photograph of the rail-track, a view of a rail-line which was photographed seen monocularly, to a binocular view of the same rail-line.

This apparent arrest of the illusory effect in the Guam sample in spite of the increase of the depth cues may be interpreted in various ways. It could be said that this population's size constancy is relatively low in "real-world" settings and hence the plateau reached shows that they have attained the ceiling level of their performance so that any further enrichment of depth cues does not affect them greatly. This would imply that in the "real world" the constancy mechanism of the Guam observers operates at an entirely different level than that of the Pennsylvanian observers. It could also be put forward that such additional cues as are provided by the photographic stimuli are simply too weak to trigger the constancy scaling mechanism in the population not used to such cues. This postulate accords with the environmental hypothesis, but the difference between the responses of the Guam and the mainland samples to the photograph of the sward suggests that one should treat it with caution. This is so because although open spaces and views of roads and railways going into the far distance may be rare in Guam, density gradients must be commonplace.

An extension of Leibowitz's studies using the four stimuli which we have just described and in addition four other variants of the Ponzo figure was carried out by Brislin (1974). The subjects were again drawn from Guam and from Pennsylvania. An age range from 3 to 22 years was explored with a large number of subjects. The results summarized briefly were: the illusory effect increased with addition of realistic pictorial depth cues, both the *sward* and the *railway line* photographs leading to greater illusory effect than the central figure, as did the abstract perspective cue. This was true of both cultural groups. There were, however, differences between these two groups, the Guam subjects showing significantly less proneness to illusion on three of the figures; the two pictorial stimuli (the sward and the rail-lines) and the control figure consisting of two equal bars. Surprisingly there was no significant cultural difference between the responses to the geometric figure. This figure too was the sole exception to the general finding that the illusory effect increases with age in the Pennsylvanian sample. No such distinct age trend was present in the Guam sample. Further presentation of the stimuli to the Pennsylvanian sample in two orientations, with the apices of the figures either upwards or to the left, led to a significant and pronounced difference in responses in all figures used, with the sole exception of the two-bar control figure. In discussing these results Brislin states that they are supportive of the ecological hypothesis.

Another study using the Leibowitz stimuli is that of Wagner (1977). His subjects were boys and youths from Morocco and came from both urban and rural environments, each environment providing both schooled and unschooled subjects. Several unexpected results were obtained. The rail-track figure which incorporates the elements of the abstract figure yields lower scores than the abstract figure for three out of four age groups in two of the populations and in the third population it does so for all four age groups. The implication therefore appears to be that enrichment of the figure leads to a *decline* of illusory effect. Such results have not been previously reported and although conceptually conceivable, for it could be that the presence of the density gradient makes the detection of perspective more difficult, they are difficult to interpret. This difficulty is augmented by the comparison of the responses to the figures showing railway track on a density gradient with those to the figure incorporating only the density gradient. The scores of most sub-groups are about equal whichever stimulus is used. The argument which could be advanced in view of these findings is that those results are probably determined solely by the density gradients and that therefore the converging track does not affect the magnitude of the illusion. Comparison of these results with those obtained from Guam college students and Ugandan villagers (Leibowitz *et al.* 1969) is instructive. In these samples there appears to be no difference in susceptibility to illusion between the geometric figure, texture photograph and perspective photograph and there seem to be no indications of greater susceptibility to geometric figures.

There are also other surprising aspects of the findings from Morocco. The susceptibility to illusion as embodied in the geometric figure appears to decrease with age between about 7 and 19 years whilst susceptibility to illusion as embodied in the track figure appears to increase. Wagner stresses the difference between responses to the two types of stimuli and points out that Brislin (1974) considered his own data, which were similar, to be supportive of the notion that susceptibility to illusion increases with age and ignored the significant age related decrease obtained with the help of the geometric figure. This criticism seems to be misplaced. There are in the case of the geometric figure significant differences between the various age groups tested by Brislin and these are reported by him; these do not, however, constitute the consistent significant decline which Wagner finds. For example, in the case of Brislin's Pennsylvanians the youngest and the oldest groups provide scores which fall below those of intermediate groups. Perhaps the wisest if somewhat defeatist attitude which one can adopt is that these two studies do not give us a definitive indication as to the nature of age changes, although in view of the greater number of different age groups used by Brislin (six) his data are probably more informative than those of Wagner based on four different age groups.

A comparison of Brislin's results obtained with the geometric stimulus with those of Leibowitz and Judisch (1967) shows a striking similarity of the development curve and hence supports his findings.

The extensive studies of the Leibowitz school are not the only studies in which the effect of variation of the strength of the pictorial depth cues has been observed. Suppose the Ponzo figure were presented in three ways, (i) in its usual form, (ii) forming a part of portrayal of an object known to be vertical, such as the side of a gymnastic jumping box and (iii) forming a part of portrayal of a road; could it yield such results as to affect the constancy scaling hypothesis? Newman and Newman (1974) believe that this could be so and that the results which they obtained using these very stimuli argue against such a scaling process. Their results showed that the effect of the standard, abstract version of the figure did not differ from the "gymnasium" version, but both these led to a weaker illusion than the road figure. Hence they argue that if the enhancement of the depth effect can be expected to increase the illusion one should also expect a decrease to follow from its degradation. Therefore the gymnasium figure should yield a weaker illusion than the standard figure. This does not happen. It follows, they argue, that the scaling mechanism is probably not involved in the process. The weakness of this argument lies, however, in an assumption that the three figures form a sequence on the scale of pictorial depth in which the gaps between the two meaningful figures and the abstract figure are both sufficiently large to cause difference in responses. This may not be so. The relative strengths of various cues, as the Leibowitz school has shown on several occasions, are not so easily assessed. It is possible that the gymnasium figure does not provide significantly poorer depth cues than the abstract figure and that the results obtained are perfectly reconcilable with the notion of constancy scaling, especially so since a gradation of depth cues in the Pennsylvanian sample (Leibowitz *et al.* 1969) does in fact evoke a gradation of the effect similar to that which was obtained by Newman and Newman.

Another problem which use of such stimuli as used by Newman and Newman presents is that of deciding to what extent recognition of a depicted object in which the illusion figure is incorporated can be taken as evidence that the entire picture embodies depth cues additional to those provided by the illusion figure. That is to say that such cues as have been provided by the portrayal are eidolic, not merely epitomic (p. 106).

In contrast with the above findings Smith (1973) found the perspective (Ponzo) effect to be fairly definite. In his study three groups of Xhosa differing in the extent of Westernization were tested on an adjustable slide version of the Ponzo figure and their susceptibility to the illusion was found to increase with acculturation. Furthermore, when these subjects were subsequently presented with a figure showing very strong perspective cues, which it was hoped would introduce a "perspective set", and re-tested the scores of both the most acculturated and the moderately acculturated groups were observed to increase significantly. This flexibility of the perceptual mechanism in the more sophisticated observers strengthens the plausibility of our explanation (p. 48) of Davies's observations on the effect of education upon perception of the Muller-Lyer illusion by the Banyakole. The resistance to such inducement of perspective by the least acculturated rural group may, as Smith suggests, show a relative stability of the perceptual mechanism and a resistance on its part to process pictorial patterns as if they had some cues to the third dimension. Yet it might be noted that even this group is prone to illusion and therefore to some smaller extent apt to engage in such processing.

THE POGGENDORFF ILLUSION

This figure is notable in the cross-cultural studies for its failure to evoke consistent results. It was included by Segall *et al.* in their test booklet but the procedural difficulties encountered by the testers yielded questionable data. The illusion is not, therefore, extensively discussed in the final report on this study.

One could reasonably postulate that this illusion will be affected by both "ecological" and "carpentered" factors. These suggestions are derived from the shape of the figure (Fig. 2.12), which could be said to

Fig. 2.12   Poggendorff figure.

consist of two Horizontal–Vertical illusion figures which ensure ecological involvement whilst acute angles made by the oblique lines suggest that carpenteredness may also affect the illusion. The ecological influence is, however, questionable because the two Horizontal–Vertical figures which are embedded in the Poggendorff figure are of a distorted T-type and they are presented on their sides, and this type of figure in this particular orientation is not appropriate for testing of the ecological effects. Therefore in terms of the two hypotheses concerned the Poggendorff illusion is probably mostly attributable to the rectification of the angles associated with the Carpentered World hypothesis. This postulate has the support of Robinson (1972) who thinks that such rectification may indeed be the cause of the Poggendorff illusion as well as of the Zöllner illusion and agrees with Parker's (1974) observation of the role of lateral inhibition in the visual system. Inhibition, according to Parker, makes it unnecessary to postulate the constancy mechanism in explanation of these illusions. If this is so, then, accepting the likely assumption that the extent of inhibition is not affected by experience, one is forced to conclude that the illusions in question are solely affected by the innate characteristics of the perceptual mechanism.

CLASSIFICATION OF ILLUSIONS

The very disparities and contradictions obtained in the inter-cultural studies of the most commonly investigated illusions reported above provide a warning against attempts to derive a taxonomy of these phenomena from a single set of stimuli used with a culturally homogeneous sample of subjects. Unfortunately many of the published studies of classification of illusions do so.

Classification of illusion figures presents the same difficulties as classification of any other phenomena which involve more than one variable. Such stimuli cannot be classified merely by the magnitude of the effects which they evoke without considering causes which are inherent in them. The dangers of such simplistic approach are apparent from the fact that adoption of such an approach would make us classify the Horizontal–Vertical illusion together with the Muller-Lyer illusion since in both of these the illusory effect takes the form of overestimation of the length of a line. Yet classification by using geometric features is equally unsatisfactory since, e.g. the fins of a Muller-Lyer figure can be gradually opened out until they are normal to the shaft and the figure arrived at is therefore an I-shaped arrangement of two Horizontal–

Vertical figures. Similarly the shape of the fins can be varied leading to figures which are clearly different in appearance.

All these figures evoke illusions and their classification would be of little import were it not for the fact that different theoretical explanations advanced do not fit all the figures equally well. The Carpentered World hypothesis, for example, seems a plausible explanation for the illusory effect of the Muller-Lyer figure, but not for an arrangement of circles.

Application of factor analysis, a certain sign of conceptual despair, cannot resolve the issues because the factors which emerge are not the same in all cultures. This is clearly shown by Jahoda and Stacey's (1970) correlation matrix between illusion scores obtained from Scottish and Ghanaian subjects. According to this Scottish responses to the Horizontal–Vertical illusions correlate with their responses to Helmholtz's square and Sander parallelogram; but Ghanaian responses to the same stimulus correlate with those to Helmholtz's square, Sander parallelogram, Muller-Lyer and Dichosection. Similarly the correlation with the Muller-Lyer responses in the Scottish sample are: with Dichosection responses, with Titchener circles and with Sander parallelogram, while the Ghanaian sample responses to Muller-Lyer also correlate with Sander parallelogram scores, and with Dichosection scores, but not with the scores on Titchener circles; on the other hand, they correlate with both the Horizontal–Vertical and Helmholtz's square. This sample of correlations clearly shows considerable disparities between the two cultural groups. One cannot obviously classify illusion figures as if they were mere physical entities since the effects associated with them are psychological. Therefore clusters which the responses to such figures form in different cultures are entirely different and do not correspond to the *a priori* notions derived from them about the features of such figures. That is to say, the explanation of such clusters lies not in the nature of the figures but in the nature of the perceptual processes triggered by these figures. In so far as these processes are influenced by culture this implies that a parallel analysis of the relevant features of culture is really needed to arrive at a fully satisfactory taxonomy.

The intra-cultural attempts at determining the relationship between illusory effects evoked by various stimuli, most notably such as those of Taylor (1974, 1976) are really attempts at deriving a more convincing taxonomy of illusions than that which can be intuited from unsystematic observations. The complex relationships which emerge from such studies are however to an cross-cultural psychologist suggestive rather than convincing. This is so for two reasons. One of these particularly close to the heart of the students of cultural differences is that the populations which were used in those factorial studies were culturally homogeneous and are unlikely therefore to present a universally valid taxonomy. Indeed the very data which we have reviewed in this chapter and which show considerable inter-cultural differences question any assumption of universality.

The second reason which can be advanced against too hasty an acceptance of such taxonomies as definitive is the fact that the intuitive element has not been entirely eliminated by the use of such techniques. This is so because each of the illusions used is represented by a limited number of figures which the experimenter chooses, presumably because he judges them to be typical of a particular illusion. By doing this he imposes an *a priori* categorization upon a phenomena which could be thought to form a continuum. (The Muller-Lyer illusion and the Horizontal-Vertical illusion do, for example, as Gregory has pointed out form a continuum, for by gradually modifying the angle of the fins of the Muller-Lyer stimulus from outward to inward pointing one passes through a point at which the fins are normal to the shaft. In this position the figure could be thought of as consisting of two Horizontal-Vertical illusions.) The taxonomy derived may therefore be tainted with arbitrariness to an unacceptable degree.

These caveats are not intended to suggest that such intra-cultural studies as hitherto have been carried out are devoid of interest to cross-cultural psychologists. They provide a rich source of hypotheses by imposing a degree of organization upon otherwise untidy data. For example, Taylor's data suggest that the perceptual mechanism responsible for the Ponzo figure, in its traditional orientation with lines converging towards the top of the figure, may be entirely different from the mechanism responsible for the illusion evoked when the figure is turned through a right angle.

The observations also on occasion support cross-cultural findings. Thus Taylor's observations also suggests unambiguously that the Poggendorff illusion seems to be an embodiment of a factor which is not shared by the other illusions commonly used in cross-cultural work. It is therefore pertinent to recall that Poggendorff was the blackest of the sheep in the Segall *et al.* flock and gave results which were found difficult to interpret.

It seems possible that such factorial studies are probably more helpful when they yield negative than when they yield positive results. As shown above, the fact that scores on two illusions share a factor does not imply that they are a result of operations of the same perceptual mechanism, although there is a modicum of probability that it is so. When, however, no common factor is shared by illusions, that is their *effects* are essentially different, there seems to be no reason for postulating a common mechanism; a point which has to be considered when evaluating data obtained on what are thought to be variants of the same illusion.

The difficulties of taxonomy of illusions, which, as we have seen, are considerable, were swept aside in a comparison of performance on two figures assumed by Ahluwalia (1978) to embody the same perceptual cues. The figures were: a conventional form of the Muller-Lyer illusion consisting of two figures, one with inward and one with outward pointing arrows and Delboeuf's illusion consisting of two pairs of equal circles and straight lines so arranged that in one figure the line connects the two circles and in the other it intersects them and forms their diameters.

The subjects were drawn from two environments in Zambia; urban and rural. The urban subjects came from a carpentered environment, the rural ones were assumed to be from a largely uncarpentered environment. Its uncarpenteredness is not, however, extreme; certainly not as severe as that of some of the environments described by Segall *et al.* Notably, Zambian rural school buildings are rectangular as are some other official buildings. Some tools and vehicles used in the area also embody strong carpentered features. Notwithstanding this contamination the two groups were found to differ greatly in their illusion scores, the rural populations being, as expected, less prone to the illusion.

If the two figures used do really embody the same perceptual cues, then the results can be interpreted as demonstrating the effect of the differential carpenteredness upon perception of figures which do not contain "angular" perspective cues. Therefore either the illusory effect is misnamed and does not really depend on perceptual perspective cues or it is due to some other more general factor of which angularity is but one manifestation. The exact nature of this effect is, however, difficult to assess because the environmental factors interact singly or conjointly with other factors (the age of the observers, the type of stimulus, the sex of the observer and the colour of the stimuli) and the analysis by Ahluwalia does not concern itself with these complications.

That such complexities arise is shown by Gregor and McPherson's (1965) comparison of two groups of Aborigines, one of which has settled and for two generations lived in the carpentered environment of a mission station and the other has lived in a reserve traditionally inhabiting circular windbreaks. Segall *et al.'s* stimuli were used. The results showed no difference between the samples on the Muller-Lyer illusion and the expected effect on women only in the case of the Sander parallelogram. This is a much more confused result than that described above, especially so since the descriptions of the groups suggest that the differences between them in terms of carpenteredness were more radical than between the Zambian samples.

Since Segall *et al's* data showed, and the Zambian data confirm, a distinct decline of illusion susceptibility with age, one could argue that the weakness of the Australian data obtained from adults could have been effected by such a decline and the same explanation could be offered for absence of a significant difference between Ghanaian and Scottish students tested by Jahoda (1970) and between different groups drawn from Ghana (Jahoda 1966). Such a simple explanation suggested by Ahluwalia is, however, suspect because the effect of ageing upon susceptibility is not simple. Both Walters (1942) and Wapner and Werner (1957) report complex development trends. The susceptibility to Muller-Lyer illusion decreases from the age of 6 years to the early teens and then increases from 15 years to 19 years. One can but agree with Wohlwill (1960) who stresses the importance of investigating the entire age ranges.

The changes of illusion susceptibility with age are central to the Piagetian theory of illusions, which, it has been suggested, might be helpful in understanding cross-cultural differences in susceptibility.

Piaget (1969) divides illusions into primary and secondary. The primary illusions are said to be those which show the following developmental characteristics. Their qualitative attributes (the location of the positive and negative spatial maxima and of the median zero illusion in relation to the proportions of the figure) do not alter with age of observers whilst the illusory effects generally decline, sometimes remain constant, but never increase with increasing age. These illusions are thought of as "simple field effects" resulting from an interaction of elements appearing well-nigh simultaneously in a single "field of concentration"; they can in consequence be evoked by tachistoscopically presented stimuli.

In contrast, secondary illusions result from stimuli which require subjects to relate centrations in space or time. Since the activities leading to the establishment of such relations change with maturation so do the resulting illusions. The magnitude of such illusions typically increases up to a certain age.

The essential difference, therefore, between the types of stimuli evoking the two types of illusion is their complexity. If the stimulus is sufficiently complex to call for active structuring, then the illusion is of Type 2, otherwise it is of Type 1.

These notions were invoked by Wagner (1977), who replicated in Morocco some of the work done by Leibowitz and his associates and described above. Wagner's findings presented a surprising effect: the Ponzo illusion evoked by simple geometric stimuli was observed to *decrease* with the age of the observer whilst the illusion evoked by the two photographic stimuli showed no such effect. This led to a postulate of an important new effect which Brislin (1974) is said to have misinterpreted, and an invocation of the Piagetian taxonomy as an explanatory concept. Unfortunately, such conclusion seems to be premature for there is a number of earlier studies showing clear *increase* of this illusion with age, when presented in a simple geometrical form; although this increase in the magnitude of the illusion between the ages of 4·5 years by Wagner *et al*. Farquhar and Leibowitz (1971) data show a very rapid increase in the magnitude of the illusion between the ages of 4·5 years (the youngest group tested) and about 8 years of age, the illusion increasing from about 2·5% to about 14·6%.

Extension of the Ponzo studies to other populations reveals further complexity of the associated effects. Ugandan subjects inhabiting the same environment but differing greatly in educational attainment also differ greatly in their susceptibility to illusions evoked by Leibowitz's stimuli (Leibowitz and Pick 1972). The results, which are plotted in Fig. 2.11, clearly show a consistent failure to respond to the illusion by Ugandan villagers and a susceptibility in Ugandan students similar to that of the Guam and Pennsylvanian students. Since both Ugandan groups live in the same environment the difference between them must be attributable to some other factor.

The possibility that pictorial sophistication might be responsible for the difference was suggested earlier when considering cultural differences in susceptibility to the Muller-Lyer illusion.

The essential element of such sophistication is the ability to perceive pictorial depth. Failure to do so implies that such cues as density gradient or perspective convergence are unlikely to be correctly interpreted and, if the illusion depends on perception of pictorial depth, the illusion is unlikely to occur.

THE EFFECT OF EDUCATION

One of the cultural variables which is intimately connected with pictorial sophistication and which might affect perception of illusions is the extent of formal education. This influence is difficult to control in Western samples since general compulsory education makes large and controllable variations in this attribute unlikely and confines them to those sub-divisions of population already differing considerably on account of other variables such as health or genetic endowment. Intra-cultural comparisons do on the other hand offer opportunities for such investigations.

The possibility that education may affect perception of illusion figures was implicit in Jahoda's (1966) comment that pictorial perception may be influenced by it. The impact of education has subsequently been investigated by Davies (1970). Segall *et al.'s* Muller-Lyer figures as well as a set of specially made Muller-Lyer figures were used by Davis with adult Banyakole subjects from Uganda. The subjects were divided into three groups according to their educational attainment, it being implicitly assumed that the process of education was not selective and therefore that the subjects within the groups were equally well endowed genetically. The results were mildly supportive of the notion that the illusory effect depends on education and implied that, contrary to Jahoda's suggestion, education tends to reduce the effect. Some uncertainty about the finding lies in the lack of consistency in the subjects' responses to the stimuli. It appears that the first set of stimuli presented evoked no definite educational trend nor did the second presentation in the case of one of the two samples tested. It was only the second and the third trials in one of the samples which showed the reported decline with education. The reason for this could therefore be that groups differing in education differ also in the way in which they react to exposure to new stimuli and perhaps to the very task of being tested. The more educated subjects adapt to such a situation with greater ease and therefore the decline of the illusory effect which is associated with repeated presentation of the stimulus begins, in their case, relatively early. The less educated do not adapt as easily and the decline, if any, is therefore retarded. This creates the difference between these groups on later trials. If this is so then the experiment could be interpreted as measuring both the effect of education on the magnitude of illusion and on experimental adaptation. Such interpretation makes a definite conclusion about the influence of education impossible.

Nor do Jahoda and Stacey's (1976) observations clarify the issue. They compared Scottish and Ghanaian subjects lacking in systematic training in drawing and allied skills and found them to differ in their responses to L-type figures of the Horizontal–Vertical illusion. The Ghanaian students were more susceptible than the Scottish, a result which accorded with the Ecological hypothesis. Counterparts of these subjects who had had the appropriate training did not, however, differ. The results thus suggest that the cultural differences in susceptibility to the illusion may perhaps be overcome by training and that they may be consequences of learning; and therefore that the environment hypothesis is plausible.

But this suggestion is also weakish for we do not know to what extent subjects' perceptual skills affected their choice of training; whether, for example, only those pupils who had outstanding spatial abilities chose to undergo training in subjects using such skills and, if so, whether this tendency was equally strong in both cultures.

OTHER HYPOTHESES TESTED INTERCULTURALLY

The main two hypotheses discussed related to the effects of the ecological exposure (the Ecological hypothesis) and of experience with rectangular objects (the Carpentered World hypothesis).

Other hypotheses have also been put forward to explain cross-cultural differences in susceptibility to illusions. Rivers' early notions have already been discussed. His suggestion that attention may be an important factor has been reviewed by Doob (1966), who thought that the more analytic attitude the non-Western populations have may be responsible for their lesser susceptibility to illusions. Segall *et al.* (1966, p. 184) made little of this suggestion since for them it lacked the support of a plausible ecological condition which would provide a functional hypothesis.

Davis and Carlson (1970), on the other hand, subjected the idea of the dominant role of attentional factors in cross-cultural differences in perception of the Muller-Lyer illusion to an empirical investigation. The procedure used by them involved two variants of instructions which differed in the extent to which they drew the subject's attention to the lines which had to be compared. The results obtained were inconclusive. The strongest and in a way most surprising effect is the significantly lower susceptibility to illusions observed in the Ugandan students than in both Western groups *and* in a sample of rural Banyakole adults. Another noteworthy finding is that the magnitude of the effect varies with types of stimuli used, an observation already reported by Bonte. Davis *et al.* regard the difference between their two African samples as being confirmatory of Davis's (1970) earlier report that more sophisticated subjects make more discriminating judgements and hence are less prone to the illusion. Granted that this is so the reported finding is in agreement with Segall *et al.'s* hypothesis, provided one can justify the lesser potency of such sophistication in the West and thus explain the yawning gap between the results obtained with Ugandan and American university samples.

Another and entirely different kind of hypothesis explored in cross-cultural studies of illusions is that based on pigmentation of the eye. This is said to affect perception of patterns and hence of illusions. Since the illusions are central, as Julesz's (1971) work has shown, such an effect cannot explain them completely but it may account for cross-cultural differences in this respect. It has too a certain attraction in that it suggests that such cultural differences as have been observed are essentially peripheral; that "we are all the same below the fundus oculi" if not beneath the skin. This factor has probably contributed considerably to the popularity of the idea. The experimental investigation has not, however, obtained unambiguously supportive evidence. Since the hypothesis involves pigmentation it is physiological rather than cultural and as such will not be discussed further here. A discussion of relevant recent findings can be found in Deręgowski (1980).

There is only one reasonably firm conclusion which the data proffer; there are cross-cultural differences in proneness to illusions and hence in the manner in which the perceptual mechanisms operate, among cultures.

One cannot proceed beyond this important but rather general statement with much certainty. The nature of the factors which are responsible for the difference remains obscure. Although the evidence inclines towards the ecological and environmental influences it does not do so with much vigour and the possibility of genetic influences remains practically unexplored. Many of the studies are mutually contradictory.

The reasons for such a confusing pattern of results lie in the nature of the stimuli and the nature of the postulated influences, and the relationship between them.

There appears to be no psychologically pure version of an illusion stimulus (with the sole possible exception of the Poggendorff illusion). Various illusion figures are correlated. Nor do there appear to be cultures which are identical but for one crucial attribute which is of especial interest to a student of illusions. Thus there is fuzziness both in the definition of the experimental populations and of the experimental measures. A great degree of ambiguity resulting from the interaction of the two need not therefore offer surprise.

The importance of the general conclusion is two-fold, it confirms that the limits within which human perceptual apparatus operates are broader than those which could be determined by intra-cultural experimentation, and it suggests that there may be other stimuli than illusion figures which are perceived differently in different cultures.

Such differences would certainly be expected to arise in the case of pictures which often incorporate illusory elements to evoke perspective, but the differences may also occur with simple patterns having neither illusory properties nor the power to represent other objects.

We shall now examine cross-cultural data pertinent to perception of such patterns.

3. Perception of Patterns

Cross-cultural studies of perception of non-illusory patterns are more recent than the studies of perception of illusion figures. They are, however, psychologically important because they enable us to compare the performance of the perceptual mechanisms in various cultural groups under conditions free from the ill-understood illusory effects, and therefore responding to stimuli which cannot *a priori* be said to be affected by some unknown factor which might be culturally specific.

Although, as our review of the illusions shows, even relatively simple stimuli are subject to complex influences it is convenient for the purpose of discussion to distinguish the dominant factors, even though such conceptually distinguishable factors might not be independent. The empirical evidence to hand is such as to suggest a two-fold division of the processes hitherto investigated cross-culturally into:

(i) problems of perception of patterns *per se*, and

(ii) problems of perception of orientation of patterns.

Investigations falling in the first of these categories derive largely from similar investigations in Western psychology and constitute their elaboration and extension. Investigations falling into the second category are, on the other hand, largely derivative of work in non-Western cultures. They are cross-cultural observations of a phenomenon which apparently was largely unnoticed and therefore uninvestigated in Western cultures, probably because the phenomenon, although present there, is relatively rare and relatively less intense than in some non-Western cultures.

PROBLEMS OF PERCEPTION
OF PATTERNS

The essence of these problems can be conceived as that of perceptual organization of the data present in the stimulus. It includes therefore the problems of categorization of the stimuli, in so far as such categorization is guided by perceptual rather than other more elaborate cognitive processes, as well as the problems of perception of the characteristics of the stimuli.

There is a close and obvious relationship between the internal organization of patterns and their classification. Patterns having similar organization tend to be regarded as in a sense similar, although their overall appearance may differ considerably. Thus the letters A and U share the common organizational attribute of symmetry but share fewer common elements than the letters K and R, which do not share this attribute.

Symmetry, as many studies show (for a review see Corballis and Beale 1976), is a very salient and influential characteristic of patterns; accordingly it figures prominently in cross-cultural investigations of pattern perception.

The very fact that in "Western" cultures symmetry has been studied for a long time and by people drawn from a variety of specializations (physicists, psychologists, biologists, mathematicians and theorists of art to name the students whose concern with these issues was greatest) has led to an involved terminology which is not always consistent. Hence, before proceeding further, I propose to eliminate possible ambiguities by choosing a number of descriptive terms from those which have previously been used by others, and define them. These terms will be adhered to throughout the book.

A plane symmetrical pattern can be thought of as being a result of rotation of one of its enantiomorphs (one of the two symmetrically arranged parts) about an axis through two right angles. Two distinct types of symmetry can thus be created, depending on whether the imaginary axis is placed in the plane of the paper on which the initial pattern is drawn or normally to that plane. In the former circumstances bilateral or "mirror" symmetry results, various forms of which are illustrated in Fig. 3.1(i)–(iii); in the latter case skew symmetry results. as shown in Fig. 3.1(iv).

Of the variants of bilateral symmetry, shown in Fig. 3.1, that which arose from placing the axis of rotation in the subject's median plane (shown in Fig. 3.1(i)) is palpably the most striking and is often erroneously labelled as vertical. Such labelling is not thought objectionable or unusual in those cultures in which translation from the horizontal plane to an inclined or a vertical plane is readily and unconsciously achieved. The reader of this book, for example, would regard a printed figure of a standing horse as upright independently of whether the book were laid in front of him, on the table or held vertically in his hand. Acceptance of the convention that when the picture is laid flat the depicted object is nonetheless seen as standing and not as lying down is,

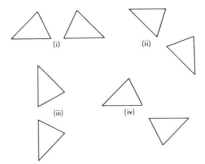

Fig. 3.1   Pairs of enantiomorphic scalene triangles illustrating the terminology used. (i), (ii) and (iii) are *bilaterally* **symmetrical. (iv) is** *skew-symmetrical.* **The three bilaterally symmetrical figures furnish examples of (i)** *median* **symmetry, (ii)** *diagonal* **symmetry and (iii)** *transverse* **symmetry.**

however, as we shall show (p. 183), not universal. Therefore whilst it is probably justifiable to regard medially symmetrical patterns as being unaffected by the inclination of the plane in which they are presented in Western cultures, wherein most of the psychological studies have been undertaken, it is not so in the case of some other cultures for which the distinctions between orientations of medially symmetrical stimuli are critical. In those cultures the term "vertical symmetry" or more strictly "median symmetry in the vertical plane" has a special meaning distinct from, say, "median symmetry in the horizontal plane". Because these distinctions are of consequence the term *median* symmetry will be used here as the more general term, references to verticality being made only when they are thought to be relevant.

A figure such as the random shape varies under normal circumstances in its perceived symmetry depending on the orientation of its axis of symmetry. When the axis of symmetry is normal to the median plane and hence lies in a transverse plane, transverse symmetry will be said to obtain. All intermediate variants can be measured in terms of the degrees of inclination of the axis of symmetry from the median, the fronto-parallel or the transverse planes, as appropriate. When the axis is set at 45° to the median plane the resulting symmetry is called diagonal symmetry. This term is illustrated in Fig. 3.1(ii). In addition to the reasons already stated this nomenclature is thought to be preferable to that sometimes used wherein median symmetry is called vertical and transverse symmetry horizontal, because it stresses the importance of the spatial relationship between the observer and the stimulus rather than that between the observer and the direction of the earth's gravitational pull. This is not to say that gravitational effects cannot influence perception of symmetry. On the contrary they can, as

c

Rock and Leaman (1963) have shown. Such influence was, however, observed under rather special conditions in which subjects could cogitate upon the task and correct their percepts accordingly; when opportunities for such adjustment are not provided and the subjects are required to respond quickly (Corballis and Rodlan 1975), the gravitational effect is absent. We are inclined to take the latter case as more typical of "perception" and hence regard Rock and Leaman's study as not affecting the proposed terminology.

Skew-symmetry presents somewhat different problems. Skew-symmetrical stimuli have not been used in psychological investigations as extensively as the bilaterally symmetrical stimuli, the entire class being typically represented by the instance created by a 180° rotation of an enantiomorph in the plane of the paper. It is not the only type of transformation possible; one can have rotations through other angles and yielding different figures. Figures so derived are also regarded by some as symmetrical provided that the rotations are pure; i.e. that they are performed about a single fixed axis. Should rotation be combined with translation skew-symmetry cannot be said to be present. (A reader wishing to determine whether a figure is skew-symmetrical as a result of such a 180° transformation may do so by connecting a number of corresponding features on the two elements of the figure by straight lines. If such lines intersect at one point the two elements are enantiomorphic and the figure is skew-symmetrical.) I shall not concern myself with transformations other than those involving 180° rotations as such have not been used extensively in cross-cultural work, and by skew-symmetry I shall mean that involving 180° rotation.

Corballis and Beale (1976) in their review of the perceptual problems call skew-symmetry *centric* and do not discuss it extensively; this is a pity for the problems associated with perception of this form of symmetry are, as Reuning and Wittman (1966) have shown, qualitatively different from those associated with perception of bilateral symmetry, and cannot be thought of as being mere variants of the latter.

It is often said that numerous instances of bilateral symmetry in nature contribute to its easy detection by human observers. Animals, it is pointed out, when looked at *en face*, many artefacts ranging from aeroplanes to whisky bottles and, perhaps most importantly, human faces are all symmetrical or very nearly so, and frequent encounters with such embodiments of symmetry facilitate detection of symmetry wherever encountered. This argument does not appear to be entirely satisfactory for several reasons:

(1) It postulates that when objects can be divided into two perceptually distinct categories, in this case symmetrical and asymmetrical,

such categories, if they occur in the environment with sufficient frequency, begin to dominate the perceptual mechanism. This seems to be an instance of an *a posteriori* argument, which is put to question by the presence of certain other criteria which on equally speculative grounds provide probably more distinctive and mutually exclusive categories in the daily environment, and which do not appear to influence perceptual processes in equal measure; e.g. *fourness*. Most animals have four legs and so have pieces of furniture, and many vehicles have four wheels; yet there is no evidence that *fourness* is more readily perceived than *threeness*, which is not found in the environment with comparable frequency. The postulate that the mere frequency with which the phenomenon is encountered is responsible for the way in which the perceptual mechanism works seems therefore implausible. This doubt grows when one reflects that although "fourness" may be readily observable whatever the point of view an observer assumes relative to an object having this characteristic, symmetry is generally observable only from a very restricted number of points of view; e.g. in the case of human beings, only when the person observed is either facing the observer or has his back turned towards him. On the grounds of pure probability there is no reason to assume that these views would be more striking than the infinite number of others. If they are, as they appear to be, then the reason for this must be elsewhere rather than in the environmental stimulation.

(2) It suggests that there is one essentially indivisible class of symmetrical stimuli. This is not so for, as will be shown, when a bilaterally symmetrical pattern is rotated in the observer's fronto-parallel plane, median symmetry and transverse symmetry are not found to lie on a simple perceptual continuum but are separated by a zone in which bilaterally symmetrical stimuli set at intermediate orientations evoke an entirely different kind of response. The two types of symmetry, median and transverse, form two distinct poles which are more easily identified than symmetries within the intermediate zone. The salience of transverse symmetry, in relation to the symmetries in the intermediate zone, cannot therefore be attributed to generalization from median symmetry and requires postulation of another environmental influence. This would be difficult to find for transverse symmetry does not appear to be as common as median symmetry.

(3) Furthermore, and this is probably the most damaging consideration, such speculations are not sustained by any empirical evidence obtained in the course of cross-cultural work. Contrary to expectations, subjects drawn from cultures where symmetrical artefacts are relatively rare show greater tendency to render bilaterally symmetrical stimuli

medially symmetrical than do their counterparts derived from cultures where such artefacts are relatively common (see p. 81).

These objections to the suggested environmental determinants strengthen, by default, the only alternative argument available; that the perceptual effects associated with symmetry are to a large extent determined by the inherent features of the perceptual mechanism.

This does not necessarily imply that culture has little influence upon perception of symmetry and hence perception of patterns because it is possible that cultures differ in the extent to which they require their members to attend to symmetry and to regard it as a critical feature. There may also exist an association between different genotypes and cultures so that the percepts may be the result of genetic determination or the interactions between the genetic and cultural vectors.

Simple matrices are widely accepted as tools for investigation of pattern perception. They consist of rectangular or square grids of cells, each of which can be either filled or left empty so that a desired pattern is created. Attneave (1955) used such matrices in one of the earliest investigations of the applicability of information theory to perceptual processing, in the course of which, just as in Paraskevopoulos' (1968) later studies, symmetrical and asymmetrical patterns were used. This work showed that although symmetry and especially median symmetry is a feature of stimuli which is readily abstracted by most perceivers, there are differences in the effectiveness of such abstraction among various groups. Children classify symmetrical figures faster than asymmetrical figures and take shorter time to find a symmetrical figure than to find an asymmetrical figure, but the differences between symmetrical and asymmetrical figures are larger in the case of older children than in the case of younger children, suggesting that the ability to perceive symmetry is correlated with age (Forsman 1967). This correlation is confirmed by Paraskevopoulos' study of reproduction from memory of simple dot patterns. Children of about six years of age were found to be capable of making use of patterns having *both* median and transverse symmetry but it was not until about a year later that median symmetry on its own provided sufficient guide to effective perceptual organization, and transverse symmetry on its own did not become effective until four years after that, i.e. at about the age of 11 years.

These Western studies suggest the possibility of a two-fold kind of inter-cultural difference. There may be differences in performance at various age levels, and there may be differences in the rate of change of performance with age.

A comparison of the responses of illiterate Kpelle children from Liberia and American school children on a simple task of estimating the number of dots either randomly scattered or arranged in patterns confirms that such differences are indeed present (Gay and Cole 1967). Fig. 3.2 shows the responses made by these groups when required to estimate the number of dots exposed for a quarter of a second. There appears little difference between the Kpelle responses to the patterned and the unpatterned stimuli. Little use seems to have been made of the organization of the pattern. This was clearly not so in the case of the American sample. Its performance was superior to that of the Kpelle, and for arrays consisting of six dots or less the regularities of patterns have practically eliminated all errors.

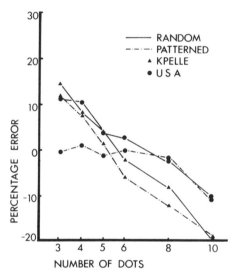

Fig 3.2   **Graph showing the percentage of errors made by Kpelle and American children when reproducing simple patterns. Kpelle responses to random and to patterned arrays are strikingly similar. This is not so in the case of the American responses.**

A dismissal of this contrast as obvious because the Kpelle were unschooled would be mistaken, not only because the experiment does not permit one to attribute the effect simply to schooling, but above all because it would miss the essential point of this cross-cultural comparison, that such observations as those reported above, derived from American samples, about the ages at which children are likely to attend and make use of symmetry do not have universal validity and therefore fail to describe adequately the capacities of the human perceptual mechanism.

More detailed evidence obtained from the Kpelle and from American subjects by the same group of workers (Cole *et al.* 1968) under essentially the same conditions confirms and extends the above observations. The responses of the two cultural groups differ to a negligible extent when made to small *and* to large numbers of random dots, (e.g. three and ten dots) presented in a random arrangement. Large differences in correctness of responses occur, however, in the intermediate range, the Kpelle making many more erroneous responses. When the two groups are compared on their responses to patterned stimuli a similar absence of large differences at the extremities of the range and their presence in the middle prevails; again, Kpelle scores are lower in the intermediate range. The results can probably be explained by the American subjects' ability to encode the patterns provided and to impose their own idiosyncratic structure upon patterns which in the experimenter's view are random. When only a small number of dots is presented such strategies are not really needed since the pattern being simple, it can be recalled anyhow, and hence the Kpelle, who do not use these strategies, perform about as well as the Americans; when the number of dots becomes large, on the other hand, the strategies can no longer offer help and hence the American performance drops to the Kpelle level. This interpretation is confirmed by considering the nature of errors. These, as the authors point out, show the influence of the patterning in the case of the responses to the patterned stimuli by the Americans but not by the Kpelle. The patterned stimuli used were symmetrical, consisting of two symmetrical rows of dots. The results can therefore be thought of as indicating a cultural difference in perception of symmetry, but they can also be thought of as indicative of a failure to realize that, in patterned stimuli, the number can be estimated by noticing the number in one of the equal rows and taking account of the number of such rows. The difference between the responses made by the two groups to random sets of dots cannot, however, be thus explained and support the notion that generally the Kpelle were less expert in the perception of the patterns used in the experiment.

If the symmetry is not taken into account, then with a task wherein a reproduction of patterns is called for, representatives of the Kpelle and similar cultures should do about equally well on symmetrical and asymmetrical patterns. An attempt to test this hypothesis by Deręgowski (1972) can only be described as inconclusive. Zambian children were presented with six types of pattern and required to reproduce them. The only difference observed was that between the medially-symmetrical and side-by-side patterns, the former being easier to reproduce. No differences were observed among these and other stimuli (transversely symmetrical, up-down repeated, random). The square matrices which were used to create the patterns were rather large (6 x 6 cells) and it may be, and the evidence below confirms this suspicion, that the task was simply too difficult; that it fell beyond the zone where structuring helped and is similar to the case with patterns having ten dots in Cole *et al.'s* experiments just described. Symmetry, it would appear, does not dominate perceptual organization under all circumstances.

Any interpretation in the simple terms of perception or non-perception of symmetry becomes even more questionable when the other variants of structured stimuli are introduced. A comparison between Scottish school children (seventh grade of primary school; mean age 11·7 years) and Bukusu school boys (first form of secondary school; mean age 18·4 years) from Western Kenya (Bentley 1977) required reproduction of patterns of dots drawn in 6 x 6 matrices. Random, medially symmetrical and transversely symmetrical patterns were used as well as patterns symmetrical about a diagonal of the matrix, and skew-symmetrical patterns.

The comparisons of responses showed a clear difference between the two cultures on two of the patterns: random and skew-symmetrical. On both of these, performance of the Bukusu fell below that of the Scots. On the remaining three types of pattern there was no such difference between the cultures.

The evidence for cultural difference on perception of pattern is thus reinforced. The Bukusu school boys, just as the Kpelle, perform less well on random patterns, which presumably call for spontaneous perceptual organization. Furthermore, they are less able to exploit the organization of the pattern when it takes the form of skew-symmetry. These difficulties cannot be simply dismissed as resulting from lack of comprehension or lack of experimental experience on the part of the Bukusu, because, as has been said, they performed about as well as the Scots on the other patterns. Indeed, the sequence of pattern difficulty is exactly the same in both groups and is as follows:

(Median symmetry; Transverse symmetry); (Diagonal symmetry); (Skew-symmetry; Random Pattern).

The types of symmetry which are bracked together in the above list were not found to differ from each other in terms of the evoked responses.

Further investigations of perceptual organization have been conducted by attempting to vary the salience of median symmetry of the stimuli and by introduction of repeated stimuli. The latter are constructed by repeating the same pattern twice; either side by side thus, LL, or in any other orientation. Such side by side repetition may be seen as being related to median symmetry, but whereas in the case of the median symmetry an enantiomorph is flipped over to create a pattern, here an element is slid along in the plane of the pattern. When the enantiomorph and the element are identical the information contained in the resulting figures is precisely determined and equal to the information contained in the initial pattern. The figures differ only in the type of transformation involved in their creation. This makes them especially suitable for investigation of perceptual processes, as the studies reported below show.

It is not possible to deduce from the reported results whether the extent to which bilateral symmetry influences the responses can be enhanced by introduction of other cues stressing or disguising its presence, or whether, once symmetry is present, it becomes by and large an overriding consideration. The Western data on this issue are ambiguous. It appears (Deręgowski 1971a) that in 4 x 4 square matrices introduction of a dividing line coincident with the axis of symmetry has no significant effect. On the other hand, when the enantiomorphs differ in colour then symmetrical patterns are reproduced less well, but so are repeated patterns whose elements also differ in colour. This can therefore be thought of as a general effect not specifically associated with symmetry.

A comparison of bilaterally symmetrical patterns and repeated patterns reported in the same study shows that the former are superior when medially symmetrical patterns and side-be-side repeated patterns were compared. No analogous effects were observed in comparing reproduction of the transversely symmetrical patterns and the corresponding repeated patterns. The superiority of performance on medially symmetrical patterns as contrasted with that on repeated patterns has been investigated further by Corballis and Rodlan (1974), whose results showed that an increase of separation between the elements leads to a change of performance, with the symmetrical pattern evoking fewer correct responses than the corresponding repeated pattern. The effect of symmetry is decreased, it seems, if the perception of the pattern as a unit is made more difficult. This is confirmed by Bentley's (1975) observation that when medially symmetrical matrices had straight lines imposed upon them this affected reproductions of the patterns made by the Bukusu school children. The imposition of lines coincident with the axis of symmetry (a condition identical with that employed by Deręgowski) led to better responses than those obtained with a simple matrix, but when oblique lines were imposed they appeared to decrease the effect of symmetry. Examination of the errors made by Bentley's subjects confirms this interpretation. Erroneous symmetrical responses constitute about 33% of the errors made in response to the stimuli in which median symmetry of the entire array was preserved, the imposed line being placed in the median plane, and only 4% of the errors made in response to the stimuli in which the imposed line was oblique.

The cross-cultural evidence pertaining to perception of patterns presented in matrices suggests the following general conclusion. The tendency to perceive inherent redundancies in the structure of the stimulus pattern is present to some degree in all cultures; but this degree varies considerably, especially in the extent to which subjects are able to encode patterns lacking strong inherent organizational characteristics such as symmetry.

PATCO STUDIES

Another method of investigating perception of symmetry has been devised by Hector (1958). It is of impressive simplicity and should probably have attracted wider attention than it has hitherto done. The Pattern Completion (Patco) test, as the method is called, consists of a series of drawings (Fig. 3.3), each drawing showing three narrow

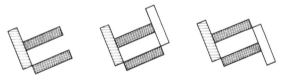

Fig. 3.3   A Patco test figure and two possible symmetrical responses. In the first response the *fiche* has been so placed as to lead to a bilaterally symmetrical pattern, in the second so as to lead to a skew-symmetrical pattern.

oblongs. The subjects' task is to place a fourth oblong, which is identical with the other three, in such a manner as to render the pattern symmetrical. This fourth oblong is provided to the subjects in the form of a thin metal fiche. Once the oblong is in the position chosen by the subject, the subject either inserts his pencil into two small holes made on the longitudinal axis of the fiche or draws around the fiche and thus records his response. He is then free to proceed to the next figure of the test. This procedure, apart from its very neatness, has the additional advantage of being suitable for group administration, and was indeed used in this manner.

The original version of Patco consisted of 60 stimuli divided into two subsets. Stimuli 1–30 were to be completed by creation of bilaterally symmetrical patterns; stimuli 31–60, on the other hand, were to be completed by creation of skew-symmetrical patterns. All figures were printed in black.

Subsequently several other variants of the test were designed. Hector (1959) himself introduced a coloured version in which the symmetrical part is printed in a different colour than the odd stimulus which has to be matched by the appropriate placement of the fiche. This version was found to be easier than the monochromatic version. Later Tekane (1963) used a variant of stimuli which would be rendered either skew or laterally symmetrical.

One can put forward an argument that subjects responding correctly to Patco patterns do so by consciously employing a purely mechanical procedure.

Such a solution of the bilateral symmetry problem could be as follows:

(1) Find the pair of rectangles which define an axis of symmetry. With three rectangles on the drawing there are three possible pairings, but only some of these may yield the axis. (In some versions of the test this step presents little difficulty since the oblong to be paired by the fiche differs from the others either in colour or by having the pencil holes marked on it.)

(2) Given the line of symmetry defined by the two rectangles chosen, place the fiche in such a position that it forms an enantiomorph of the third oblong.

An analogous mechanistic procedure can be applied to the stimuli intended to evoke skew-symmetrical responses.

However it seems unlikely that subjects, especially unsophisticated subjects, follow consciously analytic procedures. Nevertheless such theoretical analyses are useful because they suggest a possible classification of errors.

Consider Fig. 3.4: it shows a stimulus pattern as well as the distribution of responses obtained from a sample of municipal policemen from Johannesburg. Each of the lines connecting two dots indicates a position occupied by the metal oblong, the dots corresponding to the position of holes in the oblong. Therefore each line connecting a pair of such dots shows the direction in which the metal oblong was placed. There are apparently two large homogeneous groups of responders. The larger of these completes correctly the symmetrical W pattern. There is therefore a relatively large group of subjects who try to produce such a pattern. But the results also show that there is a degree of imprecision in their responses since the inclination of the axis of the metal fiche in this group of responses varies from about 32° to about 65°. Many of these subjects, it would appear, correctly identify the axis of symmetry but place their response oblong imprecisely. The second homogeneous set of responses

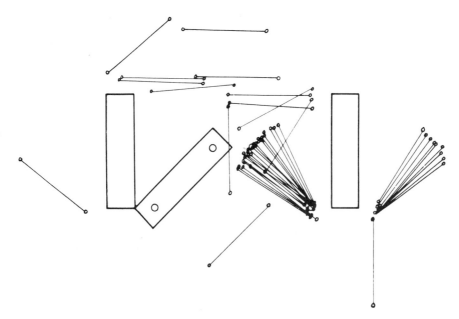

Fig. 3.4   Dr Crawford-Nutt and the National Institute for Personnel Research, policemen to a Patco test figure shown. (With acknowledgements to Dr Crawford-Nutt and the National Institute for Personnel Research, Johannesburg.)

is that which has led to the creation of a repeated pattern in the form of the sequence, LL. Here too a degree of imprecision is clearly observable, but, more importantly, these responses show that the axis of symmetry has not been identified by the subjects who reproduced the existing pattern in place of an enantiomorph. Finally, there is a number of widely scattered responses. This set shows little internal cohesion. It contains a large number of responses which are seemingly random but which on close inspection appear to be lawful, for they are either nearly parallel or nearly perpendicular to one of the oblongs forming the original pattern. Neither the axis of symmetry nor the essential unit of the pattern seems to be taken into consideration by the subjects who made these responses. Similar distinction between various types of error are presented in Tekane's (1961) analysis of error which Bantu industrial workers made in response to Patco figures.

The percentages of various types of error observed were as follows, (n = 1368):

(1) Inaccurate placing of oblong in more or less the correct position: 26·4%.

(2) Repetition of the configuration of the two oblongs of the same colour: 6·9%.

(3) Placement of the response fiche on the side of the intended symmetry line occupied by its intended enantiomorph: 13·2%.

(4) Placement of the fiche orthogonally to one of the three drawn oblongs, but excluding the three categories given above: 40·1%.

(5) Random placement: 8·2%.

(6) No response: 5·2%.

These groupings do not correspond entirely to those which we have just described in a sample of responses of Johannesburg police, but the same elements can be found in both of them. Inspection of the two sets of responses shows considerable differences in the frequencies with which various types of error were made. The low frequency of the errors of the fourth category in the responses made by the policemen in combination with rather high frequency of the errors of the second category are especially notable and suggest that the samples may differ in the extent to which they can structure stimuli: careful and detailed analysis of errors may reveal a perfect scale analogous to that described by Jahoda (1978) in his analysis of orientation errors.

Existence of inter-cultural differences in precision is implicit in Fridjhon's (1961) data. He noted that the responses which Bushmen made to Patco stimuli differed from those of white subjects by being less precise. "Bushmen . . . tend to put the fourth oblong in only more or less the right position, the white sample as members of a far more complex and demanding culture were more exacting in their performance." Similarly, but in a different context, Jahoda (1956) thought that the orientation in which Ghanaian subjects placed Kohs' patterns was primarily determined by their greater tolerance of imprecision (see p. 87). On the other hand, differences in accuracy which might arise are well illustrated by the data which we have just reviewed.

I shall now consider the important perceptual difference between bilateral and skew-symmetry, to which I have already alluded. This difference and its possible implications are discussed at some length in Reuning and Wittmann's (1963) study. The data considered by them were obtained by means of Patco stimuli from trainee teachers. These showed that the bilateral symmetry was not, contrary to expectations, found to be the easier of the two. The teachers, when asked to complete Patco patterns so as to render them bilaterally symmetrical, performed less well than when asked to complete the same patterns and rendering them skew-symmetrical. When left entirely free to choose their manner of completion subjects tended to construct skew-symmetrical solutions relatively more frequently. In addition, more skew-symmetrical responses were made in error when bilateral responses were called for than bilateral errors were made when skew-symmetrical responses were called for.

These results are contrary to those reported earlier by Tekane (1963), which showed no evidence of greater frequency of skew-symmetrical responses made by black children and black illiterate miners. When the same set of Patco stimuli as that used by Reuning and Wittmann (1963) was used with those samples the miners were found to make fewer symmetrical responses of either kind and were found to favour bilaterally symmetrical responses, whilst the relative frequencies of responses of the schoolchildren showed no definite preference. The absence of any evidence to show that skew-symmetry was preferred in either group seems acceptable, as far as the influence of ecological factors is concerned: it would be difficult to conceive of environments where subjects are exposed to skew-symmetrical stimuli with greater frequency than to bilaterally symmetrical stimuli. Reuning and Wittmann's data, showing greater frequency of skew-symmetrical responses, pose this very problem.

In order to solve the problem the authors examined responses to Patco stimuli obtained from a variety of populations, paying special attention to the relative size of scores attained in response to problems requiring bilateral, and problems requiring rotational solutions. The difference between the scores on the former and the scores on the latter, they note, is not constant in all the populations, but decreases in the following order: (i) Knysna forest workers (intellectually backward), (ii) black mine workers (unschooled and industrially inexperienced), (iii) black mine workers (random sample), (iv) Kalahari Bushmen, (v) black mine workers (schooled and industrially experienced), (vi) pupil pilot candidates, (vii) black mine workers (scoring high on a general ability test), (viii) white teacher training college students. This shows, as the authors point out, a negative correlation between development and the difference between "bilateral" and "rotational" (or skew) scores. Likewise the same data show that as the overall score increases the difference between these scores decreases.

These considerations, the authors suggest, show an essential difference in the manner in which the two types of symmetry are influenced by cultural and environmental factors. This is represented schematically in Fig. 3.5, which shows a steady increase of the "bilateral" scores throughout the development range, and somewhat more rapid changes of "rotational" scores with development. The "rotational" scores, unlike the "bilateral" scores, are confined to the upper part of the developmental range. The graph also shows a total score curve obtained by addi-

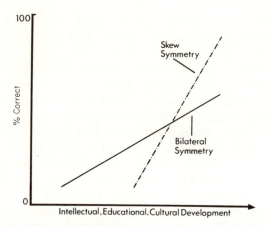

Fig. 3.5   Reuning and Wittmann's (1963) notion of the relationship between two types of symmetry (bilateral and skew) and development.

tion of the "bilateral" and "rotational" scores. The hypothetical curves inspired by the experimental data illustrate the authors' contention that: "the *bilateral* part (of the total score) is correlated with intelligence and not, or only slightly, with differences in education and cultural level; the *rotational* part is correlated with level of education, cultural development *and* with general intelligence". Bilateral symmetry, they point out, is frequent in natural and man-made environments; skew-symmetry is almost exclusively a characteristic of man-made objects. One cannot avoid being exposed to bilateral symmetry and gaining a degree of perceptual familiarity with it; on the other hand, skew-symmetry can only be commonly experienced in industrial cultures, but even there the experience is not as prevalent as that of bilateral symmetry. It is of course intellectually accessible to individuals specially gifted in this respect in all cultures.

The apparent contradiction between Tekane's results and those of Reuning and Wittmann can therefore be explained by the difference in the subjects tested. Both Tekane samples, the illiterate miners and the secondary school pupils, were less intellectually sophisticated than the college students used by Reuning and Wittmann.

Olson's (1970) observations of cross-cultural differences in ability to reproduce one of the simplest of skew-symmetrical figures, a row of dots lying along a diagonal of a square matrix, agree with Reuning and Wittmann's suggestion of considerable cultural influence upon ability to perceive such figures. All of the Canadian children tested by Olson could reproduce a diagonal by the age of six years, only about 70% of the Kipsigis and Logoli children from East Africa could do so by the age of

12. There was a distinct difference between the schooled and the unschooled Kenyan children, the schooled children being consistently superior at the task. The explanation which Olson offers for this finding is concordant with that suggested by Reuning and Wittmann: the Logoli and Kipsigis cultures do not foster the relevant perceptual skill, which is only acquired in the course of formal schooling, whilst Canadian children acquire it even before entering school.

Cross-cultural differences in perceptual difficulties associated with skew-symmetrical stimuli have also been reported by Deręgowski (1972a). These are shown by the responses made to the Kohs' type figures. Patterns D, E, G and H shown in Fig. 3.6 consist of identical elements. The subjects have to arrange these elements in order to reproduce the patterns. Figure 3.6 G is, as can be seen, skew-symmetrical. When tested on this task Zambian and Icelandic samples built correct patterns (i.e. patterns having correct arrangement of tiles but not necessarily correctly oriented) in the proportions given in the table below. It is apparent from the table that for this series of stimuli the skew-symmetrical forms present the greatest difficulty to the Zambian subjects, but no such effect is observed in the Icelandic sample, which seems to have reached a "ceiling" as far as these particular stimuli are concerned.

Related work on pattern reproduction which shares the elements of both the Patco and the Kohs' Blocks tests was carried out by Bentley (1975) in Scotland and Kenya. The Kenyan subjects were of the Bukusu tribe. The patterns used were similar to those of the Patco test. The essential difference between the standard Patco procedure and that used by Bentley was that whilst in the former a single member has to be placed to complete the pattern, in the latter the entire pattern of four members had to be reproduced by a subject who was shown the stimulus array for three seconds. Three types of pattern were used: random, symmetrical about a plane intersecting subjects' median plane at 45° ("diagonally symmetrical") and symmetrical about two planes intersecting subjects' median plane at 45° ("symmetrical about both diagonals"). The main differences between Scottish and Bukusu school children were that the Scots made fewer reproduction errors and that their erroneous responses contained fewer errors of rotation than those of the Bukusu of the same age. When the samples were equated in terms of years of schooling, however, the difference in the number of errors made was found to be no longer statistically significant. This result can be explained by postulating the importance of schooling or of relatively different rates of maturation of the two samples, or perhaps by an interaction between the factors of age and schooling. There were also

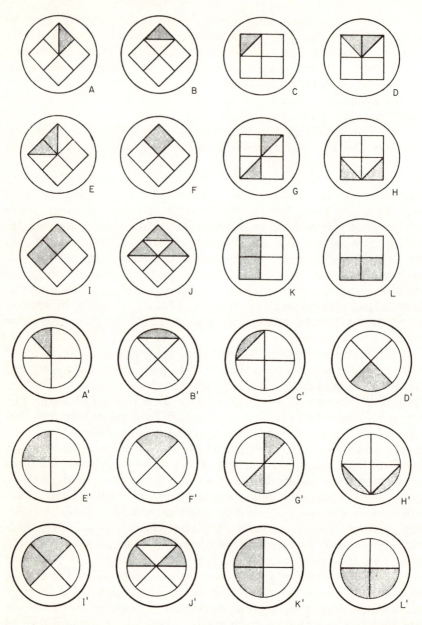

Fig. 3.6   **Kohs type patterns used by Derçgowski (1972). A–L show traditional square patterns. A'–L' show circular patterns introduced to eliminate the effect of stability.**

Table I. *Percentage of correct responses to each of the stimuli used.*

Stimulus (Fig. 3.6)	Sample Icelandic (n = 6)	Zambian (n = 24)
D	83	46
E	100	50
G	100	17
H	100	42
D′	100	92
E′	100	88
G′	100	63
H′	100	92

striking similarities between the responses of the two groups. In both groups the number of errors made decreased with age and schooling and in both the orientation errors made are such as to lead to median, transverse or "wrong-diagonal" symmetries. The combined approximate ratios of frequencies of the three types of erroneous settings of otherwise correct responses were Median: Transverse: Wrong-diagonal— 14: 5: 1.

There appears to be little variation of the frequency of errors of orientation with age in the Scottish sample within the investigated age range of five to over 11 years. The Bukusu responses do not appear to differ greatly from the Scottish responses in this respect in the two younger groups, but unlike Scottish responses their number of orientation errors continues to increase with age and is greater than the Scottish both for the 9–10 years group and the 11+ group. This cross-cultural comparison which şhows that, unlike the errors of reproduction, errors of orientation cannot be eliminated by taking number of years of schooling into account, raises the general issue of the relationship between a pattern and its orientation. Is the orientation an attribute of a pattern which is encoded inseparably as such, or is it perceived independently of the pattern?

Bentley postulates that Rock (1973) is in error in suggesting that the description of a pattern includes its orientation. Both the orientation errors observed, which suggest that the pattern has been remembered although orientation has been forgotten, and reproductions of wrong shapes which are so placed as to preserve the nature of symmetry of the original stimuli argue, he maintains, for a degree of independence between these factors.

Another distinct group of perceptual studies in which perception of symmetry has been said to be a major factor comprises studies of discrimination learning.

Mach (1897), one of the earliest students of symmetry and associated phenomena, remarked that the two enantiomorphs are easily confused because they probably evoke similar sensations, the sensations being similar because of the symmetry of the human visual apparatus. Corballis and Beale (1976) disagree with this. They do not think it probable that salience of symmetry and comparison of mirror images are closely related. They argue that "If an observer were actually confused about which way round each half of the pattern was then he should confuse symmetry with repetition, or at least perceive them as similar. Yet symmetrical patterns do not look like repeated ones." Now, it is palpably true that the repeated patterns are strikingly different from symmetrical patterns, but it is also true that the elements of these patterns differing in orientation are similar, as indicated by the notorious b–d–p–q confusions, which children often experience and to which Mach refers. Such difficulties show unambiguously that as far as the perceptual mechanism is concerned there must be a degree of similarity between b and d, say, to create uncertainty as to how one should respond to each of these symbols presented on their own. Derȩgowski and Ellis (1974) have suggested that the distinction between the similarity of the elements forming a pattern and the symmetry of the patterns formed of such elements is important to understanding of subjects' performance in traditional experiments on discrimination learning. Their data showed that when Zambian children were presented with random polygons for two seconds and then required to identify the polygons which they have seen in a set of similar polygons including both the figures originally used and their enantiomorphs, the errors, when these were made, were not random: enantiomorphs are chosen more frequently than one would expect by chance. The tendency to confuse enantiomorphs was thus confirmed with stimuli and on a population different than those hitherto investigated. A further experiment compared the ease with which discrimination is learned between a pair of traditional medially symmetrical shapes forming a set, such as that used by Rudel and Teuber (1963) and Serpell (1971), and between a pair of asymmetrical enantiomorphic figures. The former of these two sets was used because it provided a link with earlier studies and because figures forming it were each medially symmetrical, but when presented to the subjects formed asymmetrical arrangements thus contrasting with the other set, wherein individual figures were asymmetrical but formed medially symmetrical sets (Fig. 3.7). The traditional discrimination learning procedure was followed. Two enantiomorphic plaques were presented to each subject, one of the plaques being arbitrarily denoted as "right"; the child then had to recognize this "right" plaque on a series of presentations, on each of

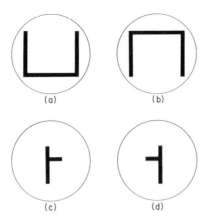

Fig 3.7   **Discrimination learning stimuli used by Deręgowski and Ellis (1974). The stimuli were used in pairs. The upper pair was presented either in the "a–b" arrangement shown or in the "b–a" arrangement. Analogously the lower pair was presented either as shown ("c–d") or in a transposed order "d–c".**

which it appeared in one of the two different arrangements. The subject was told whether each of his responses was correct or otherwise and was judged to have learned discrimination if he reached an arbitrary criterion defined in terms of a length of run of correct responses before making 50 responses. The number of responses he made was taken to be his learning score. The total number of responses allowed was also arbitrarily limited to 50, and subjects who had failed to reach the criterion by their fiftieth response were said to have failed to learn. Scottish children, it was found, learned to discriminate between the symmetrical stimuli with greater ease than between the asymmetrical stimuli. These data in combination with other published data led Deręgowski and Ellis to argue that in a discrimination learning task of the kind generally used the ease of learning is affected by both the nature of the individual elements and of the entire array. The sequence of symmetries – median, transverse and skew – correlates, they contend, positively with the ease of learning when it pertains to individual stimuli and negatively with the ease of learning when it pertains to the arrangements of the pairs of stimuli presented at each trial. The two factors thus oppose each other. A table of their interactions can be drawn (Fig. 3.8), which shows the effect of each of the possible combinations of the factors upon learning.

    The ease of learning can thus be seen as depending on two factors, (i) the ease with which the "correct" figure *per se* can be encoded and subsequently recognized and (ii) the effect of the combination of the

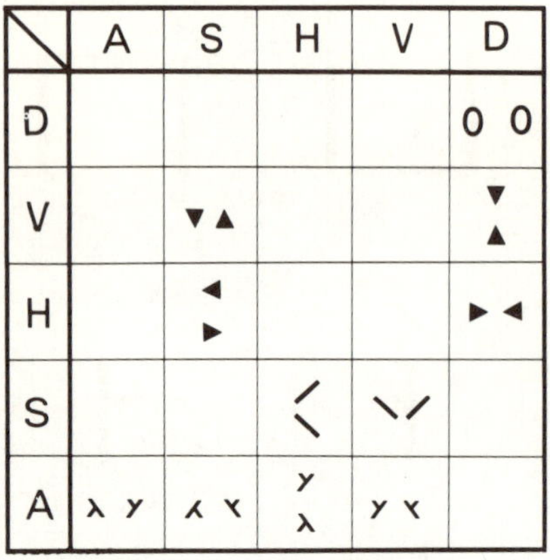

	A	S	H	V	D
D					0 0
V		▼ ▲			▼ ▲
H		◄ ►			► ◄
S			<	\/	
A	λ ʏ	ʌ ʏ	ʏ λ	ʏ ʏ	

Fig. 3.8   A table summarizing the relationship between the symmetry of the enantiomorphs and the symmetry of the patterns which they form, as postulated by Deręgowski and Ellis (1974).

"correct" and "incorrect" figures, which are always presented together, on the ease of recognition. Medially symmetrical figures are easy to encode and therefore one would expect them to yield better performance than, say, asymmetrical stimuli. Thus, *pari passu*, "U" should be easier to recognize than "R". On the other hand, symmetrical arrangements of two figures will present a greater obstacle to identification of the "correct" stimulus than an asymmetrical arrangement.

The effectiveness with which a stimulus is encoded can also be described in terms of interaction between the individual forms of stimuli and the three basic enantiomorphs associated with them. These three enantiomorphs of a stimulus are such that together with the stimulus they form a pattern symmetrical both medially and transversely. The three enantiomorphs are: one which would render the stimulus medially symmetrical, one which would render the stimulus transversely symmetrical and one which would render the stimulus skew-symmetrical. In the case of a simple asymmetrical figure such as b the corresponding enantimorphs are (Type 1) d; (Type 2) p and (Type 3) q. This scheme when applied to symmetrical figures yields some enantiomorphs which are identical with the initial stimulus and some which differ from it. Thus in the case of a stimulus symmetrical about the observer's median plane, such as U, the enantiomorphs are (1) U, (2) ∩ and (3) ∩; in the case of a stimulus symmetrical about a transverse plane, such as C, the corresponding enantiomorphs are (1) Ɔ, (2) C and (3) Ɔ ; whilst in the case of a skew-symmetrical stimulus such as / the enantiomorphs are (1)\, (2) \ and (3) /. Studies of discrimination learning suggest that the confusions are most frequent in the case of the two stimuli forming a pair which is identical with the combination of the stimulus and its enantiomorph of Type 1, less frequent if the pair of stimuli is identical with the combination of the stimulus and its enantiomorph of Type 2 and least frequent when it is identical with the combination of the stimulus and its enantiomorph of Type 3. Accordingly one would expect those enantiomorphs, which we postulate to be created when stimuli are presented on their own, to decrease in magnitude of their effect in the order: Type 1, Type 2 and Type 3. Furthermore, it appears plausible that when such an enantiomorph is identical with the stimulus it reinforces the stimulus; when it is not, it does not do so but reinforces an appropriate alternative pattern. Therefore in the case of a pattern, such as b, there are no reinforcing enantiomorphs, but each of the enantiomorphs suggests a different alternative and these alternatives decrease in their strength as follows: d, p and q. For the other patterns considered above the corresponding effects are as follows:

Figure U.

Reinforcing enantiomorphs: Type 1

Non-reinforcing enantiomorphs. Type 2 and Type 3

Figure C.

Reinforcing enantiomorphs: Type 2

Non-reinforcing enantiomorphs: Type 1 and Type 3

Figure /.

Reinforcing enantiomorphs: Type 3

Non-reinforcing enantiomorphs: Type 1 and Type 2

This suggests that patterns exemplified by U are likely to be remembered better than those of the C type and much better than those of the / type. Furthermore, this schema shows that in the case of the oblique line the original stimulus and the identical enantiomorph are finely balanced by the other two enantiomorphs, which agrees well with the difficulties normally experienced when discrimination between two obliques is called for.

Since, however, ail the relevant data have been obtained from children, the schema may not be generally applicable. Indeed in view of Reuning and Wittmann's Patco studies which we have just described, it would be surprising if such generality were to prevail, for one would expect the subjects who detect skew-symmetrical patterns with greater ease than bilaterally symmetrical patterns to be relatively more influenced by the former type of symmetry than the subjects, such as children, who incline towards bilaterally symmetrical patterns.

The above discussion suggests a relationship between symmetry and confusion of "mirror images", and a theoretical mechanism responsible for the perceptual phenomena in question. In so doing it inclines towards Mach's rather than Corballis and Beale's view of the problem. It treats the problem as essentially that of perception rather than, as Corballis and Beale would, of labelling. It is not intended, however, to imply that labelling is of no consequence whatsoever, for there may be several factors influencing responses. The clearest indications of the effect of labelling are perhaps those reported by Barosso and Braine (1974), who required subjects to complete an array by placing a missing picture of a pair. The pictures were meaningful representations of single objects (e.g. a doll) and were used to match either (i) identical or (ii) *other* (e.g. a tree) meaningful pictures. The results show a similar pattern of errors under both conditions and this is used to sustain an argument that as "mirror-image" errors can occur with non-enantiomorphic image stimuli; *ergo*, the *mirror* image confusions do not really arise. The explanation by the authors that young children, aged about three years, match meaningful pictures by considering their clearly definable tops or bottoms is plausible, but the extension of this argument to abstract figures seems questionable, not only because it is difficult to argue that, say, dot matrices or random polygons have equally unam- biguously defined "top" and "bottom" features, but also because the combination of two such matrices, for example, forms a perceptual unit of much greater coherence than a juxtaposition of two self-contained drawings. The observed performance on the meaningful figures can be thought of as an instance of *perceptual* separation of the two figures similar in its effect to that of both physical and perceptual separation of two geometric patterns. When such patterns are well separated the fact that they are enantiomorphic remains unnoticed (Corballis and Rod- lan 1974). Similarly when the two enantiomorphs differ in colour, the number of errors occurring when the matrix is being reproduced increases (Deręgowski 1971a).

It thus seems plausible that the use of representational stimuli removes the effect of basic perceptual organization almost entirely and that other factors including labelling then hold sway.

Serpell (1971) was probably the first to investigate discrimination learning cross-culturally. His procedure was derivative from that of Rudel and Teuber (1963) and was in principle similar to that described in the introductory paragraphs of this section. The stimuli used were simple geometric figures on square plaques. The figures, which formed pairs, were: (i) a short vertical line and a short horizontal line, (ii) two short mutually orthogonal diagonal lines, (iii) two U-shaped figures which could be presented either so that they were medially or trans- versely symmetrical. These stimuli were arranged in a variety of ways.

The vertical and the horizontal lines (i) when paired, yielded asymmetrical arrangements; the diagonal lines (ii) when paired, yielded arrangements symmetrical about either the median or transverse plane and the U-shapes (iii) could be arranged to form either patterns symmetrical about both median or transverse planes, or skew-symmetrical patterns. Serpell compared his data obtained from urban Zambian children with those obtained by Rudel and Teuber. The order of the difficulty of patterns was the same in both groups. The horizontal and vertical bars were easier to discriminate when they formed a skew-symmetrical pattern than when they formed a pattern symmetrical about both major planes. However, the samples differed considerably (by about two years) in the age at which they reached comparable performance, the Zambian children being consistently behind the American children. Furthermore, Zambian rural children tended to lag behind Zambian urban children by a similar amount. This lag, Serpell suggests, may be a result of a difference in "intellectual stimulation" which the children experience in their homes and nurseries. Such explanation is unfortunately difficult to verify, unless some of the relevant stimulation is more closely specified, and such specification is by no means obvious, as shown by the difference on the easiest of the discrimination tasks involving the vertical and the horizontal bar. At the age of 4·5 years the American children required about 15 trials to learn this discrimination and this number of trials remained reasonably constant throughout the age range extending from 3·5 to 8·5 years. Zambian children required just under 40 trials at the age of 4·5 and the experimental curves suggest it was only between 6·5 and 7·5 years of age that their performance reached that of the American sample.

The most obvious implication which these observations contain is that the performance of the American children on the task in question cannot be regarded as representative of human behaviour and that a broader cross-cultural view needs to be taken if the nature of the perceptual mechanisms is to be understood.

There are also other aspects which merit consideration. One of these is the relationship of Serpell's results to Reuning and Wittmann's observations on the nature of skew-symmetry. Serpell's results show that the skew-symmetrical *arrangements* are a relatively easy obstacle to discrimination learning. One would indeed expect this to be so in the samples observed, for, according to Reuning and Wittmanns, relatively unsophisticated subjects do not perceive this kind of symmetry readily and are therefore unlikely to experience any difficulty in seeing the pattern they are looking for in such an array. One would expect such difficulties to occur in more sophisticated subjects, who, given appropriate stimuli, should find discrimination between enantiomorphs forming bilaterally symmetrical patterns relatively more difficult than discrimination between enantiomorphs forming skew-symmetrical patterns; a problem which has not, as far as I know, been investigated.

Another aspect is that of the relationship between Serpell's study and studies specifically concerned with perception of orientation. The results of his experiment provide data pertinent to this issue but unfortunately in such a restricted manner that no definite conclusions can be derived from them. This is so, both because the settings of the individual figures used are perceptually unique, differing in orientation by either 90° or 180°, the zone between such angular settings being left unexplored, and because individual figures are always presented within more complex arrays. Yet it is in the *terra incognita* lying between the perceptually unique orientations used by Serpell that the most striking examples of cross-cultural differences in perception of orientation are to be found, and the interaction between the characteristics of the individual stimuli and the array which they form that determines the difficulty of discrimination.

THE PROBLEM OF ORIENTATION

One of the earliest recorded observations made on a population belonging to a cultural group, which was in later years to contribute considerably to the investigation of perception of orientation, must be that made by Dr Laws.

Laws was a Scottish medical missionary in, what was then and still is, a remote part of the African continent, the Livingstonia Mission in Nyasaland (now Malawi). In a slim booklet adressed to women's associations in Scotland he wrote of various problems associated with missionary work and of the population with which this work was undertaken; and in this context of the difficulties which the local servants had in attending to orientation. Unlike the Scots maids, Malawi maids seemed to have difficulties in setting the table. The outstanding and striking difficulty was that of putting various items in correct alignment: "In laying a table, there is . . . trouble . . . for the girl. At her home the house is round, the baskets are all round, a straight line and a right angle are things unknown to her or her parents before her. Day after day, therefore, she will lay the cloth with the folds anything but parallel with the edge of the table. Plates, knives and forks are set down in a corresponding manner, and it is only after lessons often repeated, and much annoyance, that she begins to see how things ought to be done and tries to do them." (Laws 1886, p. 15.)

Such observations as these are sometimes dismissed as being anecdotal, a term taken to imply that they are devoid of scientific interest. This is unfortunate for it suggests that the critics are incapable of perceiving that observations made by such men as Dr Laws have as much validity as do the ethological studies and that such "anecdotal" observations offer a fecund field for more precise hypotheses.

Had such anecdotal reports received the attention they deserved much subsequent planned and serendipitous rediscovering would not have been needed. We shall see later how observations by the same Dr Laws anticipated Hudson's findings on pictorial perception by about three-quarters of a century (p. 108). The observations on the behaviour of the maids anticipated a systematic investigation of the problems of reproduction of orientation by about as many years. This investigation was carried out using a standard test on a sample of a population drawn from the same part of Africa by Shapiro in 1960, and similar results were reported.

The extract of Laws' booklet which we have quoted also alludes to the possible cause of the difficulty. This is said to arise because the girls are unfamiliar with notions of orthogonality and parallelism as no examples from which such notions could be derived are provided for them by their surroundings. We have already encountered this very idea of the impact of the man-made environment upon perception when discussing the intercultural investigations of Campbell, Segall and Herskovits in their classical study of visual illusions. We have but to note that Laws' observation antecedes it by about 70 years.

Finally, the quotation implies that simple instruction is not a very efficient way of remedying such perceptual difficulties. Here too, as we shall see, strikingly similar findings have since been reported.

Spatial orientation in the most complex form pertains to perception of relationships within the three-dimensional space. In a simpler form it pertains to the relative setting of objects within the same plane, a phenomenon which we have already encountered when discussing Serpell's work on discrimination learning, and to which Laws' housemaids' errors in placing the cutlery in an erroneous orientation upon the table approximate. In the context of psychological testing it is most often measured by tasks in which subjects are required to reproduce settings of stimuli.

Several investigators working with non-Western subjects have noted *en passant* surprisingly large rotation errors made by their subjects when engaged in tasks not specifically designed to test orientation.

Thus Sousou children were found to rotate abstract designs when asked to copy them (Nissen *et al*. 1935). It might be that the subjects' unfamiliarity with pencils influenced their responses, but this is unlikely for the following reason. Had the difficulty in drawing *per se* been responsible for the orientation errors one would have expected those groups of subjects which draw correct patterns relatively infrequently to make more orientation errors than the groups which draw the patterns correctly. One would also expect the number of reproductions in incorrect orientation to be less in the less expert group. The empirical data do not form such a neat pattern. The two groups of children tested differed in age. The younger group (spanning from five to nine years) and the older group (spanning from 10 to 13 years) differed considerably in the frequencies with which they drew the test pattern (Fig. 3.9) correctly in any orientation. The corresponding percentages of correct responses were 50 and 83 respectively. The groups also differed considerably in the frequencies with which they drew the pattern in the correct orientation (4% and 33% respectively). There was however no such difference between the frequencies with which correct pattern was reproduced in an erroneous orientation. The percentages were 46 and 50. Commenting on these results Nissen *et al*. suggest that for these subjects the "extensity of the designs was the more important feature, the direction being secondary" (p. 329).

The difference in frequency rotations between the younger and the older of these groups is noteworthy because it may be seen as supporting Biesheuvel's (1952a, b) contention, derived from his extensive work in Africa, that spatial abilities, which include that of reproducing orientation correctly, are much influenced by experience, and that given suitable experience the children's performance on the tasks taxing such abilities can be greatly improved. The same argument has been put forward much later by McFie (1961) and was, in this case, based on the

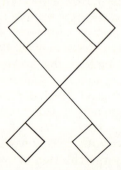

Fig. 3.9   A stimulus figure used by Nissen *et al*. (1935) in West Africa.

observed improvement of scores on the two tests of spatial ability: Wechsler's Block Design test and Terman-Merill's Memory for Design test. This improvement which was observed in Ugandan technical school pupils at the end of two years of training was not associated with parallel improvement of their scores on verbal skills. This was interpreted as showing that training rather than maturation was responsible for the change. Such a conclusion, although it presents an interesting hypothesis, is not however sustained by the data for it makes assumptions about the relationship between verbal and spatial skills and the rates of development of those skills in the population in question which the data do not justify.

A marginal but a very influential remark about the orientation difficulties was made by Jahoda (1956). He noted that rotation of reproductions of Goldstein–Scheerer patterns was very common in his Ghanaian subjects, and furthermore, emphatic instruction was quite successful in removing these orientation errors. Thus Jahoda, working with a different population and using a very different task, seemed to have succeeded where the combined efforts of Dr and Mrs Laws have failed.

All the above observations agree on the presence of surprisingly large orientation errors in certain cultures. They do not indicate the precise nature of such difficulties nor tell us whether the observed errors are random or systematic; i.e. whether in Jahoda's phrase the designs are left "at whatever angle they happen to be completed" or whether there is some systematic tendency towards favoured orientations in which subjects set their responses, and if there are such favoured orientations what their defining attributes are.

All the workers whose research has been briefly reported above inclined towards the random error hypothesis. A subject having reproduced a pattern geometrically similar to the stimulus regards such reproduction as satisfactory and his task as done.

On the other hand, Maistriaux's (n.d.) work in the Congo led him to suggest that the most typical orientation error was a production of a mirror image of the stimulus, a highly lawful transformation. He observed this phenomenon in responses to several tests, including Test de Niveau General (a task similar to that used in the Kohs' Block test) and Le Test des Batonnets (a derivative of the Goldstein–Scheerer Stick test). Such transformation may of course be the result of indifferrence, as Maistriaux suggests, but it is a very specific type of indifference confined to two enantiomorphic alternatives. It differs radically from the "indifference" suggested by Jahoda.

Shapiro's work helps to resolve these conflicting views. Unlike many of the observations previously mentioned it was concerned directly with the problem of orientation and relied on an established psychological procedure, deriving its impetus in part from the studies of brain-damaged patients. It had been well known for some time that such patients make a variety of errors when reproducing simple geometric patterns such as those used in the Kohs' Blocks test, most notably that they often reproduce the patterns in a different orientation than that of the stimuli. Two characteristics of the stimulus pattern which influence the orientation of the response are: (i) the orientation of its axis of symmetry (if any) and (ii) the orientation of its boundary. When one of the axes of symmetry is presented in the observer's median plane so that median symmetry results, the tendency to rotation is much reduced. It is also reduced when the stimulus pattern is presented so that it appears as a square resting on one of its sides (that is in a *stable* setting) rather than as a square resting on one of its corners (that is in an *unstable* setting). Shapiro's motives for studying the problems of rotation in a non-Western culture appear to have been purely heuristic. The resulting study in spite of certain methodological weaknesses turned out to be one of the most successful studies inspired by the heuristic approach; if success be measured by the number of experiments which it inspired.

Two groups of African subjects were used in Shapiro's study: primary schoolteachers and illiterate road-sweepers. Both groups were tested in Rhodesia but the latter consisted almost exclusively of Malawian immigrants. The subjects were shown patterns similar to those in Fig. 3.11, one at a time, and asked to copy them. The orientation of scorable drawings made was measured and the data used in comparisons among the two African groups and a variety of English groups of which that of normal healthy subjects is of the greatest interest in the present context. The rotation scores showed considerable variation; they were lowest for the normal English controls, intermediate for literate Africans, and highest for the illiterate Africans. The rotations of the illiterate group were also higher than those obtained from other English groups: low and high grade mentally defective subjects, and brain-damaged subjects. Thus the cross-cultural testing showed that, as far as could be ascertained, healthy and normal, but illiterate Africans had a tendency to rotate which exceeded that of not only normal but also subnormal individuals from the English sample.

The stimuli used by Shapiro can be placed in a 2 x 2 classification depending on whether the symmetry considerations are such as to foster or inhibit rotation, and whether stability is such as to foster or inhibit rotation. The four categories thus obtained were not, however, represented by equal number of stimuli. Furthermore, the data presented permit discussion on the observed rotations only in terms of 30° zones and does not allow one to determine the *sense* of the responses, i.e. whether they were clockwise or anti-clockwise.

There are three stimuli rotation of which could have been influenced by both stability and symmetry; 41 out of 42 responses did show the expected rotation. A further group of three contains those stimuli which could be affected by instability. Thirty-seven responses did indeed show such rotation whilst two failed to do so (there were also three ambiguous responses). On the other hand the stable stimulus, the median asymmetry of which one would expect to induce rotation, yielded no evidence of such rotation at all; of 13 illiterate responders 11 did not rotate their responses appreciably, whilst the remaining two did so in a manner unrelated to the hypothesis. The only stable and medially symmetrical stimulus shows only one 90° rotation; of the remaining 13 subjects eight reproduced it correctly and five upside down. All these 13 subjects, therefore, preserved both the stability and the symmetry of the design. This analysis clearly suggests, and a more detailed analysis of data (Deręgowski 1977) confirms, that the stability is the main determinant of the rotation. Symmetry, it appears, plays but a small role, if any.

It is possible, however, that under the circumstances of Shapiro's experiment such perceptual effect of symmetry as might have been present was simply swamped by the much stronger effect of stability. The effect of symmetry should be more readily observable in responses made to stimuli free from the influence of stability.

A study by Deręgowski (1972) attempted both to investigate more thoroughly the competing influences of symmetry and stability and to examine the effect of symmetry alone. To investigate the competing effects a special set of stimuli was made. It contained 12 figures (see Fig. 3.6), three of each of the four possible types: (i) mediately asymmetrical and unstable, (ii) mediately symmetrical and unstable, (iii) mediately asymmetrical and stable, (iv) mediately symmetrical and stable. Shapiro's data just reviewed lead one to expect that the tendency to rotate will decrease with types of stimuli in the order given above. Replacement of square stimuli by circular stimuli bearing similar patterns, as shown in Fig. 3.6, eliminates the stability effect and provides patterns differing in their symmetry only. Mediately asymmetrical of these should lead to greater rotations than the symmetrical ones.

Three groups of subjects, two of which were drawn from the same part of Africa as Shapiro's sample, and the third, a control group, which was drawn from an isolated rural, Western population, reproduced such stimuli using plastic tiles. The African groups were Zambian school children and Zambian unskilled workers. Icelandic school children provided a European control group. The use of tiles for reconstruction of the stimuli was thought preferable to drawing (because drawings are on occasions difficult to interpret and because unskilled draughtsmen may find it difficult to draw such patterns) and to traditionally used wooden blocks (because pilot studies showed that inexperienced subjects often spend considerable time turning individual blocks over in search for an appropriately coloured face).

Comparison of the groups on those responses in which the tiles were so arranged as to produce a geometrically correct (albeit not necessarily correctly orientated) pattern showed a striking difference between the Icelandic sample and the Zambian samples. The incidence of errors in the former group was so low as to make some of the statistical comparisons unnecessary. This was not so in the Zambian groups. This difference between groups is clearly seen from Table II, where the responses are divided into the following categories:

(i) *Nil*: No rotation, i.e. rotation within $11.25°$ of the setting of the stimulus.

(ii) *Towards stability or median symmetry*: Rotation predicted from the stability or symmetry of the figure, i.e. reproduction falling within $11.25°$ of one of the stable positions.

(iii) *Other*: other settings.

Of the stimuli used (Fig. 3.6) two (E and I) are such that rotation towards stability could also be rotation towards symmetry, whilst in three others (B, F and J) these two influences are opposed to each other so that rotation towards stability would inevitably result in loss of median symmetry. Comparison between the responses to these two groups of figures should therefore reveal the influence of symmetry.

The table shows percentages and absolute values of each type of response made by the three experimental groups. It is readily apparent from the data presented that effects of symmetry are not readily noticeable in the responses made to the stimuli, which are clearly subject to the influence of stability. However, when the effect of stability is removed, as in Fig. 3.6, A′, C′, E′, G′, I′ and K′, the effect of symmetry becomes apparent as shown in the bottom row of the table. This incidentally also shows that under these circumstances the Icelandic children, although less subject to influence than the Zambian subjects, are also prone to the anticipated effect. The hypotheses derived from Shapiro's findings are thus confirmed.

Absence of consistent differences between the performance of Zambian adults and Zambian children is especially interesting, since it shows that whatever the perceptual experiences which the former have undergone and whatever the effects of maturation might have been these have not ensured their superiority on the task. It could be argued, therefore, that the data support the contention that experience is not important. Such an argument, however, suffers from the same fatal flaw as McFie's data: a selected sample without a proper control group.

The most important finding of the study is perhaps that the errors of orientation on this task are systematic. The effect of this is presented in Fig. 3.10, which portrays distribution of responses due to various types of error. Line AB represents a continuum of responses available to the subject. In our case it represents the range of angular settings at which the stimulus can be placed. An entirely random response would lead to a rectangular distribution such as that shown in Fig. 3.10b. Any non-random responses would lead to deviation from such a distribution, and possibly, to subdivision of the continuum. There is an infinite number of ways in which such a continuum could be divided. It is possible, for example, that a subject regards a given orientation of a stimulus as being unique, a condition polarly opposite to that described above. Such a circumstance is shown in Fig. 3.10c. Theoretically the bar shown should be of no thickness but the combination of random errors, such as are commonly made in responding and in measurement, give it some body. Neither of these extreme cases describes the reported data. Neither entirely random nor almost perfect responses prevail in the Zambian samples; the performance of the Icelanders, on the other hand, can be said to approximate to the perfect responder paradigm.

A further clarification of the processes involved was provided by Jahoda (1976), who demonstrated that those Kohs type patterns which took longer to construct and which were therefore presumably found by

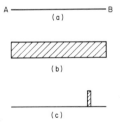

Fig. 3.10   Possible distributions of responses. (a) a perceptual continuum, (b) a distribution of responses which would obtain if the subjects responded at random or thought all the responses within the range to be equivalent, (c) a distribution of responses which would obtain if only one type of response were made.

Table II.   *Distribution of orientation of correctly reproduced patterns. (Figures without brackets give percentages; those within brackets give absolute values.)*

	Sample and type of error								
	Icelandic children			Zambian children			Zambian adults		
Hypothesized influence and stimuli	Nil	Towards the character-istic shown	Other	Nil	Towards the character-istic shown	Other	Nil	Towards the character-istic shown	Other
Stability (+) Symmetry (+) (Fig. 3.6, E and I)	75 (9)	Stability 0 (0)	25 (3)	13 (3)	Stability 62 (15)	25 (6)	17 (2)	Stability 58 (7)	25 (3)
Stability (+) Symmetry (−) (Fig. 3.6, B, F and J)	100 (17)	Stability 0 (0)	0 (0)	15 (4)	Stability 70 (19)	15 (4)	37 (6)	Stability 44 (7)	19 (3)
Symmetry (+) (Fig. 3.6, A′ C′ E′, G′, I′ and K′)	78 (28)	Symmetry 14 (5)	8 (3)	27 (21)	Symmetry 31 (24)	42 (33)	18 (8)	Symmetry 24 (11)	58 (26)

his subjects, Ghanaian school children, to be more difficult, were reproduced at greater deviations from the position of perfect stability in which they were presented. The errors observed were relatively small, the means ranging from just over 4° to about 14°, and therefore the data do not challenge the role of the major determinant of orientation, the stability of the stimulus; but it does define another factor, that of the subjective difficulty of the stimulus. The extent to which the understanding of the concept of horizontality affects the error was also investigated by Jahoda. He found that the grasp of the concept as measured by a Piagetian procedure, which requires subjects to indicate on a drawing of a flask the surface of water in a similar flask which is shrouded by an opaque cover and presented to the subject in various orientations, related directly to the orientation errors of the patterns, but weakly. A *post hoc* examination of the data suggested to Jahoda that since the rotation error and the pattern reproduction error show a highly significant *inverse* relationship this might indicate that both errors are associated with the extent of psychological differentiation.

This hypothesis was investigated and the relationship between pattern difficulty and errors was further explored in another experiment (Jahoda 1978) involving both Scottish and Ghanaian school children. The results confirmed the influence of subjective pattern difficulty upon orientation errors and showed that both groups of children were so influenced. They also showed a considerable difference between these two groups, the Scottish errors being much smaller. A comparison of scores on the Embedded Figures test, which were taken to indicate the extent of differentiation, did not, however, show a direct relationship with the deviations from correct orientation.

The notion of dividing the perceptual continuum can, alternatively, be thought of as the variation of the concept of sameness. It is possible, for example, that in some cultures stimuli are regarded as being the "same" as long as the patterns displayed remain the same, notwithstanding their orientation, whilst in others only a narrow zone of deviations in orientation between two figures is allowed if they are to be considered the "same". Studies of sameness are complicated by the fact that two polarly opposite notions of the concept can be entertained by subjects, things may look the same even if they are not and the observers know that they are not, and things may be the same although they do not look the same. In addition to these contrary notions the observer may of course happily experience one of the concordant notions of things being what they seem to be. The concordant notions do not present special problems but the discordant do, as they make it difficult to define the nature of a cross-cultural difference.

Such differences may arise because of the difference in *perception* of stimuli, but they may also arise because of the difference of conscious knowledge about the stimuli. A subject who wilfully and contrarily to his percept allows, in making his response, for the illusory distortion provides an instance of such an effect.

Under such circumstances the notion implied in the experimental procedure influences the results greatly and should carefully be borne in mind when evaluating them.

In his investigations of *sameness* Jahoda presented subjects with pairs of stimuli. The stimuli, which were Kohs type patterns, were either identical and identically orientated, identical and differing in orientation, entirely different but in the same orientation, or entirely different and in different orientation. Each pair was judged by the subject as being the same or different. It was hoped that this would reveal the differences between the two cultural groups which, it was postulated, might be present because children from a less "carpentered" environment would have, as a result of limitations of experience, less

D

well defined concepts of orientation than their counterparts from more "carpentered" cultures.

Indeed, the results obtained strongly support the notion of cultural difference; about 25% of Scottish and 75% of Ghanaian children misused the term "same" by applying it to stimuli which differed in orientation. Furthermore, analysis shows that all those Ghanaian children who called rotations of 90° or more "different" failed to regard rotations of 45° as the same. Jahoda describes this as showing a perfect scale. Since the orientation matching errors are associated in both the Scottish and Ghanaian samples with the magnitude of angular deviation in the pattern reproduction task, it is argued that the "perfect scale" presents an argument against the notion that such association may be the result of simply a greater tolerance for angular variation, and that it presents a systematic effect. This interpretation can be questioned because it implies that the orientation used in the experiment lies on a simple perceptual continuum. It follows from such an implication that if one were to plot discriminability of the stimuli against the difference of orientation relative to each other one would obtain a monotonic relationship, discriminability gradually increasing from 0° to 180°. This, however, is unlikely to be so, for other data suggest that there are certain orientations of stimuli which are more readily confused and which, if used in an experiment such as that now discussed, are more likely to evoke the response "same". This is most likely to happen when two patterns to be compared are so arranged that the overall pattern is medially symmetrical, as our considerations of discrimination learning show. The angular settings at which such symmetry occurs are directly dependent upon the stimuli used. In Jahoda's experiment it occurs with skew-symmetrical chessboard patterns, and may also affect responses made to two stimuli which would form a pair symmetrical about an oblique axis had they not been mutually displaced. In the latter case the effect may well be strengthened by the fact that the patterns are set in an unstable orientation and hence the movement towards stability and the movement towards symmetry are here acting in unison.

The different patterns of Scottish and Ghanaian responses suggest that the sources of confusion about the notion of *sameness* may not be the same in these two cultures. The Scottish subjects, may be more influenced by the considerations of symmetry of the arrangement of the two patterns, but the Ghanaian subjects may, in addition to being more tolerant of deviations from the modal settings (of 0°) in which the stimuli are in the same orientation, be less prone to such influence. In addition, it is possible that the Scottish responses were affected by the fact that in the 45° orientation (as in the 130° orientation) one of the stimuli was in an unstable position, and the other in a stable position. The perceived difference could therefore arise from considerations of stability of the stimuli rather than from the considerations of orientation of their patterns. The findings reported previously and showing primacy of stability over median symmetry agree with this suggestion.

Another finding reported in Jahoda's paper is the lesser concern with the orientation of the Ghanaian children as shown by the fact that they were more likely than the Scots to leave the patterns in whatever orientation they completed them. In the procedural variant in which subjects were reminded of the importance of the angular setting by the experimenters, more corrective adjustments were made by the Ghanaian subjects than in the variant where no reminder was present. No analogous difference was observed in the Scottish sample. Such an effect of unconcern with orientation, when present, is by its very nature non-directional, i.e. it increases variance of the errors made, but does not affect systematic biases such as those due to stability and symmetry which we have discussed. It is however possible, but this is yet to be demonstrated, that the method of *construction* of certain patterns which subjects use is such as to promote a systematic bias.

When model settings of the stimuli such as the "stable" and the "unstable" orientations of Kohs' patterns are used in an experiment there is a risk of imposing a binary division where none exists. Thus rotations towards stability, such as discussed above, may be purely artificial. It might be that the "unstable" 45° settings used are inherently less stable than the 0° "stable" settings and therefore evoke a wider range of responses, and since such responses cannot but tend towards increased stability an artificial trend to stability is observed. If this were true, such a trend would not be observed if, say, 22·5 settings of stimuli were used, since they would evoke about equal proportions of rotations towards stability (i.e. towards 0°) and towards instability (i.e. towards 45°). Identical propositions can also be advanced with respect of the influence of the symmetry of stimuli. When the axis of symmetry is so orientated that it lies in the subject's median plane an analogy to a stable setting is obtained; when it lies outside that plane the setting is analogous to an unstable setting.

The applicability of this argument to both stability and symmetry was examined by Deręgowski (1977), who obtained from Rhodesian Shona school children a sequence of responses as follows. Each subject was presented with an initial stimulus (S1) to which he made a response (R1) by adjusting a pattern identical with the stimulus, but set in a random orientation on a turntable. The angular setting of R1 was recorded. The turntable was upset to a random setting and a new setting of the stimulus S2 presented which was identical with the preceding response (R1). The procedure was thus continued, eliciting a series of ten responses which can be symbolically described thus:

S1 – R1
   S2 – R2
      S3 – R3
         S4 – R4
            S5 – R5
               S6 . . .
                  . . . R10

In the above schedule the physical characteristics of the responses and stimuli which lie in the same columns are identical.

In investigating the effects of stability square stimuli were initially either a zero or a 45° setting. In investigating the effects of symmetry the two analogous settings of circular patterns were used.

The results obtained are shown in Fig. 3.11. The stable setting of the stimulus evokes a series of responses meandering near the zero value, with the largest mean deviation of about 2° (these are not shown on the graph), whereas the unstable stimulus evokes a curve which drifts rapidly away from the initial setting; in the case of six of the subjects in the clockwise sense and anticlockwise in the other six. The unmistakable trend towards stability appears to be present in both groups and is clearly shown in the plot of combined results.

The scores obtained with the circular stimuli which were intended to investigate the effect of symmetry do not yield such a neat pattern. The responses made were less consistent, some subjects deviating in their successive responses now this way, now the other, both when responding to the symmetrical stimulus and when responding to the asymmetrical stimulus. Nevertheless, as expected the curve of group mean responses made to stimuli whose initial setting was symmetrical mean ders about the symmetrical setting. The corresponding curve begun by an asymmetrical setting does not do so, but the trend shown is weaker than that of the analogous stability curve. This relative weakness of the effect of symmetry could have been anticipated from previous results. The significance of the finding lies not only in the weakness of the mean trend but also in the way it arises, for it is not a result of consistent weakening in all the subjects but rather of large individual differences. Of the 12 subjects used only five rotate their responses with any consistency and in the expected sense. Three subjects adjusted their with

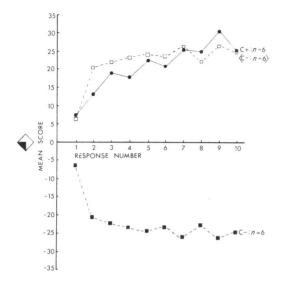

Fig. 3.11 A trail of sequential responses the first of which was made to the stimulus in the orientation shown. The continuous line and the dotted line represent clockwise and anti-clockwise rotations respectively. Superimposition of the latter curve on the format shows the similarity of their shapes.

All the subjects were found to be "consistent" in their responses rotating them in the same sense on at least nine of the ten trials.

equal consistency in the opposite sense whilst the remaining four show low consistency in their responses. Both these groups, as Fig. 3.12 shows, tended to reduce the mean scores.

The gradual drift towards stability which all the subjects showed and the somewhat less certain drift towards median symmetry argue against simple dichotomies on either dimension. The stimuli are, it seems, perceived not simply as unstable or asymmetrical but as more or less unstable or asymmetrical. Alternatively it could be said that the pull towards stability (or symmetry) is not constant but is a variable affected by the orientation of the stimulus and that this pull decreases as the stimulus approaches a stable (or symmetrical) setting. It seems probable therefore that the response "same" made by Jahoda's subjects to pairs of stimuli do not necessarily indicate perfect mutuality of the relationship between the stimuli forming the pairs. This can be illustrated by considering percepts which, evidence suggests, one would derive from a hypothetical pair of stimuli A and B, set at 25° and 35° respectively, and presented to one of Jahoda's subjects who said "same" in response to the same stimuli set at 0° and 45° respectively. Such a

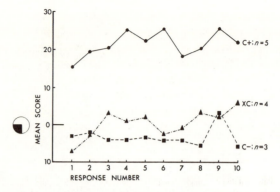

Fig. 3.12   **An analogous graph to that shown in Fig. 3.11, but obtained with the circular stimulus, which embodies only bilateral symmetry. The relative weakness of the tendency to rotate is readily apparent both from the shape of the curves and from the presence of four "inconsistent" responders (marked "XC").**

subject would respond similarly to the A–B pair, and since each of these stimuli is likely also to be seen as "same" as a stimulus "C" at 0° setting one would expect a perfect perceptual identity (expressed by =) to prevail among   e three stimuli, thus:

$$A \ (25°) = B \ (35°) = C \ (0°)$$

However, the curves showing the effect of stability, for example, (Fig. 3.11) do not support such interpretation, as a reproduction of stimulus A leads to a much smaller rotation of the adjustable stimulus towards stability and hence towards stimulus C than does reproduction of stimulus B. On the other hand, reproduction of stimulus C does not evoke systematic rotation towards the settings of the stimuli A and B.

Three conclusions follow from these considerations.

(1) It appears that setting C is the "idealized" purified form of A and B settings and hence the similarity relationship is not symmetric. That is to say, A and B are similar to C because they are both regarded as approximations of C. C, on the other hand, is not a perceptual approximation of A or B. There are no other orientations to which it could approximate.

(2) The difference in the strength of attraction exercised by the ideal setting C upon stimuli A and B is not the same in both cases, being larger in the case of stimulus B, which is set further away from C. Thus although the response to stimulus B may not result in a closer approximation to C than that of stimulus A the angular change evoked is on average likely to be greater.

(3) It is noteworthy that instant changes from one of the most unstable settings to the stable zero setting was not observed, although there were individual differences in the rates of approach to the ideal (0°) setting. It seems therefore that the transformations cannot be thought of in terms of a flip-flop mechanism such as that suggested by Attneave (1968, 1974) for transformation of simple triangular figures, but are probably better considered in terms of a balance resulting from interaction of several vectors acting in opposition, some towards the original stimulus setting and some towards the "ideal" setting. The response setting is a resultant of these two sets of vectors and, the data show, occupies an intermediate position between the two extremes, and moves as the stimulus moves along the continuum towards the "ideal" setting. Once this setting is reached the vector responsible for the retention of this position dominates.

This rationale, *mutatis mutandis*, can be applied to the considerations of both stability and symmetry.

The main theme of this book is the importance of cross-cultural work and to this theme we once more return. In Jahoda's experiment both Scots and Ghanaian subjects were shown to experience the same difficulties in reproduction of orientation. This is an important finding showing a generality of the phenomenon but even more important is the difference between scores of the two samples and especially very low scores of the Scottish sample, so low on occasions that had the results not been presented in the context of cross-cultural comparison the presence of the effect in the Scottish sample would probably not have been noticed, or thought of as trivial. This supports my claim advanced in the introductory section that cross-cultural work may lead to elucidation of a general perceptional mechanism, by enabling workers to investigate such a mechanism in populations in which it is most readily observable, and may bring to their attention the mechanism which would have been neglected because of its inconspicuousness within a population, which they traditionally study.

The notion of stability which has been repeatedly used in this discussion presents no difficulties and calls for no elaborate definition when such radically different orientations of a square as that with its base horizontal and that with one of its diagonals horizontal are contrasted. However when more complex figures are used, the discrimination between stable and unstable figures becomes more difficult and a more precise definition is therefore called for. The definition which we shall advance here is derived directly from the very basic concepts of mechanics and corresponds well with the daily experience acquired by handling objects.

Two factors determine stability of a solid object resting on a flat horizontal surface: (i) the shape of the base and (ii) the position of the centre of mass. Assuming that the observer, in the absence of contradictory evidence, conceives that the figure at which he is looking rests also on a flat horizontal surface the analogous determinants in the case of simple non-representational figures will be: (i) the shape of the lower boundary of the figure and (ii) the position of the perceived centre of mass. The first criterion is therefore quite simple: "horizontal" lines, and lines concave upwards and having their extremes at the same level (rather like the bases of claret bottles) lead towards perception of stability; other lines do not do so.

(Such simple outlines may not, however, be predictive when a drawing is perceived as depicting a solid object, for under these circumstances a concave downwards outline may be perceived as an edge of the base or a cylindrical object resting on a flat surface. We shall not concern ourselves with the perception of stability of such clearly representational figures.)

The second criterion is more elusive because it involves perceived mass. In some cases, such as that of a drawing of a horizontally divided square whose bottom half is filled in black and the top half left "empty", the notion that this orientation is correct because the darkened area is heavier seems intuitively obvious and is indeed supported by experimental evidence (Serpell 1971a).

An additional important factor influencing perceived stability is likely to be the extent to which a subject sees a pattern as representing, however crudely, some other object or symbol which has a characteristic orientation.

In contrast with the notion that stability and symmetry affect perceived orientation, Ghent/Braine postulates that figures have features which are focal (focal points) and that children tend to prefer figures to be so orientated that the focal points are at the top and the longitudinal axis of the figure in subjects' median plane. According to Braine (1978) such features of stimuli as stability or median symmetry are descriptive terms which "serve more to cover ignorance than to uncover the process underlying judgements made" (p. 11); but this may be an overstatement. Both symmetry and stability patterns appear to be more easily *a priori* determinable characteristics than the position of the focal point and of the longitudinal axis, and hence appear to offer a superior source of information for predicting how the perceptual mechanism will respond to a stimulus in question, whether it will be seen as upright or otherwise. In elaborating her ideas further Braine argues for a developmental sequence in perception of orientation which begins with a simple distinction between upright figures and figures in other orientations. At this initial stage all non-upright figures are thought to be equivalent. The data adduced to foster this argument have been obtained in experiments involving simple pictures of such commonplace objects as dogs and houses, which in the "real world" have their specific orientations with which subjects were certainly familiar. These data cannot therefore be taken as offering unambiguous support. Especially as Watson's (1966) experiments comparing infants' perception of abstract and non-abstract drawings show, these are not treated identically. He observed that whilst his subjects clearly discriminated, in terms of fixation intervals, between upright and upside-down schematic representations of faces, they did not do so when viewing simple disc bearing eccentric dots either at the top or the bottom, or the upright and inverted versions of letter T. The latter of these patterns has been used by Ghent in her earlier research.

Furthermore, examination of responses to abstract figures reported in psychological literature does not afford much support either; confusions between enantiomorphs reported by the students of discrimination learning, the monotonic scale of similarity reported by Jahoda (1978) and just discussed, and the analysis of the responses made to Kohs' patterns all argue against such dichotomy of percepts.

It can be postulated that the orientation of the figure is an inherent feature of the figure and not an independent dimension which may or may not be taken into account in comparing figures, just as one might do with, say, colour. Such a relationship has been thought to prevail by several workers, notably by Wohlwill (1960). Gibson (1969) also argues that since objects do not change with the change of their spatial orientation, "what a child learns (if learning is necessary) is to perceive their permanence despite change in position" (p. 415). Only on encountering digits and letters later in life has a child to recognize the importance of orientation and to learn to attend to it. This view has been current in psychology for some time.

In Ghent's (1961) experiment children were presented with pairs of simple symmetrical geometric figures. Within each pair one of the figures was "upside-down" relative to the other. The subjects were required to indicate that figure which was the upside-down picture in the pair of pictures shown to them. A remarkable consistency of choices, made without any hesitation, was observed. It was attributed to the presence of the "salient feature at the top of the figure, and a vertical orientation of the main lines (or long axis) of the figure" (Braine 1973).

The alternative possibility that stability of the figures might have affected the responses was thought to lack support of the data. This, however, is a debatable point.

Application of the criteria of stability which we have just discussed to the patterns used by Ghent yields in most cases predictions identical to those derived from the notion of the "focal point". This is so in the case of ten of the figures (Ghent 1961, p. 179). Two further figures are letter-like. This leaves four figures to which one could not apply the stability principle directly, but which could be described, *post facto*, in terms which would justify the responses observed; a lollipop-like figure if labelled as such by a child could, for example, be claimed to have a very definite preferred orientation.

Such *post facto* analysis is not really acceptable, although it clearly shows a need for eliciting verbal responses in order to ensure that the stimuli are truly abstract. However, the small number of figures to which such analysis had to be applied shows that the "focal point" may not be a dominant influence in perception of orientation. Serpell (1971a) thought that stability may be the principal determinant of orientation *preference*, the location of the focal point being an additional factor which becomes critical when a choice has to be made between two equally stable orientations.

It is important to notice that the responses in these experiments are said to indicate preference. The process involved is therefore seen as involving an aesthetic element. Nevertheless, such aesthetic choice is made on considering perceptual features of the stimuli, in this case such features as affect the judgement between two alternative and polarly opposite orientations. It is for these reasons that cross-cultural explora-tion of the Ghent/Braine notion of a focal point is of interest. There are two pieces of research of importance; Antonovsky and Ghent's (1964) replication of Ghent's study carried out in Iran, and Serpell's (1971a) investigation carried out in Zambia.

Antonovsky and Ghent's data show the same preference as that pre-vailing in the original American sample and the data which they pro-vided are subject to the same general critique as the original data. In addition, the preferences in the Iranian sample are consistently weaker and indeed in the case of two of the stimuli there is no evidence of preference.

The stimuli used by Serpell in his Zambian study were more varied than the Antonovsky and Ghent set and have yielded results which can be said to incline towards Antonovsky and Ghent's argument, but such inclination is far from definite. Notably, responses to two of the stimuli are such as one would expect, according to Antonovsky and Ghent's results, from children much younger than the Zambian ones, whilst to two other stimuli the responses are such as one would expect from older Zambian children. Had the discrepancy between the two groups been systematic and in the same sense as the results obtained by Antonovsky and Ghent, one would be inclined to seek the source of the effect in some factor common to both Iranian and Zambian cultures, but absent in the West. Such discrepancies between Western and non-Western responses are not uncommon and are exemplified by Serpell's (1971b) study of difficulties in discrimination learning.

Further, on an angular U-shape (consisting of three sides of a square) the preference of Zambian children was the inverse of the American preference. Zambians thought ∩ and the Americans thought U to be the right way up. The Zambians did so even though they labelled the figure as a "U". This failure to find an agreement between the labelling and the preferred orientation indicates that our earlier suggestion that subjects should be asked to name the patterns, so that any representational value therein may be detected and its effect upon preferred orientation assessed, may not provide an ideal solution of the problem. It does not nullify such a suggestion because the naming which followed the indication of preference was done by subjects familiar with both orientations of the stimuli and it is therefore possible that the name was derived from the stimulus in the more "nameable" orientation, notwithstanding the fact that the orientation of the less "nameable" stimulus was preferred.

In sum, cross-cultural studies of orientation do not simplify the problems being investigated; on the contrary, they complicate them – but such complications as arise simply show that the investigations conducted solely in Western cultures did not do justice to the phenomena.

Unfortunately cross-cultural studies have not concerned themselves with the two important factors which, as Rock (1973) has shown, dominate perception of orientation of plane figures: the retinal orientation of the figure and orientation of the figure within the environment. One would suspect that the effect of the latter of these two factors may be especially worthy of investigation, because the environmental determinant of the phenomenal shape is said to operate by effectively labelling various parts of the stimulus as "top", "bottom", "left" and "right". This labelling is thus dependent on the relationship between such background and the figure. The influence of background is, of course, central to one of the measures of field effects inspired by Witkin's theory of field dependence, which has shown considerable cross-cultural differences (Witkin and Berry 1975).

Comparison of responses made in various cultures to the stimuli differing in the degree of internal coherence, such as Patco and Kohs' patterns or simple figures used in discrimination learning, has so occupied psychologists that work on less clearly structured patterns has not been extensively attempted.

Yet stimuli of such a kind may prove rewarding. Maistriaux (n.d) in his Congolese studies used modified versions of several standard tests including that of the Goldstein–Sheerer stick test. In the modified version which he called "Le Test des Batonnets" the subjects were presented with geometric patterns of varying difficulty extending from a single straight line to a double rhombus. The task was to reproduce these figures by an appropriate placement of wooden splinters on a white surface. A selection of such splinters was provided. The errors made by the Congolese children while not unique were more pronounced than the errors normally encountered in "Western" populations. Apart from the "mirror" responses which we have already discussed the Congolese children also showed the usual errors associated with such tasks; production of "approximations", influence of the shape of the field upon which the stimulus was presented, failure to analyse the stimulus properly, syncretism, inability to handle concurrently all the information provided by the stimulus and reproduction of proportionally wrong figures. Although Maistriaux does not analyse the nature of these errors in detail but merely provides overall scores for various groups, his general observations sustain our contention about the value of cultures as natural laboratories for investigation of perceptual processes.

4. Pictorial Perception

Cross-cultural studies have probably contributed more to the understanding of problems associated with perception of pictorial materials than to any of the other problems dealt with in this book.

We shall for the purpose of the present discussion define a picture as follows. A picture is any surface pattern which is such that it evokes an ambiguous percept, the ambiguity resulting from the mutually exclusive notions of the pattern as it stands and of the pattern as a representation of an object. This definition clearly excludes any considerations of the origin of the picture. The artist's intent, his subconscious motives and the possible influence of his cultural setting, which occupy so much space in the discussion of works of art are not taken account of at all and the definition is tautologous in the sense that we require an observer's cooperation to be able to say whether a given pattern constitutes a picture as far as that observer is concerned because only he can inform us how the pattern is perceived, and whatever he defines as a picture is a picture. The pictorial nature of a stimulus, just like beauty, lies in the eye of the beholder. The definition is also both too wide and too narrow to be acceptable in a book on art because it expressly classifies Rorschach inkblots as pictures but denies that *trompe-l'oeil* pictures are pictures when they are viewed under such conditions that they are mistaken for real objects. Similarly anamorphic pictures cease, according to the definition, to be pictures when viewed at an inappropriate angle.

The illusion figures according to the definition do not form a unified group. Those whose deceptive properties escape the observer's *perceptual* awareness are not pictures. The Horizontal-Vertical illusion and the Muller-Lyer illusion do commonly fall into this category. Those which do not escape it (e.g. as the Necker cube or the "two-pronged trident" seldom do) are pictures. Both kinds of illusions however can be incorporated in pictures to provide a vehicle for evocation of a grander pictorial ambiguity.

Although in daily experience the recognition of a depicted object and perception of depth are intimately related such a relationship is not universal and it is possible for a picture to represent an object without evoking perception of pictorial depth, just as it is possible for a picture to evoke perception of depth without the observer's being able to associate the image with any particular object. We shall call the cues embodied in the former pictures *epitomic*, as such pictures epitomize the concepts of particular objects although they do not evoke perception of depth, an attribute which objects obviously have. We shall call the cues embodied in the latter pictures *eidolic* (a term derived from the Greek term for ghost) since they, in spite of not having any clearly attributable characteristics associated with real objects, evoke perception of pictorial depth.

Most pictures contain both epitomic and eidolic elements; there are, however, pictures in which only one of the two elements is present. Thus silhouette drawings or silhouette cut-outs which were so popular in the late eighteenth and nineteenth centuries are instances of purely epitomic pictures. One willingly accepts that Fig. 4.1 shows a lady in a crinoline but one does not see pictorial depth and arrives at no notion of the width of the garment. Similarly one can see all manner of things in a Rorschach inkblot although one does not perceive pictorial depth.

The most striking example of purely eidolic pictures are the impossible figures in their elementary form. The well known two-pronged trident (Fig. 4.2) is seen as three-dimensional in spite of the fact that the depth cues are contradictory and cause the perceptual mechanism to oscillate between the two possible percepts. The figure has no specific meaning and its perception as a mere flat pattern would rid the mechanism of the conundrum which it is unsuccessfully attempting to solve—yet such a solution is not generally attempted. One can even doubt whether it is at all possible in pictorially sophisticated observers. Other

Fig. 4.1   A silhouette of a lady in a crinoline provides an example of an epitomic percept. Although the viewer is provided with no cues evoking perception of the third dimension sufficient information is presented in the figure to enable him to label it correctly.

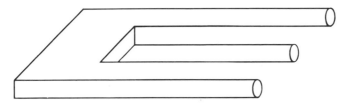

Fig. 4.2   The eidolic "two-pronged trident". The figure is only seen as confusing because the perceptual mechanism attempts to interpret it as representing a solid. No confusion would prevail if the eidolic cues were disregarded and the figure treated as a flat pattern.

examples of eidolic cues are provided by other illusion figures which likewise depend for their effects on involvement of the mechanisms associated with the perception of depth; the Muller-Lyer illusion, the Vertical-Horizontal illusion and the Sander Parallelogram are said to fall into this category.

The notion that illusions constitute an important element in Western painting has been explored by several workers most notably by Gombrich (1962) and Arnheim (1966). The former of these reports an observation made by a Japanese artist Yoshio Markino, whose father on first encountering a drawing made in accordance with the rules of perspective thought it showed a distorted box. Such a report is of course inconclusive because it could mean that the viewer thought the figure was not in the style of representation which his previous cultural experience had led him to accept as correct, that is that the conventions of drawing which he had learned have been violated. It could also mean that the perceptual processes involved were in this case different from those found in the observers who perceive such perspective drawings as correct. If this were so one would expect this difference not to be confined to drawings but to be also present in the "real world". Finally it could also mean that perceptual skills used by those normally viewing "perspective" and "non-perspective" drawings differ, there being a discrepancy in the manner in which individual cues as well as assemblies of cues presented in the pictures are treated. Although superficially similar the first and the last of those possibilities are fundamentally different. The first merely presupposes a knowledge of conventions, the last requires modification of the manner of *seeing*, which is confined to a specific realm of experience, namely to dealing with pictures.

The extent to which a human observer can judge correctly a shape of an inclined lamina has preoccuppied students of perception for considerable time. An inclined square lamina may cast a retinal projection identical with that which would be cast by a rhomboidal lamina free of any inclination, yet generally the perceptual mechanism does distinguish between two such figures. An explanation of the remarks made by Marikino Senior may be sought either in the very nature or in the manner of operation of the perceptual constancy mechanism, which in the above instance ensures that the former of the two laminae is seen as being more squarish.

There is evidence that there are cross-cultural differences in perceptual shape constancies. Thouless (1933) compared shape constancies of students drawn from the Indian continent to those of British students. The subjects were presented with a thin inclined lamina and had to choose from a series of response laminae presented in their fronto-parallel planes, a shape identical with that of the stimulus. The Indian students showed greater constancy than did their British counterparts, an observation in agreement with the styles of drawing typical of the two cultures. One is tempted therefore to postulate that the "distorted" style of Indian art is the result of the greater tendency towards constancy of Indian artists. To do so however would be to overlook the "chicken-and-egg" conundrum with which the data present us, for from them one can argue with equal justification that the difference between the two groups of students is due to the exposure to the two different forms of art, or even simply to the differential exposure to pictorial materials. The second of these hypotheses seems the more plausible of the two because Beveridge (1935), working with Glaswegian and west African students, observed that the latter, like the Indian students of Thouless, showed greater tendency to phenomenal regression to real objects.

However Winter's (1967) observations of the influence of the *size* of the retinal projection upon percepts in various South African cultural groups rank them as follows: Kalahari Bushmen, South African Whites, South African Bantu, Bantu locomotive drivers, white students of optometry; with the Bushmen being least influenced and hence showing least *size* constancy. If *size* and *shape* constancy are influenced by the same forces, this evidence questions the above conclusion.

The cultural differences in the magnitude of the Ponzo illusion reported by Brislin and Keating, which were observed when real objects served as stimuli, argue, however, against the view that the differences observed when drawings are used as stimuli are unique to such stimuli. Further, to anticipate some of the data on a phenomenon of the implicit-shape constancy, which appears, *prima facie*, to be related to the constancy investigated by Thouless and Beveridge, there are intra-cultural differences between children drawn from different social strata and probably from different genetic pools. The possibility of an involvement of a hereditary element in determining the operation of the perceptual mechanism in dealing with illusions is also suggested in a recent paper by Coren and Porac (1979) showing familial resemblances in illusion susceptibility to the Muller-Lyer illusion and to a lesser extent to the Ebbinghaus illusion.

Thus the problem which initially appeared to concern the relationship between culture and perception as defined by the artistic activities and perceptual responses characteristic of different cultures, may involve a variety of unexpected variables such as general perceptual differences between subcultures and heritable traits. Fortunately our prime concern is with the nature of the perceptual mechanism, and this permits us to skirt both these issues and the equally complex problems which would arise if we were to consider sophisticated and immensely intricate works of art.

The relationship between perception of depth in pictures and the illusory effects can be clearly demonstrated by requesting subjects to perform two different tasks; one of which indicates the extent of their skills of perception of pictorial depth and the other the extent of misinterpretation of an illusion figure (Deręgowski 1976b). Buale school children from the Ivory Coast were required to build Plasticine and bamboo models of the three figures shown in diagram 4.3, after being carefully instructed how to use such materials and after building a tetrahedron similar to that which was displayed in front of them. Each of the three figures can, theoretically, evoke one flat response and an infinite number of "3D" responses. Fortunately differentiation within the latter group need not concern us here. We have merely to decide whether the model built is flat, having all the members in approximately the same plane and hence can be taken as evidence of two-dimensional perception of the figure, or whether it is not flat and therefore shows that the figure is perceived as portraying a three-dimensional framework. This decision is generally easy, the constructions falling unambiguously into one of the two categories. Thus classified responses can be used for classification of individual subjects with each response contributing one 2D or one 3D score.

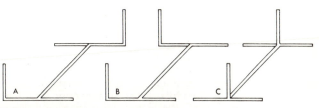

Fig. 4.3   Figures which were used as construction stimuli with Ivorean children.

All the schoolboys were subsequently tested on the implicit-shape constancy task. This involves recognition of simple geometric figures. The figures were presented initially either on their own (Fig. 4.4) or surrounded by a network of lines suggestive of a cube (Fig. 4.5), and the schoolboys were requested to attend to them because they were told they would be required to recognize them later. The same figures were subsequently presented for identification embedded in an array of distractor figures. The distractors belonged to the same family and represented the stimulus figure as it would appear in orientations different from those in which it was originally shown. These orientations were derived as follows: the original figure was derived from a figure glued to a side of a cube whose relevant face lay in a plane making an angle of 45°

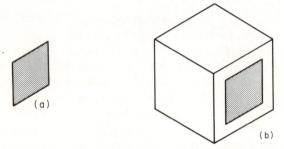

Fig. 4.4 Examples of (a) control stimulus, and (b) experimental stimulus, used in the implicit-shape constancy studies. The latter figure is likely to be seen as the more squarish of the two, by most subjects.

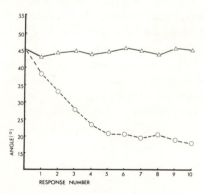

Fig. 4.5 Implicit-shape constancy drift curve. The continuous line shows a sequence of responses obtained by presenting figures on their own without the background of a "cube", the dashed line responses obtained with the use of such a background.

with the observer's median plane. The other figures were derived by altering this angle. A set of figures was thus obtained extending from a simple frontal projection, in which the face of the cube and hence the figure were in the observer's fronto-parallel plane, to inclinations greater than 45° and hence involving greater distortions of the figures than those present in the original stimulus.

Comparison of the choices made after looking at the stimulus presented on its own with those made after looking at a stimulus presented on the background of a drawing of a cube shows that latter choices approximate more closely to the frontal view of the figure than do the former. The subject's behaviour is similar to that observed in the shape constancy experiments, suggesting that similar laws govern human perception when dealing with real and with implicit shapes. A comparison of the scores on the implicit-shape constancy tasks of those schoolboys who built no three-dimensional representations of the three simple drawings on the modelling task just described, with those who built at least one such model, shows that the latter tend to be more prone to the influence of the implicit shapes, their responses showing greater constancy effect than those of the pupils who built flat models. This is not a startling finding, for pupils who are influenced by depth cues in their interpretation of pictures would be expected to be so influenced both when reproducing the depicted figures and choosing what they consider to be correct reproductions of figures.

The interest of this finding lies in the relationship it shows between pictorial perception and the illusory effect. The subjects who perceive depth in pictures more readily are, it appears, more prone to the illusion which the pictures evoke. The relationship between perception of illusions and perception of pictures is thus demonstrated. One would expect to obtain further support for it from a cross-cultural comparison of subjects drawn from pictorial and non-pictorial cultures. A comparison of Scottish school children with rural African school children such as the Bukusu and the Buale whose performance has just been described should show the greater trend towards constancy in the former group. The data obtained do indeed show such an effect. The implicit-shape constancy prevails in both groups and whilst the two groups do not differ in their responses when the stimuli are presented on their own, they do differ in their responses to the stimulus drawn on a background of the drawing of a cube. The Scots as expected are more influenced by the cube than their African counterparts.

An essentially analogous comparison of children in Nigeria by Makanju (1967) shows that children of university staff are more influenced by the implicit-shape constancy than working class children.

It is important to consider the nature of responses which lead to these differences. The responses are not of the *either/or* form. They do not suggest that a subject either sees a drawing of a cube as a cube and therefore treats the stimulus as if it were drawn on a cube so that his response shows perfect constancy, or that the subject sees the entire figure as flat and hence chooses a geometrically congruent response figure. If such responses were obtained they would suggest a very simple process indeed; namely that verbal labelling might determine responses. On being presented with the initial stimulus the subject who perceived a drawing of a cube as a cube would say to himself: "This is a drawing of a cube with a pattern on one of its faces to which I am required to attend. I shall therefore treat the stimulus as if it were a cube and under such circumstances the pattern shown as a diamond here would be a square. I shall choose a square as my response." He would then pick up a square and show perfect constancy. On the other hand, a subject who did not perceive the drawing as depicting a cube would ignore the pattern of lines and choose a geometrically congruent diamond.

In practice subjects choose responses somewhere in between those showing perfect constancy and those showing no indications of constancy. They respond as if their decision were influenced by a number of vectors, some of which are towards the perfect constancy, but others oppose them and the final response is therefore the result of a balance.

An analogy with the speculations concerning the determinants of reproduced orientation of plane geometric patterns (p. 76) is readily apparent, and is further strengthened by the application of an experimental procedure similar to that used in investigating orientation errors and involving sequential presentation of stimuli. In the present case the procedure used was as follows. Each subject was presented with a stimulus drawing and made his choice of appropriate responses as in the experiments just described, but unlike those experiments the procedure did not end there but his choice determined the next stimulus with which he was presented; he then made his next choice and the cycle was repeated. This was done ten times. Symbolically the procedure can be represented as shown below.

Let $S1, S2, S3, S4 \ldots S9$ be the stimuli drawn so that the orientation of the relevant face of the cube appears to lie in a 45° setting in figure $S1$ and in the fronto-parallel plane of the subject in $S9$. Let $R1, R2, R3 \ldots R9$ be the corresponding drawings of the stimulus on its own from which the responses are to be chosen. Then typically the following procedure obtains.

Trial 1: S1 —— R3
Trial 2:   S3 —— R5
Trial 3:   S5 —— R6
    etc.

A plot of responses obtained from a group of Scottish children in such an experiment is shown in Fig. 4.5. The curve shows clearly a steady drift towards fronto-parallel orientation of the pattern. This drift is absent in the case of the curve obtained by using two sets of stimuli on their own in an otherwise identical procedure. The latter procedure merely yields a curve wavering about the correct setting.

The essential factor in the implicit-shape constancy appears to be the same as that involved in the Sander Parallelogram illusion; a perceptual hypothesis is suggested by some characteristics of the stimuli and leads to a non-vertical percept. In so far as the above description implies a casual chain it is probably incorrect; for it thereby suggests perceptual separation of the distorting and distorted elements, whilst it is probably more justified to consider the organism as attempting to make sense of the entire stimulus.and transforming all the inter-related elements so that they make generally better "sense" than they do without transformation. The noteworthy element of the particular percepts just described is that they imply perception of the third dimension in a picture.

Such implication is also said to be present in the Muller-Lyer illusion, but the effect there is much more subtle and not as readily apparent. On the other hand, the stimuli used in the implicit-shape constancy studies, being drawings of parallelopipeds, seem to evoke perception of pictorial depth with greater intensity than the Sander Parallelogram. The three stimuli can therefore be ranked in terms of increasing degree to which they overtly evoke perception of pictorial depth as follows: (i) Muller-Lyer arrows, (ii) Sander Parallelogram and (iii) drawings of parallelepipeds.

The simplest hypothesis is that subjects who are prone to perceive pictorial depth are also more influenced by the effects associated with perception of those stimuli which create illusions, dependent upon the perceptual mechanisms normally involved in perception of depth; this includes all the illusions discussed in this book: the Horizontal–Vertical, Muller-Lyer, Sander Parallelogram and Ponzo.

Therefore it is likely that whatever the factors affecting perception of illusions, the very same factors also affect perception of pictures. Such simple relationships between pictures and illusions may, however, be obscured by another cultural effect: that of drawing skills. Segall *et al.*

(1966) think that drawing skills diminish the illusory effect. If this is so then as the comparison of African and Scottish samples on the implicit-shape constancy task clearly shows any diminution brought about by such an instruction in the Scottish children is more than compensated for by other factors. On the other hand Thouless (1932) observed that artists show greater shape constancy. This may seem to suggest that persons who have undergone training in drawing will be more suscept-ible to illusions. In addition it has been suggested that general sophisti-cation of subjects leads to a decrease in the illusory effect (Davis and Carlson 1970).

Thus three possible influences are put forward, the third of which is so broad as to include the other two, which in general are so intertwined in any given culture that they are difficult to separate.

Further exploration of those tangled hypotheses, although difficult, could be undertaken by studying cultures differing in the dominant artistic style, especially following Thouless' (1933) example by inves-tigating the representation of perspective, in combination with intra-cultural studies of people with different degrees of training in drawing. Differentiation on the latter dimension would probably be quite easy to achieve, for drawings made even by highly educated people coming from a highly pictorial culture often reveal astounding incompetence (Came-ron 1938).

The importance of the distinction between epitomic and eidolic recog-nition is sometimes, perhaps under the influence of linguistic usage, overlooked even by experienced experimenters and in the circums-tances in which it is likely to affect results. Thus Greenfield *et al.* (1966) expect children who sort pictures by the form of the portrayed object, to group together a picture of an orange and a picture of an alarm clock since both are round. Indeed the drawn shapes are round although they are projections of entirely different solids; a sphere and a cylinder. The judgement of similarity of such pictures is therefore subject to three influences which are to some extent inter-dependent, and which in their pure form are as follows:

(i) Epitomic influence: the observer labels the picture and in judging similarity uses the shape which a particular label evokes.

(ii) Eidolic influence which rests upon the three dimensional notion of the object to which the picture gives rise.

(iii) The influence of the geometric shape of the *pictures* which is independent of their eidolic or epitomic value.

A particular judgement of similarity may thus be affected, in one of a variety of ways in which these influences may be evoked, by the stimuli to be compared. Consider, for example, a *drawing* of a car which is geometrically almost congruent with a *drawing* of a hat. The geometric shapes would therefore be clearly thought of as similar, but not so the epitomic shapes. Furthermore, if, for example, a car is represented in silhouette (and therefore evokes a purely epitomic response) and a hat is drawn in perspective (and therefore evokes an eidolic response) the difference in shapes is *perceptually* apprehensible and the notion of similarity may be rejected in spite of striking geometric congruence of the drawings; as might indeed have been the case in Greenfield's study.

The inability of an observer to respond to the epitomic cues is clearly easier to observe than his inability to deal adequately with eidolic cues. It requires no sophisticated experimentation or even detailed questioning but a simple indication on the part of the observer that he does not see a picture as portraying an object. When a woman presented with a photograph turns it this way and that, examines it and fails to see in it the picture of her own son, as a Bush-Negro woman is reported by Herskovits (1948) to have done, we may suspect the presence of epitomic difficulties.

On the other hand, detection of eidolic difficulties calls for more elaborate procedures since such difficulties may be obscured by the observer's familiarity with the depicted actions and objects. Thus if a picture shows a mouse and a cat, say, seated on a road drawn in perspective, the cat being drawn smaller, correct recognition of both the animals (an indication of the ability to deal with the epitomic aspect of the picture) and hence a deduction that the cat is further away from the observer than the mouse does not tell us anything about the observer's ability to perceive pictorial depth. A much more refined procedure is needed to assess it.

It is not surprising therefore that the epitomic difficulties were the first to attract the attention of students on inter-cultural differences, and speculations upon this issue were already current in the last century; whereas it was only about 25 years ago that Hudson's serendipitous discovery of misperceptions of pictorial depth led him to investigate such eidolic difficulties in some detail, in a paper (Hudson 1960) which was to prove seminal to practically all the work done in this area.

We shall deal with these two types of problem in the historical sequence.

EPITOMIC AND EIDOLIC DIFFICULTIES

Reports of such difficulties are to be found both in missionary and anthropological literature. These are sometimes dismissed as anecdotal although what such a term means is not clear. It seems unlikely that it is intended to question the veracity of the observers nor can it be taken to imply that their procedures were unsatisfactory. It seems, more likely, to convey a vague disapproval or outright rejection passed without much reflection or experience of the populations tested and not resting upon any data whatsoever.

I consider such "anecdotal" evidence to be of value and it will therefore be examined here.

Perhaps the most often quoted report (besides Herskovits' observation of a Bush-Negro woman) is that of Dr Laws, whose observations of the difficulties which orientation of objects presented to Nyasaland maids we have already described. He also noticed a striking inability, especially in older people of Nyasaland, to perceive pictures when first confronted with them. Here is his description of the problem:

> Take a picture in black and white, and the natives cannot see it. You may tell the natives: "This is a picture of an ox and a dog"; and the people will look at it and look at you and that look says that they consider you a liar. Perhaps you say again, "Yes, this is a picture of an ox and a dog". Well, perhaps they will tell you what they think this time. If there are boys about, you say: "This is really a picture of an ox and a dog. Look at the horn of the ox, and there is his tail!" And the boy will say: "Oh! yes and there is the dog's nose and eyes and ears!" Then the old people will look again and clap their hands and say, "Oh! yes, it is a dog!". When a man has seen a picture for the first time, his book education has begun! (Beach 1901, p. 468).

Observations of similar difficulties were also made by others; Fraser (1932), another physician, noted them as did Larken (1927), an administrator in the Sudan. Later they were also reported by several psychologists working in a variety of cultures. Nadel (1939) noticed that Yoruba boys (in northern Nigeria "could not identify outline drawings on paper of a man or even of common objects as a hut or crocodile or a pot *although exactly the same* figures were all once identified when they appeared in carvings or on native leatherwork, i.e. in their familiar, established cultural context" (p. 190). Another observation was made by Warburton (1951), when he tested Gurkha recruits for the British Army. These recruits were occasionally unable to recognize pictures of objects with which they were thoroughly familiar. Forge (1970) found similar difficulties in New Guinea: Cole and Scribner (1974) found them in Liberia amidst the Kpelle, two of the photographs which they used are reproduced in their book and appear, to a Western eye, perfectly clear. This short list of reported difficulties can of course be balanced by reports of extremely dramatic responses to pictures described by other observers. Thompson (1885), a prominent nineteenth century explorer, describes how Wataveta women, when looking at photographs of "some of their charming white sisters", thought them "to be living beings".

And here is a description of what must have been one of the earliest slide shows in Uganda by A. B. Lloyd (1904):

> When all the people were quietly seated the first picture flashed on the sheet was that of an elephant. The wildest excitement immediately prevailed, many of the people jumping up and shouting, fearing the beast must be alive, while those nearest to the sheet sprang up and fled. The chief himself crept stealthily forward and peeped behind the sheet to see if the animal had a body, and when he discovered that the animal's body was only the thickness of the sheet, a great roar broke the stillness of the night.

Such dramatic data do not permit us to dismiss the reports of failure but merely suggest that even "remote" populations may differ in their ability to perceive pictures and, more importantly, that some stimuli probably are more effective in evoking the appropriate response than are some others. Thus a transparency projected in the dark with all the usual environmental cues which tend to contradict the pictorial cues hidden by darkness, and with only the cues contained in the picture left to sway the observer, combined with the size of the projected image being closer to the real size than those of ordinary photographic depictions, may evoke an illusion of reality so strong that it may become, as we have just seen, overpowering. The variation in effectiveness of various ways of portraying objects need not surprise us. There is ample evidence from Western studies showing such variation, just as there is evidence showing that Western children sometimes fail to recognize pictures. This somewhat trite observation has to be made because it is easy to make an erroneous assumption, both in relation to the epitomic and in relation to the eidolic abilities, that in any particular population these abilities are either present or absent. In fact they differ from individual to individual and from one group to another just like any other ability. To make this point perfectly clear and to provide a link with the mainstream of psychology we shall now describe some of the relevant Western studies.

Systematic research of the ability to deal with one kind of pictorial difficulty at various development stages has a relatively long history. Binet described in 1890 the frequent failures of young children to recognize drawings of various parts of a face, e.g. a nose or an ear presented separately, although they were recognized with no difficulty when presented in the context of the face. The mutual support which various elements of a picture derive from each other is clearly important, and the ability to deal with the difficulties which reduction of such support entails has long been thought to be psychologically significant. It is measured, for example, by the Street Test, and has recently been investigated by Gollin (1960, 1961) using special "interrupted" pictures.

When objects are drawn in interrupted lines the gradual increase of the size of the gaps and the corresponding decrease in the size of the line segments make such drawings increasingly more difficult to identify. A set of such drawings (Fig. 4.6) can therefore be used as a measure of the difficulty encountered in recognizing the depicted object. Gollin found that there was, in American children, a gradual decrease with age of the completeness of pictures required for recognition. Younger children appeared to be less able to fill in the gaps. An interesting extension of this investigation (Spitz and Borland 1971) involved presentation of a series of stimuli differing systematically in the quantity of information they retained. This variation was achieved by variation of the extent of deletions from the line drawings. As one would expect the probability of correct identification decreased with increase of deletion and increased with age and education of the subjects, so that with 60% of the drawings deleted, the nursery school children identified correctly about 25%, the children from the second grade about 52%, and superior adults about 72% of the depicted objects. These results do not reflect familiarity with the depicted objects because all the subjects were able to identify them when additional information was provided in the drawings: the results clearly reflect subjects' ability to handle degraded drawings. According to Spitz and Borland this ability does not vary linearly with age and schooling but increases sharply up to the age of about eight years and thereafter continues to increase but at a much reduced rate.

An alternative way of looking at the problem is to consider the problem of pictorial perception, not as one which can be solved by an observer extrapolating from the data present so as to complete the percept, but as one in which he has to disentangle the relevant informa-

Fig. 4.6   A set of three figures differing in completeness and similar to those used by Gollin (1960) and others.

tion from the obscuring noise. Here, too, data show (Elkind and Scott 1962) that younger children find it more difficult to identify a drawing embedded in a set of other drawings than do older children.

Such observations do not apply solely to line geometrical figures or line drawings but extend also to photographs blurred in a systematic manner. Potter (1966) has demonstrated that younger children took much more time to recognize depicted objects, indeed on occasion some of the children, aged between four and nine years, failed to recognize some of the pictures even with the experimenter's help. This failure ought to be remembered when similar failures in non-Western cultures are discussed.

A specific error to which children and, as we shall see later, some pictorially unsophisticated adults, are prone is that of syncretic perception. This expression is used to describe "pars pro toto" perception, wherein the depicted object is described in terms of only part of the information provided in the picture.

Segers (1926) carried out a systematic investigation of the phenomenon using to this end specially prepared *syncretic* drawings of animals made, e.g. by drawing a cow's body with a dog's head. Children under seven years of age had no difficulty in naming such animals. They appeared simply to label the entire syncretic animal by the name appropriate to one of its parts ignoring the inherent inconsistency of the beast.

Further work on syncretic figures was done by Elkind (1969) using stimuli inspired by Meili-Dworetzki's earlier studies. These consisted of meaningful and familiar elements forming syncretic assemblies in which, unlike in Segers' pictures, the elements were not joined together but merely carefully arranged. Such absence of connections between elements introduces into Elkind's pictures an additional problem, that of supplying the missing elements, which was the object of Gollin's studies. A figure of a man formed by appropriate juxtaposition of an apple (head), a pear (body), two bananas (legs) and two bunches of grapes (arms) may serve as an example of Elkind's stimulus. Children of different ages, Elkind observed, responded differently to such stimuli; the youngest children named only the constituent parts (in our case an apple, a pear, a banana, etc.); somewhat older children were "able to schematise wholes but in so doing lose the significance of parts" (i.e. in our case the man is perceived). At a yet higher level of sophistication the two types of percepts apparently alternated and either a coherent whole or simply a collection of independent items was seen; at a higher level still both percepts were entertained simultaneously.

The two different perceptual processes, that of supplying relevant additional information and that of rejecting irrelevant information, can be thought of as opposite ends of the continuum. Independently of this continuum, one can postulate a continuum describing the extent to which various elements of the picture affect the perceptual process. Thus, for example, in such pictures as those used by Gollin, integration of all elements is necessary for recognition of the depicted object. Both the shape of horns and the shape of the tail may be needed to identify the animal on the other hand, integration of elements is not called for at all in the case of, say, a class photograph wherein individuals can be recognized and the entire assembly labelled correctly as Class X without considering the mutual relationships between the individuals. The syncretic stimuli such as those used by Elkind are of especial interest in this context. Clearly the important characteristic in the case of such integrations is not the specific epitomic nature of the particular elements involved but rather their most general characteristics, such as shape or colour. In addition the relationship with other elements is crucial. This has clearly been demonstrated in the reports on Vicker's studies of the economy principle, implicit-shape constancy studies and indeed in all illusion studies. Such relationships can derive from any characteristic of the stimuli, such as similarity of shape, size or colour, but they can also be derived from their placement or orientation in relation to each other. These are the factors which determine the manner of integration and hence the nature of the percept derived. The role of any single element in such circumstance can be likened to the strength of a single animal in a pack and Kipling's saying, familiar to every cub scout, that the strength of the pack is the wolf and the strength of the wolf is the pack, can be used to describe the process.

The performance of Western subjects on the tasks occupying different positions on these continua shows that a degree of sophistication is needed before such strange percepts as a man made of fruit can be derived from pictures. The gradual changes in pictorial perception described above and their presence in Western populations demonstrate that a single kind of picture cannot be regarded as a valid measure of epitomic ability either within or between cultures, and that it is erroneous therefore to use, for example, Hochberg and Brooks' (1962) data showing instant recognition of one kind of picture by a single infant as evidence for the universality of pictorial perception.

Analogously, claims that groups do not differ in pictorial perception because of similarity of their responses to a particular set of pictures is also palpably false. On the other hand, demonstration of a difference between such groups on a single picture does, if methodologically sound, demonstrate a true difference in perception.

One may conclude by adducing a linguistic analogy. The ability to ask a waiter for a cup of coffee, although an indication of an ability to express one's wishes in, say, Danish, does not mean that the ability extends to asking the same waiter for a glass of lemon tea, nor does it imply that everyone is able to order coffee in Danish.

Let us now consider some relevant observations from non-Western cultures. Muldrow working in Ethiopia on a remote tribe of Me'en (Mekan) observed difficulties similar to that reported by Dr Laws and others. She noticed that when the Me'en, most of whom were probably entirely unfamiliar with pictures, were given a page from a children's colouring book they would smell it, examine its texture, listen to it while flexing it, even attempt to taste it, but they would entirely -ignore the picture. (Similar behaviour has been reported earlier by Bitsch (1970) who conducted his informal observations on Ituri pygmies in 1949.) These strange responses might, however, have been due merely to unfamiliarity with paper. It is possible, Muldrow thought, that on being presented with an entirely novel material the Me'en examined it thoroughly but ignored surface markings, thinking them to be of little consequence; a hypothesis consistent with Nadel's observations on Yoruba which we have quoted. To check on this hypothesis new pictures were printed on coarse cloth, a material with which the Me'en are familiar. The new pictures were much larger than those printed on paper and originally used, being about 50 cm x 100 cm in size. Two of the pictures showed single animals; the dik-dik and the leopard (Fig. 4.7). When these pictures were shown, the number of people who responded "I don't know" when asked what they saw in the picture decreased dramatically. Such response could no longer be thought of as modal in the population, as shown by the following figures giving the responses of 34 Me'en of both sexes–adult and juvenile–drawn from the isolated section of the tribe (Deręgowski *et al.* 1975).

Stimulus : *dik-dik*. Responses   : Correct   :   22
                                       Other   :   7
                                       "Don't know" :   5

Stimulus : *leopard*. Responses   : Correct   :   32
                                       Other   :   2
                                       "Don't know" :   0

The "other" responses consisted entirely of attribution of wrong names to the animals, e.g. of calling a leopard a giraffe; responses naming a similar animal, e.g. calling a dik-dik a goat or a buck, were recorded as

Fig. 4.7 **Greatly scaled down reproductions of two of the figures used for testing subjects who where unfamiliar with pictures. The drawings represent (a) a dik-dik and (b) a leopard. The subjects were familiar with both these animals.**

correct. It therefore appears that the difficulties in recognizing an indigenous animal clearly depicted on familiar material were not overwhelming, a conclusion agreeing with Nadel's (1939) results, although there was clearly a proportion of subjects for whom even these pictures proved obscure.

The nature of this obscurity is hinted at in the verbatim reports of those of the Me'en who succeeded after some struggle in naming the animal, or who after careful consideration of the stimulus gave up the uneven struggle against, to them, a strange contrivance. Consider the following comments made in response to a picture of a dik-dik.

(1) Man, about 35 years old, looks at the picture:
    Experimenter: (Points to the picture): "What do you see?"
    Subject: "I'm looking closely. That is a tail. This is a foot."
    E: "What is the whole thing?"
    S: "Wait. Slowly, I am still looking. Let me look and I will tell you. In my country this is a water-buck."

(2) Man, about 25 years old:
    E: (Points to the picture): "What do you see?"
    S: "What is this? It has horns, leg . . . front and back tail, eyes. Is it a
        goat? A sheep? Is it a goat?"
(3) Man, aged about 35 years:
    E: (Points to the picture): "What do you see?"
    S: "I don't know." Is it a man? It looks like a cow. (As E outlines the
        animal): "That is its horns, legs, tail, ear. It is a cow."
(4) Woman, aged 20 years:
    E: (Points to the picture): "What do you see?"
    S: "I don't know." (As E outlines the animal): "I don't know. Those
        are legs, horns, ears, tail. I don't know what it is."

The dramatic improvement obtained by the introduction of the pictures printed on cloth shows that the implicit suggestions of the importance of the familiarity of the medium made by Nadel and Muldrow's are probably correct.

The subjects' verbalizations help us to define the nature of the residual difficulties after the change to a more familiar medium. The difficulties encountered cause the observers to assemble the information by slowly accumulating all the data required, as it were, to decode the collage of smaller meaningful units. Sometimes, as the last report shows, such final synthesis of all the information fails to emerge. Sometimes, too, subjects seem to jump to a conclusion on the basis of only part of the available information. This happened to the third of the subjects whose protocol is given above, who replaced his suggestion that the figure is that of a man by the suggestion that it "looks like a cow".

Such syncretic guesses have also been observed by Shaw (1969) in a study conducted in Kenya. A small percentage of observers misidentified Fig. 4.8a, calling it an elephant, presumably because of the shape of its feet; a snake, probably because of the shape of its head; and a crocodile, perhaps because its shell has a pattern of lines similar to the crocodile's scales. Similar "pars pro toto" responses were obtained to some of the other stimuli used.

However, an instance of holistic erroneous perception obtained from the same sample of subjects ought also to be noted. Fig. 4.8b, which was intended to represent a cob of maize, was variously perceived as that of a man, a bird or mosquito. Such interpretations of the figure become intuitively more obvious when it is presented in various orientations. It might be, therefore, that the observers, unable to derive any meaning from the figure as originally shown mentally rotated the entire figure until they arrived at an orientation in which a meaning could be derived. The possibility of such processes is supported by the data

(a)

(b)

(c)

Fig. 4.8   Stimuli which were unsuccessful in conveying the intended meaning (a) a tortoise, (b) a cob of maize. Misperception of the latter is found easier to grasp by the pictorially sophisticated observers when an allowance is made that the percept could have been rotated. The figure in the middle could be that of a bird in flight and the figure on the right that of a man wearing a long cloak. (Courtesy of the Flying Doctor Service.) (c) a family scene. (Courtesy of UNESCO.)

obtained using Kohs type patterns which, it will be recalled, showed considerable rotation of patterns by observers derived from populations similar to that used by Shaw. This epitomic type of difficulty is exacerbated, as one would expect from consideration of the Western studies which we have discussed, by presentation of drawings of isolated elements such as an arm or some other part of the body. One of the pioneers of studies in communication, Doob (1961), noted that Fulani villagers when presented with such drawings found them difficult.

There are two levels of epitomic difficulty therefore: the basic level, at which the observer fails to make any sense of the picture whatsoever and behaves like pictorially sophisticated subjects sometimes do when asked to say what they see in an inkblot; this type of difficulty might have faced some of the five Me'en observers who are categorized as "don't knows" above. The second, lower level of difficulty is encountered by those observers who realize that the figures represent something but are not certain what, and hence do on occasion make unusual guesses. The responses of this group present a peculiar problem because they may derive from two entirely different cognitive states of the observer. One of those is similar to that generally experienced on inspection of a Rorschach blot. The observer regards the stimulus as essentially meaningless and is aware of the variety of ways in which it can be interpreted and hence, on request, offers one of the interpretations available to him. The alternative state is that of precise and unique perception of the figure combined with the inability to label it accurately, and hence use of broad categories such as "an animal" or erroneous sub-divisions of the correct category such as "a cow" in response to a figure of a dik-dik. A Western cultural parallel may apply when an observer shown a picture of an isosceles triangle calls it "a triangle" or "a scalene triangle".

The laborious perceptual process in which subjects engage as the evidence suggests, can be interpreted in two polarly opposite ways. It can be said to consist of a slow accumulation of elements from which a recognizable figure is built; or as a slow emergence of the entire figure rather as if the picture were first displayed out of focus and therefore blurred and focussed slowly so that the blur gradually disappears. The verbal evidence quoted is ambivalent. It could be said that such enumeration of parts of the animal as that made by the first of the observers quoted ("that is a tail", "this is a foot", and so on) is just what would be expected from an observer who slowly gathers elements together. The response of the fourth observer who successfully identified various elements ("those are legs, horns, ears, tail") but who failed to integrate them into a cohesive whole also supports such an interpretation. On the

E

other hand, the type of response exemplified by the protocols of the second and the third observers could be seen as supporting just the opposite, holistic point of view. The figure is perceived as being that of a man but after further examination it is thought to be that of a cow, and a cow it remains. Such gradual changes of opinion about what the depicted object might be were reported by Potter (1966) in her study of responses of American children to increasingly clearer projections of pictures.

It has been argued that neither of these two polar paradigms is satisfactory because each of them postulates a perceptual unit, the chief characteristic of which is that it is perceived in its entirety and is homogeneous in so far as its perception is concerned; that is to say, all the contents of such a unit are perceived equally well.

If the unit is large, so large indeed as to constitute the entire picture, one would expect the viewer to perceive all the details with equal lucidity: this, as studies of recall of pictorial material show, is clearly not the case.

If the units are small elements requiring synthesis, they must be some *a priori* undefinable, yet recognizable elements of the picture; a horn, or a foot of a depicted animal, say. If so, one can ask "why do these particular elements constitute units? If a foot, why not a toe? Why not a claw?"

Such reductionism can best be described in Swiftian terms:

> So naturalists observe, a flea
> Hath smaller fleas on him to prey;
> And these have smaller fleas to bite 'em
> And so proceed *ad infinitum*.

It seems more probable that a blend of both processes described is used and that the observer proceeds by putting forward perceptual hypotheses on the basis of some of the data present and by verifying them against other data available until he reaches a satisfactory solution. Such a solution need not be the "correct" solution, as shown by Segers' study of recognition of syncretic animals by children. A dog's head mounted on a body of a cow may be called a dog because the initial hypothesis derived from the shape of its head was not disconfirmed by the inspection of the quadruped body to which it was attached, which was perhaps too superficial to reveal the incongruity. On the other hand, removal of the *nose* from the context of the face leads, according to Binet, to a failure in recognition because there is probably insufficient material even to form a hypothesis. It seems that gradual removal of features from a depiction of an object, say eyes and eyebrows from one of Binet's faces, would finally lead to such a poor remnant of representation that it no longer would be recognized as a face.

One can probably safely conclude from the scarce data obtained from remote cultures, that such acute difficulties in perception of pictures as an inability to see that a pattern on a plane surface represents something else or gross misperception of the represented objects are relatively rare when clear pictures printed on familiar material are used. Such difficulties do not occur in great frequency even in populations which as far as can be ascertained have practically no contact with pictorial materials, such as the Me'en. It follows that such difficulties would be even rarer indeed in the populations which have some minimal contact with pictures. Most of the so-called remote, pictorially deprived, populations fall into this category. There are two guises in which pictures reach them most frequently: (1) Certain products, such as matches or patent medicines, are now practically universally available and these products are often packed in wrappers with especially bold figures intended to convey their nature and to serve as brand names for the illiterate public. (2) Local men of destiny (or ill fate) ensure that their portraits have the widest possible distribution in their countries, so much so that these often penetrate (sometimes as wrapping materials) to quite remote areas.

Let us now consider some evidence obtained from populations subject to such pictorial exposure. Illiterate men and primary school children from remote rural Zambia were, in the main, able to identify models of animals on display given photographs of such models (Deręgowski 1968a). There was, apart from the obvious difference of age, a difference in the extent of schooling between these two groups, the mean number of years of schooling being for school children 4·0, for men 1·6. These two factors might have contributed to the following findings. Men were somewhat superior to school children on recognition of familiar animals (e.g. elephant, lion, zebra, hippopotamus), school children were somewhat superior to men on recognition of unfamiliar animals (e.g. polar bear, kangaroo, walrus, tapir). It would seem that the greater experience with pictures in general gave the school children an overall advantage but the more extensive experience with local animals gave men superiority over the children in the relevant range of stimuli. Such experimentation implicitly relies both on the capacity of the picture and the capacity of the model to evoke the relevant concept. If the concept is not evoked by either of these two stimuli the subject fails. It is possible, therefore, that because the children were relatively less familiar with local animals they found the stimuli to be less evocative as far as the relevant concepts were concerned. Ideally one would wish to check this conclusion by showing the subject real animals and their pictures. Such an experiment involving a travelling menagerie would, however, be difficult to conduct.

A study (Jahoda *et al.* 1976) carried out in pictorially relatively deprived environments on Ghanaian and Rhodesian children aged above three years showed that they were, in an overwhelming majority of trials, perfectly capable of recognizing familiar objects depicted in colour photographs, and indeed that their responses did not differ in accuracy from the sample of children from a small town in Ghana who had attended a nursery school. The results obtained are comparable with those obtained by Kennedy and Ross (1975) from a sample of Songe and Papua. The Songe tested were both older and more experienced than the Ghanaian and Rhodesian subjects. They were tested mostly on clear if somewhat stylized line drawings, the main exception being some figures intended to represent men which were but lightly outlined. Since, however, these peripheral figures are arranged around a central figure which is a clear depiction of a man, the meaning attributed to them may be, in part, derived by contagion from the central figure, and the result obtained cannot be thought of as showing ready perception of abstractions.

The frequency of identification of the Kennedy and Ross stimuli was found to vary with age. The frequencies obtained from subjects aged less than 40 years were comparable with those reported by Jahoda, but the group aged over 40 made fewer correct identifications. The high scores in the earlier groups need not surprise us greatly since Hutton and Ellison (1970), in an earlier study conducted on a sample drawn from the population of Port Moresby, noted that "after six years of schooling Papuans and New Guineans can correctly interpret . . . simple line drawings".

These findings contrast with a number of observations made by Forge (1970), which were obtained incidentally in the course of an anthropological enquiry. The population studied was the New Guinean tribe of Abelam which has an elaborate and ritualized pictorial art. This serves to decorate ceremonial houses by portraying on them figures composed of stylistic elements with no apparent attempt to establish correspondence with either nature or three-dimensional arts. Occasionally such decorations incorporate elements derived from Western culture such as colourful advertisements. These appear to be used primarily for their colour for the Abelam seem to have no idea of what is represented in them. Even more surprisingly the Abelam are incapable of recognizing familiar persons in photographs, other than those taken in a very specific circumstance in which those photographed stand at attention in front of a white sheet. In such highly conventional photographs recognition is precise. "Even people . . . who came specially because they knew of the photograph of a relative who had subsequently died and were often pathetically keen to see his features were initially unable to see him at all, turning the photograph in all directions", reports Forge and continues, "Even when the figure dominated the photograph I sometimes had to draw a thick line round it before it would be identified and in some cases I had the impression that they willed themselves to see rather than actually saw it in the way that we do. Photographs of ceremonial houses and objects were easier, . . . people could identify a house as a ceremonial house although it was photographed in black and white, rather than say which house it was" (p. 287).

Forge postulates that the effects observed are a result of "socialization of vision. . . . The Abelam lack of understanding of photographs even after twenty years of contact remains almost absolute and provides possible support for the hypothesis that they have very definite and limited expectations about what they will see on any two-dimensional surface made to be looked at" (p. 287).

This report on the manner in which the Abelam treat pictures contains a number of notable points:

(1) The nexus of the phenomenon is said to lie in the expectancy; presumably it is not conscious expectancy because some of the Abelam fail to perceive correctly a photograph which they have a particular desire to perceive and have indeed made a special journey to do so. The expectancy "filter" must therefore work without the observer's awareness as a part of the essential perceptual mechanism.

(2) The difficulty, it appears, is absent when figures are presented on a clear white background and in an established pose appropriate to the photographs. Under these circumstances recognition of individuals is faultless. Familiar ceremonial houses are not identified with equal ease, perhaps because photographs of these are less common than those of men, and therefore more difficult to perceive.

(3) Outlining of a figure appears to assist correct perception. One unfortunately cannot determine whether outlining is efficacious because it facilitates separation of the figure from the background, i.e. because it helps the observer to solve a perceptual riddle similar to that inherent in the embedded figures so extensively used by Witkin and others; or whether it is efficacious because it, as it were, pulls the figure together, in which case the problem which it helps to solve is similar to that embodied in the Gollin figures which we have discussed. Whatever

the reasons for these and other erroneous responses one can only conclude that the epitomic difficulties appear to be present in a variety of populations, including some populations with limited exposure to pictures; although their extent might indeed have been, as Doob observes, exaggerated because the sophisticated observers are likely to note and to remember the striking and surprising effects such as the responses of a Fulani villager calling "an extremely clear photograph of an aeroplane: a fish" (Doob 1961, p. 274).

However, even when there are no identification difficulties at all it does not mean that the drawings are regarded as equivalent to objects in those tasks in which such equivalence could reasonably be expected.

Children from a richly pictorial culture, such as Klapper and Birch's (1969) subjects, do not mime actions to show how particular tools are used when shown pictures of such tools as vigorously and well as they do when shown the tools themselves. Since the children label the depicted objects correctly it cannot be said that the pictures are less well recognized than the objects; it seems rather that the pictures evoke but a muted response. The discrepancy between models and photographs as representations is also apparent in the responses obtained from four groups of largely illiterate (mean number of years of education, 1.2) Zambian women. They were required to match toy animals and their pictures. Two of the experimental groups matched stimuli within the same representational medium: pictures to pictures and models to models. Two other groups matched pictures to models and models to pictures. Only four out of 40 women made errors when matching within the same medium but 19 out of 40 made them in intermedial matching. (Deręgowski 1971c).

The discrepancy between the treatment of objects and the treatment of pictures is also apparent in the studies of sorting. American Negro children from a nursery described as serving the "underprivileged" (Sigel 1968) found it more difficult to categorize pictures than to categorize objects although they had no difficulty in naming the depicted objects. A comparison between Scottish and Zambian children inspired by Sigel's work, showed that these populations do differ. They performed about equally well when sorting models of motor-cars and of animals but when sorting photographs of these very models the Zambian children performed less well than their Scottish counterparts (Deręgowski and Serpell 1971). Such differences between responses to various modes of representation can also be observed within adult populations well acquainted with pictures, on a task involving memory, as shown by the following experiment. A subject is presented repeatedly with a series of stimuli until he has learned to associate each stimulus with an arbitrarily designated place on a table. If various types of stimuli do not differ among themselves one would expect the locations to be learned with equal ease whether the series consists of written words, pictures or objects. When this test was used with a group of Scottish women (Deręgowski and Jahoda 1975) it was however found that there were considerable differences. Locations of objects were learned better than locations of their photographs and locations of photographs better than locations of cards bearing appropriate words (such as "knife", "book", "matches"). This occurred although the subjects had no difficulty in recognizing the depicted objects and in reading the descriptive terms. By noting how often after placing the stimulus correctly a subject made an error on one of the subsequent presentations, one can trace how often the errors made were a result of forgetting. Such analysis shows that the locations of pictures were indeed forgotten more often than locations of objects.

Even highly sophisticated subjects, such as those who served in Ekman and Junge's (1961) psychophysical investigations do not scale drawings of cubes and metal cubes in the same manner. It appears that although such drawings, as the implicit-shape constancy studies show, do to some extent evoke perception of depth, this perception is not sufficiently intense to affect the psychophysical function describing the perceived volume of the solid. As a result it differs from the corresponding function derived from the metal cubes.

There is thus a considerable body of evidence showing that pictures, when correctly identified and used in a task wherein they can be treated in a manner similar to that in which the depicted objects are treated, are not entirely efficacious substitutes for objects.

Furthermore, when pictures are used to depict a dynamic scene, young children tend to regard them as mere static displays. It was not till they reached Grade 6 that groups of American children investigated by Travers (1973) were unambiguously biased towards correct interpretation of portrayed motion although correct identification of depicted objects was the dominant response already in the kindergarten.

But whilst not equivalent to the depicted objects, pictures are clearly not arbitrary conventional signs. Such statement as that by Herskovits (1959 that "in truth even the clearest photograph is a convention; a translation of a three-dimensional subject into two dimensions with colour transmitted into shades of black and white . . ." clearly begs a question about the manner in which the word *convention* is used. As the experiment described above shows descriptive terms must be more conventional than pictures of objects, since position learning became more difficult when the former were used in lieu of the latter.

Animal studies too confirm the essential relationship between the objects and their depictions; e.g. animals which have been conditioned by operant procedures to discriminate between objects transfer readily to discrimination between drawings of these objects (Zimmerman and Hochberg 1963).

Further evidence that a picture can evoke in animals a response indicative of recognition of some elements of the depicted object as being the same as those possessed by the familiar object itself is also to hand. Monkeys taught to open a foodbox when shown even such a degraded stimulus as its schematic picture became excited and chattered (Marton *et al*. 1971). It is impossible to say, of course, to what extent this response indicated recognition of the box and not some specific aspect of it. Syncretic recognition is not unknown in animals as seems, for example, to be the case with a bird frightened by the eye-spots on the wings of a butterfly. Nevertheless it cannot be denied that this evidence shows that some animals are capable of perceiving epitomic cues in the pictures.

The tasks used for assessing pictorial perception are three-fold. The subject may be exposed to a picture (P) of an object (M) with which he is familiar, either because he has encountered it frequently in the course of the normal daily experience or because he has been exposed to it in the course of an experiment. This is by far the commonest situation both in the laboratory and the naturalistic settings. The counterpart of this procedure, exposure of a subject to an object which he has only previously seen in pictures, is much rarer but is of course relatively common in the pictorially rich societies wherein pictures are often used as means of communication, and therefore pupils and students and others are exposed to portrayals of objects which they have not previously encountered. The third type of task involves recognition of a depicted object by a subject familiar only with the depictions of this object. This again is more commonly encountered in the educational setting. A Scottish child may, for example, be able to recognize a kangaroo in a picture although he has never seen a real kangaroo but only other pictures of the animal. Summarized schematically the three types of task can be described thus:

$$(1) \ M - P$$
$$(2) \ P - M$$
$$(3) \ P - (M) - P$$

The fact that in the third condition the concept of the actual object may or may not be involved in the task is indicated by the bracketed "M".

The animal studies described above belong to the first category. The second category is interesting because it requires abstraction of the key features from a picture in spite of the hindering effect of pictorial surface. It also generally calls for an ability to transform the percept of the object derived from the picture since it is unlikely that the test object when encountered will be in exactly the same spatial setting relative to the observer as it was shown in the picture. In this respect it differs radically from the first condition wherein presentation of the object first enables the viewer to see it from a variety of settings one of which is likely to approximate to the pictorial setting. However the second category has not, to our knowledge, been widely used in animal experimentation. The third approach has, on the other hand, been explored by Salzen and his co-workers in a series of studies concerned with habituation to and discrimination between pictorial stimuli by squirrel monkeys (Salzen *et al.* 1980). Both effects were found to be present, but as indicated schematically above their presence does not indicate that they are necessarily a recall of an association of the initial and test stimuli with a real object, which they both schematically represent, rather than a direct association of the stimuli with each other. Such association may, however, be affected by some general similarity of the stimuli to a three-dimensional object or may even rely to some extent on the special significance of some configurations, such as the "eye" configuration in the case of birds which we have just mentioned.

On similar grounds it can be suggested that the title of the De Laroche *et al.* (1979) paper "Picture perception in infancy" is a misnomer. This paper demonstrates that babies aged five months show unambiguous novelty preference for both colour and black-and-white photographs of an unfamiliar doll when paired with those of the familiar doll. An analogous transfer from colour photographs of a human face to black-and-white photographs and to line drawings was also found, as was infants' ability to discriminate between two stimuli, such as a doll and its photograph. Although the nature of these findings is quite unambiguous their significance is not, for it can be questioned whether perception of similarity between various types of stimuli, which these results demonstrate, can be taken as indicating pictorial perception any more than a bird's startled response to the eye-spots of a butterfly can be thought of as such. Perception of similarity between a model and a picture is of course necessary for pictorial perception; but it is not sufficient, especially when no other evidence of perceived similarity than visual matching is provided. In this respect Hochberg and Brooks's (1962) data are more to the point for the vocalization by the child tested by them demonstrates that higher processes than simple visual matching were involved.

The presence in some cultures of perceptual difficulties with interpretation of such simple pictures as those hitherto considered would lead one to expect more widespread difficulties involving more complex pictures. The nature of the possible difficulties is well illustrated by Fig. 4.8c showing a family scene.

When subjects from east Africa were invited to say what they saw in this simple drawing, they described it as a family group in which a young woman was carrying upon her head a four-gallon tin–a common sight in those parts. Such an interpretation occurs to but a few "Western" observers, who generally see the drawing as portraying an indoor scene with a rectangular window behind the young woman's head. The artist presents observers with two cues: the "corner of the room" and the "tin/window". To a Western observer, the "corner" complements the cue of a rectangular window. Not so to some of the African observers. Some African subjects, it appears, do not respond to the pictorial depth cues as strongly as Western subjects do. Moreover, the intended cue of a "window" was to them irrelevant to the depth cue provided by the "corner", since it is not a window at all but a four-gallon tin. (The reader, if of a Western cultural background, may wish to try to "Africanize" himself for a while by covering the Y-shaped representation of the corner of the room with a piece of paper, thus leaving himself with only the ambiguous cue of the four-gallon tin/window.)

Such misinterpretations of pictorial depth or eidolic cues are, as has been said, more difficult to detect than are the misperceptions of epitomic cues, and although the former might have contributed to some of the misperceptions of pictures reported by the early observers they were not really noted and convincingly reported before Hudson's (1960, 1967) observations were published.

He noticed that some of the responses which he obtained to pictures of the Thematic Apperception test were such as to suggest that the responders did not perceive pictorial depth. A figure of a speaker standing with his hands outstretched, so that in the plane of the picture they appeared to be above two factory chimneys, was interpreted as depicting an insane man who had climbed on the chimneys, contrary to the artist's intention, which was to indicate by the use of perspective that the chimneys were far behind the speaker. Such observations led Hudson to design a special test part of which is reproduced in Fig. 4.9. The aim of this test is to elicit from the subject whether he perceives the man to be closer to the elephant or to the duiker. The subject is first asked: "What do you see?", in order to check that he can identify correctly various

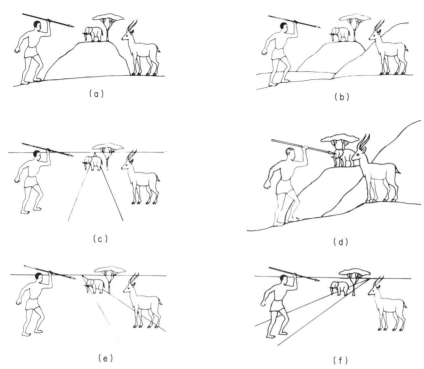

(a)

(b)

(c)

(d)

(e)

(f)

Fig. 4.9   Six of the stimuli of Hudson's Test. The seventh stimulus of the test which takes the form of a photograph showing an essentially similar arrangement of toy figures, is not shown here.

items in the pictures; i.e. that he has the basic epitomic ability. If he is successful, then two questions are put to him, one direct, "What is closer to the man, the elephant or the duiker?", and the other less so, "What is the man doing?"; with a subsidiary question, "What is the man doing with his spear?", if his answer does not indicate which animal the man is hunting.

The answers indicating that the elephant is seen as being closer to the man than the duiker are taken as showing that the observer fails to perceive pictorial depth.

Comparison of Bantu and European subjects carried out by Hudson showed that the former tended to see the elephant as being closer to the man more often than the latter. Of the two populations tested the Bantu could, therefore, be described as more frequently two-dimensional in their perception (2D-perceivers) than the Whites, who were largely three-dimensional in their responses (3D-perceivers).

Bearing in mind our observations that a particular test is likely to measure the difficulty at a particular level one would not expect scores obtained from alternative tests of perception of pictorial depth to agree in their assessment of the individuals but one would expect the results of such tests to correlate positively.

The experiment described below arises from a specific and fundamental critique of Hudson's stimuli, that the individuals tested need not *perceive* pictorial depth in order to respond "three-dimensionally". All that is required of them is the ability to evaluate the stimuli rationally. They may, for example, come to a correct conclusion by speculating as follows:

(1) Elephants are bigger than duikers and men,

(2) One conventionally draws things smaller the further away they are,

(3) Here the elephant is drawn smaller than either the duiker or the man,

Ergo, the elephant is far away and the man and duiker are close together.

Whether such a rational solution occurs or whether the subjects actually see depth in such pictures can be tested by using an apparatus in which the perceived depth of each of the crucial figures of Hudson's pictures (the elephant, the man and the duiker) can be measured without asking direct questions involving comparisons amongst them. "Pandora's Box" is an instrument eminently suitable to this purpose. It is shown in Fig. 4.10 and is described by its designer as follows:

> The figure is presented back-illuminated, to avoid texture, and it is viewed through a sheet of polaroid. A second sheet of polaroid is placed over one eye crossed with the first so that no light from the figure reaches the eye. Between the eyes and the figure is a half-silvered mirror through which the figure is seen but which also reflects one or more small light sources mounted on an optical bench. These appear to lie in the figure: indeed optically they do lie in the figure, provided the path length of the lights to the eyes is the same as that of the figures to the eyes. But the small light sources are seen with both eyes, while the figure is seen with only one eye

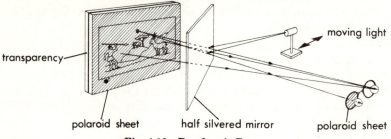

Fig. 4.10   Pandora's Box.

because of the crossed polaroid. By moving the lights along their optical bench, they may be placed so as to lie at the same distance as any selected part of the figure (Gregory 1968).

When a Hudson's test picture embodying pictorial elevation, familiar size and overlap cues (Fig. 4.9b) was made into a transparency and presented in this apparatus, African observers, drawn from a population stratum known to consist largely of 2D-perceivers on Hudson's test, did not show perception of pictorial depth (Derȩgowski and Byth 1970). The distance at which they set the movable light was not systematically influenced by whether they were asked to put it just above the elephant, just above the hunter or just above the duiker. In contrast with these responses, sophisticated European observers set the light further away when setting it over the elephant than when setting it over the other two figures, showing that not merely were they interpreting conventional cues but they actually saw depth in the picture. On the other hand, the responses of these two groups of observers did not differ when a transparency of another of Hudson's figures that contained only pictorial elevation and familiar size cues (Fig. 4.9a) was used. Neither group of subjects saw the elephant further away than the other two figures. These results are presented graphically in Fig. 4.11. The results need not surprise us since the pictorial depth cues in the latter picture are relatively weaker and may be too weak even for sophisticated Western observers. Thus it appears that the Western observers who interpret both these pictures three-dimensionally, do so for different reasons. They actually see depth only in the picture which has the pictorial elevation overlap as well as familiar size cues; when only the pictorial elevation and familiar size cues are present, the 3D-perceivers appear to rely primarily on interpretation rather than perception. Both the ability to interpret the artistic conventions and to perceive pictorial depth appear to be absent in the Zambian observers in our sample as far as these particular stimuli are concerned.

This difference between the responses of the two groups to the two types of stimuli can be interpreted in the terms of epitomic and eidolic qualities of the cues contained in the pictures. In those terms apparently addition of overlap introduces a new eidolic quality into a purely epitomic collage for the Western observers but does not do so for the Zambian observers. This interpretation seems plausible for one would not expect, as the data on illusions suggest, equal eidolic sensitivity in all populations.

Correlation between performance on various tasks involving pictorial interpretation was investigated in the following two experiments, in both of which tasks were introduced in which the verbal responses

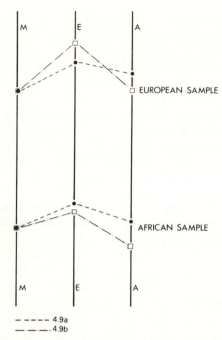

Fig. 4.11   **Graph illustrating results obtained with two of Hudson's pictures (Figs 4.9a, b) placed in Pandora's Box from European and African subjects. The vertical lines etc. represent positions of the man (M), the elephant (E) and the antelope (A). Only the relative depths within each sample are meaningful. The position of the man has been arbitrarily chosen as a point of reference within each group.**

which are used in Hudson's test were replaced by performance measures.

In the first of these, in order to eliminate the verbal element for which Hudson's procedure has been criticized, simple geometric drawings (see Fig. 4.14) were presented and the subjects requested to build models of them. Performances of the same subjects on Hudson's traditional test and on the construction task were compared, the bamboo and Plasticine models built being simply scored as flat or three-dimensional. The overall result obtained showed that although a proportion of subjects, who were judged to be 2D-responders on Hudson's test, were classified as 3D-responders on the Construction test, there were very few subjects whose responses formed the opposite pattern (i.e. who were 2D-responders on the Construction test and 3D-responders on Hudson's test). Practically all the subjects who were 3D-responders on Hudson's test were also 3D-responders on the Construction test. The most parsimonious explanation of these results is probably that the Construction test is the easier of the two tests, and that the two tests rank in the same manner as do linguistic tasks expounded in our analogy of the conversation with a Danish waiter. Those who can order lemon tea (*citron te*) can also order coffee (*kaffe*), but those who can order coffee may not be able to order lemon tea.

The obvious and the intriguing question which the above results suggest is: "Why are abstract drawings such as those used in the Construction test easier to perceive three-dimensionally than the relatively more realistic Hudson's drawings?".

Before discussing this question let us consider another experiment (Deręgowski 1969a) in which an entirely different type of stimulus and a different performance measure were used. The stimulus was one of the "impossible figures", the "two-pronged trident" (Fig. 4.2). It was used on the assumption that such a figure is difficult to remember because the observer's perceptual mechanism tends to perceive it as three-dimensional and such a percept is self-contradictory. A perceptual mechanism devoid of such a tendency and which therefore perceives the figure as flat does not encounter the contradictions. Hence encoding of the figure is facilitated and this in turn ensures superior recall.

This hypothesis was put to test by dividing Zambian schoolboys into two groups, one of 2D-perceivers and the other of 3D-perceivers as judged by the criteria of the Construction test. Children in both groups were asked to copy the impossible figure as well as a control, "flat" pattern.

The figures to be copied were displayed in a special apparatus so made that the subject had to lift a lid to look at them. The procedure required the subjects to close the lid after they had seen "enough" and wait for the signal before beginning to reproduce as much of the figure as he could. A subject could lift the lid again and repeat the entire cycle as often as he wished till he was satisfied with his drawing. The total time spent on inspection of the figure was recorded and used as the basic score.

The interval between the closure of the lid and the signal to draw, which was variable, proved crucial. When this interval was 0·1 s, that is when copying could begin immediately after the closure of the display, the "2D" and the "3D" perceivers did not differ significantly in their relative scores on the two figures, but when the interval was increased to 10 s there was a significant difference between the groups, the 3D-perceivers requiring relatively longer time to inspect the impossible figure than the 2D-perceivers, just as one would expect from considerations of the nature of the difficulty involved.

Thus the results of Hudson's test, of the Construction test and of the task involving copying of an impossible figure are mutually reinforcing in so far as they indicate difficulties in perception of pictorial depth. The nature of this conclusion is not put to question by the alternative interpretation of the difficulties experienced when the two-pronged trident is copied. This explanation is that the 2D-perceivers may find the task of copying such figures relatively easy, not because they do not perceive the depth cues present in the figure, but because they do not integrate the cues present in various parts of the figure and hence do not notice their contradictory nature. On the other hand, the 3D-perceivers attempt such integration and find it impossible. Such an "integration" hypothesis is attractive because it can also be applied to meaningful pictures such as those of Hudson's test, as was suggested by Deręgowski (1968c). According to this interpretation, individual items which are portrayed in Hudson's stimuli may well be perceived as eidolically three-dimensional (not merely as epitomic drawings standing for three-dimensional objects), yet the failure to relate them to each other may hinder perception of the three-dimensionality of the entire scene which the test measures.

This explanation is, however, more difficult to apply to the Construction test stimuli as they have to be processed in their entirety to evoke perception of the third dimension, and hence it seems more plausible that a simple failure to take account of depth cues may also in the case of these figures contribute to the frequency of 2D-responses. This rider is sustained by the difference in sensitivity to representations of right angles between populations. A theoretical curve derived by Perkins (1972) (Fig. 4.12) shows the expected distribution of responses to the figures of parallelepipeds such as those in Fig. 4.13. American data

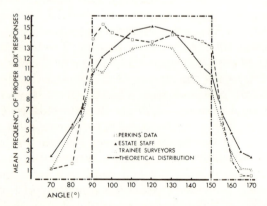

Fig. 4.12   Perkins's theoretical curve and some empirical data. The results provided by the American sample seem to differ from those obtained in Rhodesia.

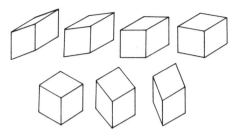

Fig. 4.13 Stimuli used in Perkins's and Rhodesian studies. Subjects were asked
to judge whether each of the figures portrayed a rectangular parallelepiped.

obtained by Perkins are superimposed upon this curve and fit it closely.
This is not so with data obtained from a sample of Black estate workers
and trainee surveyors from Rhodesia, which are also superimposed.
Instead of the sharp drop indicating a clear distinction between the
rectangular and non-rectangular solids shown by the Perkins data, the
Rhodesian curves show rather gentler slopes characteristic of wide
transition zones in which the observers appear uncertain of how to
classify stimuli.

The suggestion of differential difficulty in perception of pictorial
depth in responses to single cues therefore remains, even though it
cannot be said to be the only reason for failure in perception of pictorial
depth of more complex pictures. It is still possible that when the stimuli
calling for integration are viewed, the ability to integrate becomes the
dominant influence. This interpretation agrees with the relative ease of
the Construction test as well as with the ability of Rhodesian subjects to
detect pictorial depth whilst responding to Perkins' test, neither of the
tests stresses integration.

The reproduction techniques described above need not be confined to
geometric figures but can also be used with realistic representations.
Arrays of toys can be photographed and the correctness of the reproductions made from the photographs judged. Such a technique when used
with Western children shows a gradual change of the type of reconstruction from predominantly random at about three and a half years of age
to predominantly systematic at about eight years (Brown 1969).

A reproduction technique was also used by Page (1970), who required
his subjects to arrange drawings showing the heads of the three figures
of Hudson's test in a manner which would indicate how the scene shown
in Hudson's fifth picture (see Fig. 4.9) would appear when viewed from
an aircraft. The subjects were Zulu youths drawn from an urban
primary and secondary school with average ages of about 14 and 17
years respectively. The arrangements which they produced were as

follows: (i) the younger group placed the man and the antelope about 8 inches apart and the elephant at about 3 inches from the line joining the elephant and the man; (ii) for the older group the corresponding distances were, to the nearest inch, 7 inches and 4 inches respectively. These results can be compared with the measurements of pictorial depth obtained by the use of Pandora's Box, which we have already discussed in general terms.

Page used his data to argue that perception of pictorial depth may be compatible with the response that in Hudson's pictures the hunter is closer to the elephant than he is to the duiker. The data provided in Page's paper are however unfortunately insufficient to evaluate this postulate.

Pandora's Box data, on the other hand clearly show that Page's contention is right, provided that it can be assumed that such reproductions do indeed reflect exactly what the subject perceives. The implicit-shape constancy observations would incline one to treat such an assumption *cum grano salis* because one could argue that, just as in the case of the implicit shape constancy the response indicates a compromise between various cues available, so here the absence of certain common depth cues ensures that the reproduced depth is also a result of perceptual compromise. Furthermore the differences between responses made to Hudson's test by subjects drawn from different cultures are not explained by Page's observation. These cautionary notes are strengthened by Jahoda and McGurk's results to which we shall now turn.

Since scoring of such reproduction arrays as those obtained by Brown and by Page in their experiments is obviously difficult a simplified scheme involving only two figures developed by Jahoda and McGurk (1974, a, b) was used by these workers for a cross-cultural comparison between Scottish and Ghanaian school children. The stimuli used as well as the results obtained bear heavily on the theoretical considerations just put forward. The procedure consisted of two steps: training and testing. The subjects were trained on pictures showing two figures: one large woman and one small girl both drawn in the same plane, that is to say, with their feet at the same distance from the bottom of the picture. The subjects were required to respond by placing simple wooden tokens on a response board placed in front of them. These tokens were available in two sizes and could be placed two at a time in any combination of two out of four positions marked on the board and forming a rectangle with two of its sides in two of the subject's fronto-parallel planes. In the case of the training picture just described the correct response would be to place a large figure opposite the "woman" and the small figure opposite the "girl" both at the same distance from the subject, thus showing awareness of their depicted coplanarity. Furthermore when the two figures are drawn towards the bottom edge of the picture one would expect the tokens to occupy the pair of spots nearer to the subject, since they are nearer to him on the pictorial space, and analogously one would expect them to occupy the pair of spots further from the subjects when they are equidistant from the subject and further away in the pictorial space; that is when they are both moved equally towards the top of the picture.

The reader will have guessed by now that the testing of the subjects is concerned with their ability to match the arrangement and the size of the tokens to the depicted figures. The pictures used in the test show both the woman and the girl at either of the two pictorial depths which are indicated both by pictorial elevation and by the size of the figures, and may in addition be stressed by the introduction of additional cues such as density gradients, for example. In the experiment reported by Jahoda and McGurk (1974a) the heights of figures used were: girl, 3·3 and 5·0 cm; woman, 5·0 and 7·5 cm. Hence when the two figures were portrayed at the greater distance their relative sizes were 3·3 and 5·0 cm; when the "woman" was closer to the observer than the "girl" they were 7·5 and 3·3 cm and when these relative distances were reversed both figures were equal in size (5 cm). A subject's perception is thus judged by his placement of the "woman" and "girl" tokens on the response board.

The test was administered together with Hudson's test to children in Scotland and Ghana. As one would expect from an earlier detailed report on Ghanaian children who were tested on selected figures of Hudson's test (Mundy-Castle 1966) there was a significant difference between the two groups, the Scots being consistently more "3D" on both tests, although this trend was greater on Hudson's test. In addition the scores of both samples were higher on Jahoda and McGurk's test than they were on Hudson's test. The pattern of results obtained here is strikingly similar to the results obtained in the Construction test, which also showed that a large number of subjects who failed to respond three-dimensionally to Hudson's test pictures did so in response to the Construction test stimuli. In their interpretation of these results Jahoda and McGurk suggest that their test measures perceptual skills which are acquired relatively early, unlike Hudson's test, which requires some inferential skills and a considerable verbal comprehension. This, it is claimed, explains the significant increase of scores with age on Hudson's and an absence of such change on Jahoda and McGurk's test. The increase with age/schooling is not, however, uniform in both samples, there being no difference in scores in the Ghanaian pupils from second and fourth grades of primary school and only between the fourth and sixth grades, whilst the Scottish sample shows a steady increase throughout the range. The data could therefore be interpreted as showing that Hudson's test is inherently more difficult so that children who have reached the "ceiling" on Jahoda and McGurk's test may yet remain at the "floor" level in the case of Hudson's test. Such argument is, however, not acceptable to Jahoda and McGurk, who suggest that there is a qualitative difference between the two tests, that Hudson's test "taps merely one specific aspect, and probably not the most important one, of a complex cluster of abilities".

It has been argued before that there is no specific pictorial ability which a single test can determine and that the practical value of any level of ability can only be judged in the contexts in which a subject may find himself. Ability to do well on Jahoda and McGurk's test may be associated with the more basic aspects of perception. We shall try to show that this is indeed so, and to press the argument further to show that the notion of pictorial perception implicit both in Deręgowski's (1968c) and Jahoda and McGurk's stimuli is so fundamental as to relate more closely to the illusions than to pictures; that is to say, they embody in a particularly strong form those illusory effects which are commonly incorporated in pictures.

Comparison of the figure showing the stimuli used by Deręgowski (Fig. 4.14) with Jahoda and McGurk's stimuli (Fig. 4.15) shows their essential similarity; the difference between them being not so much in the nature of cues as of their form. The role which in Deręgowski's stimuli is played by a square is in the case of Jahoda and McGurk's stimuli played by the two figures. In both sets of stimuli *geometrically similar* elements are placed at different heights in a picture and perception of pictorial depth evoked by them measured and therefore both partake of the elevation effect which is independent of the epitomic value of the stimuli.

Elevation in the field of view is one of the most firmly established of the depth cues used by the painters and draughtsmen working in the European tradition. It is also the cue which is employed in some oriental schools of art, such as the traditional art of Persia, India and Pakistan, in which perspective convergence is not used. The absence of convergence cue with elevation cue present makes a Western observer see pictures of these schools as distorted. The entire composition looks either by introducing the elements of perspective where these are missing or by changing the elevation of the offending elements as shown in Fig. 4.16.

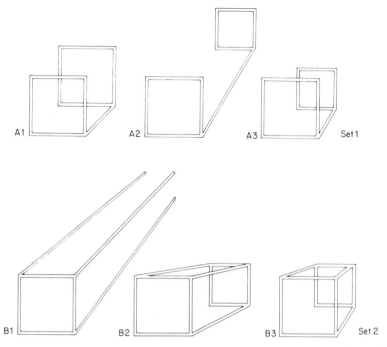

Fig. 4.14 Stimuli used in Deręgowski's (1968) construction task. Note that with a sole exception all figures incorporate the element of two squares differing in pictorial elevation.

Fig. 4.15 One of the figures used by Jahoda and McGurk (1974a).

(a)

(b)

(c)

Fig. 4.16   Three figures derivative from oriental art. (a) A tracing of the essential elements of an oriental picture. (b) and (c) "corrected" pictures. The only depth cue provided is that of elevation. This implies, to a Western viewer, that the two gardeners should either differ in size, the one higher up being relatively smaller, as shown in (b), or that they should be placed closer together, as shown in (c).

The ubiquity and effectiveness of elevation as the cue to pictorial distance is not surprising as it is one of the most frequent environmental cues. For any observer whose line of sight makes an angle with a horizontal surface on which he is standing those objects on this surface which are further away from him will also appear higher in his visual field. This experience is transferred to and established in pictorial perception in early childhood as shown by Jahoda and McGurk (1974a) in a paper in which perception of Scottish children aged between four and 11 years was investigated. The children, it is reported, even in the youngest group showed perception of pictorial depth. This increased both with age, and with the addition of further depth cues. The basic picture used contained only one pictorial depth cue, that of elevation. The picture was not however entirely devoid of information other than that presented by the two critical figures. There was a horizon which divided the entire picture into a homogeneous grassy ground and the sky with a single floating cloud. When these cues were removed so that only the two figures appeared on an entirely uniform white background the effect still remained, albeit at a much depleted strength. It seems implausible that the horizon and the uniformly green grass on which the figures stand in the picture and the sky provide pictorial depth cues. These elements do not possess any traces of either perspective or density gradients enabling them to do so. The only effect which they can probably have is that of unifying the picture. When the two figures are portrayed on a distinct common background the picture is probably integrated more effectively than when no such background is provided and in consequence there is greater perceptual tendency to compare the two figures. When no unifying background is provided the two figures are likely to be seen as two separate pictures; the resulting illusory effect is therefore likely to be much less.This element of integration has already been discussed in connection with Hudson's pictures. In the other two pictures used by Jahoda and McGurk, further cues were incorporated. They were those of linear perspective, which was introduced by including in one of the pictures a path along which both figures walked and, in another picture, in addition to the perspective of the path a density gradient was introduced and the perspective strengthened by drawing a fence running along the path. This graduation of the richness of pictorial cues of their stimuli led the investigators to observe that the effect of the added cues, "though cumulative and significant, was relatively slight compared with that of elevation alone" (p. 146). An observation which is clearly consistent with the dominant influence of elevation as a depth cue.

The general sensitivity of children to the basic pictorial cues has previously been reported by Newman (1969), who found that six-year-old children are affected by a stimulus which consisted of accumulation of pictorial gradients similar to those embodied in Jahoda and McGurk's third stimulus. The experiment which yielded these findings parallels Jahoda and McGurk's work so closely that it will be considered in more detail. In it three groups of children aged about six years, ten years and 14 years respectively were shown the stimulus figure, which was so designed that the "nearer" of the two vertical bars compared could be adjusted in height by means of a simple mechanism. The subject's point of subjective equality was determined by using this device. This was followed by elicitation from each child of a description of the picture which could be used to judge whether the array was perceived as three or two-dimensional. The two aspects of the percept were thus measured within each group and the groups compared. Now whilst there was no evidence of difference among the three groups in their susceptibility to illusion, all groups showing the expected illusory effect, there was a noticeable and significant difference among the frequencies with which children provided such descriptions as to indicate that they saw, or failed to see, pictorial depth in the scene. This is shown clearly by the ratios of "3D" to "2D" perceivers, which were:

for 6 year olds	4:12
for 10 year olds	16: 0
for 14 year olds	16: 0

If both responses, the oral description and the physical adjustment, are considered to be equally valid measures of pictorial depth perception, then the discord between them in the youngest group calls for a special justification.

Newman's experimental results agree with those of Leibowitz and Judish (1967) obtained with a much poorer stimulus, the traditional Ponzo figure. They found that of children required to identify the longer of two lines those aged above five years showed a distinct tendency to respond in accordance with the expected illusory effect and call the upper line longer, and that this tendency increased rapidly to adult levels. However children younger than five years of age showed no susceptibility to the illusion. Similarly when children were first taught to identify the larger of two squares and were subsequently asked to find the "larger" of two squares presented on a picture which provided a background rich in pictorial depth cues, those aged about three years showed no systematic influence of the background whilst those aged about nine showed the expected influence in about three quarters of their responses. This frequency is fairly close to the average adult rate, of about 80%, obtained under identical circumstances.

A further variation on the same paradigm was employed by Yonas and Hagen (1973). The instructions again required the subjects to identify the larger of the two triangles presented either on a pictorial background or on a stage. Both types of background were viewed binocularly and monocularly. The most important findings were that children showed less influence of the pictorial cues than adults and that elimination of binocular cues affected responses of children much more than adults. Olson *et al.*(1980) in their comprehensive review of recent research of children's perception stress that the results show a decline in the number of correct responses owing to the surface cues provided by the motion parallax and binocular disparity in a sample of children but that no similar decline was obtained from a sample of the adults under analogous conditions. The surface of the picture seems therefore to affect perception; a result to which we shall have occasion to return.

Two characteristics of the stimuli used in all the experiments of this family ought also to be stressed. First, that in all the experiments the stimulus to be identified was described in terms of size and, second, that in all of them the two stimuli were geometrically similar. The latter characteristic is common to figures used in investigations of perception of perspective and was also, as has been said, present in Jahoda and McGurk's stimuli. Use of such matched stimuli is widespread and for a very good reason, as it serves to eliminate the unwarranted variable of the nature of the figures being judged. This manipulation does, however, force the experimenters to run the risk of falling into the deep blue sea whilst dodging the devil, for geometrically similar figures do exercise a greater mutual influence than figures which are not similar. This is clearly so in the case of the variants of the Titchener illusion figures. When these are made up of geometrically similar elements the illusory effect is much stronger than in figures constructed from elements which are not geometrically similar (Coren and Miller 1974). The same impression is conveyed by Figs 4.17 a, b and c. The two rectangles in the first figure form a spatial arrangement identical with that formed by trapezia and rectangles in the the the other two figures, and the perception of depth is stronger in the case of the latter two figures. This effect is absent in Hudson's pictures, which use three different figures: it is, however, present in several other studies inspired by Hudson's work. It is found in Hagen and Johnson's (1977) comparison of American subjects' responses to a set of pictures modelled on Hudson's test, and to a set of pictures of their own devising "constructed to duplicate as nearly as possible" those inspired by Hudson's test, but with animal figures

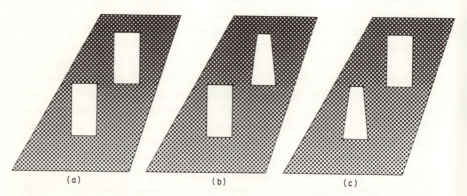

(a)   (b)   (c)

Fig. 4.17   **The effect of the difference in elevation is to induce such a perception that the upper of the two rectangles in (a) is taller than the lower. Since its discrepancy is less in figures (b) and (c), in both of which one of the rectangles has been replaced by a trapezium, the similarity between the two figures compared must augment the illusory effect.**

replaced by human "Western" figures; the place of the hunter taken by a boy throwing a ball. In this "Western" version the two figures replacing the elephant and the duiker are geometrically similar. However unlike in Jahoda and McGurk's case where the drawings had to be similar to permit similarity of tokens, such similarity has been introduced here without any apparent reason and may well be responsible for the observed discrepancies between the responses to the two versions. (It may also parenthetically be noted that the discrepancies between Hagen and Jones' "Hudson's" stimuli and the true Hudson's stimuli, for example, in the relative size of the hunter and the elephant, are such as to render any comparison of their data, with those which would be obtained with Hudson's original stimuli, questionable.)

A much earlier study of Omari and McGintie (1974), which uses the conceptually identical notion of adaptation of Hudson's stimuli so as to increase their acceptability to the subjects of a particular culture, and of comparing subjects' responses to such a test with those obtained from selected stimuli of Hudson's test almost escapes such strictness, because the experimenters have chosen to replace the elephant and the duiker by a cow and a goat respectively. The geometrical similarity effect does not therefore arise but there are unfortunately other questionable influences. One of these is that the familiar size difference within the pairs of animals may be perceived as less in the case of the modified stimuli. The other is the difference in the size of the figures, especially of that of the man. Omari and McGintie's hunter is taller than Hudson's, not only in objective terms as measured with a ruler, but also in relation to the "farther" animal. Both these factors would tend to enhance perception of pictorial depth and could therefore explain the more "3D" scores obtained by Omari and McGintie with their own than with Hudson's stimuli.

One should also mention a similar lapse in one of the important publications (Lloyd 1972): pictures which were presented as typical of Hudson's test do in fact deviate greatly from Hudson's stimuli in many ways but most importantly perhaps in that in all of them the alignment of the hunter's spear with both the elephant and the duiker is absent and the relative sizes of figures are entirely different.

A striking feature of the first set of the Construction test figures (Fig. 4.1) is that they could be thought of as incomplete Necker cubes and therefore presumably subject to the same perceptual transformations as the Necker cube; namely the characteristic reversals which make the percepts of the cube alternate, now the upper fronto-parallel face, now the lower fronto-parallel face appearing to be closer to the observer. One would also expect the difference in pictorial elevation of the faces of the cube to affect perception: the percept of the cube with its lower face near to the observer should be more probable than the percept of the cube with its upper face near to the observer.

Such reversals are of course not unique to the Necker cube, as Fig. 4.18 showing a triangular prism and its derivatives demonstrates. The five figures shown differ in their refersal propensities. Figures (i) and (iv) reverse readily, (ii) and (v) somewhat less readily whilst only very slight tendency to reverse can be detected in (iii), which incorporates an unambiguous overlap. Of these figures (v) is of particular interest, the others being included primarily to indicate the continuity of the phenomenon. This figure is similar to those used in the experiments on perception of size and distance which we have described, and also to Jahoda and McGurk's stimuli. Its reversals reinforce the impression that a common effect usually associated with reversible figures can perhaps be said to be contributory to both the Construction tests and Jahoda and McGurk's results. It ought to be noted that it is not important for perception of pictorial depth which of the two possible reversals is perceived, but that a tendency to reverse be present. Therefore the relative distance of the two triangles in Fig. 4.18 from the observer may be misperceived, although the presence of depth is perceived correctly just as was the case in Jahoda and McGurk's experiments. The perceived size of the two elements is not always affected by the reversals as Gregory (1970) has shown. But it is affected by much more stable and unambiguous density gradients, by linear perspective and by pictorial elevation. The blend of these influences is present in most realistic pictures and is jointly responsible for evocation of pictorial depth. Correctly perceived pictorial depth is thus postulated to be a vector quantity having both magnitude and direction whilst the depth derived from the reversible figures *qua* reversible figures has only magnitude and can therefore be thought of as a scalar quantity. It is therefore unlike the

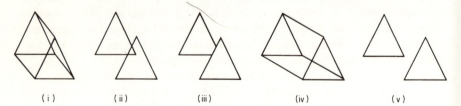

(i)   (ii)   (iii)   (iv)   (v)

Fig. 4.18   **The reversibility of the percept of two similar triangles. Either of the triangles, in each of the figures, can be seen as being closer to the observer. Such reversibility of elements of which the Necker cube is the best known example, is a factor associated with perception of depth in pictures.**

vectorial percepts of depth derived from, say, overlap or from density gradients. A combination of the scalar reversal effect with any of these factors yields a magnified vector quantity.

In their investigation using the apparatus already described, Jahoda and McGurk (1974a) found that Scottish children make two types of error, that of choice of a token of inappropriate size, and that of wrong placement of the tokens, with different frequencies. The "size" responses were more often correct than the placement responses. In terms of the experimenters' observations this meant that often the tokens were matched correctly, so that the larger token stood in front of the apparently larger figure (the "woman") and the smaller token stood in front of the smaller figure (the "girl"), but instead of being placed disgonally so as to indicate pictorial depth they were placed in a fronto-parallel plane. Jahoda and McGurk attribute the response to children's inability to recreate three-dimensional percepts, and support this claim by data showing that such difficulties are experienced by children required to reproduce spatial arrays. Their attribution is also in accord with observations on Zambian subjects, who built 3D responses to Construction test drawings, sometimes with models which, although unmistakably three-dimensional, diverged greatly from those depicted, which they were asked to reproduce. "Many of the models", it is reported, "were incomplete . . .; some could only be described as 'gothic' in that they contained many superfluous members sometimes in an extremely strange array". Some of the constructions had unsuspected distortions (Deręgowski 1968, p. 203).

Interpretation of these results, as showing that pictorial depth is perceived yet placement responses made do not show this, may however imply too rigid and generalized a distinction between ability and inability to perceive pictorial depth, especially so since a similar pattern of difficulties was, as reported above, observed by Newman, who did not require his subjects to build models but merely to describe the stimulus. The demands of construction of depicted arrays may therefore present an obstacle additional to the essential difficulty of perception of pictorial depth and hence be an invalid explanation of all the perceptual difficulties.

An alternative explanation is suggested by the analogy to our analysis of picture recognition. This is that just as in the case of studies of recognition a picture shares some characteristics with an object yet does not always evoke the same responses as objects do; so here pictorial depth is not a robust effect which evokes an appropriate response whatever the task. It is rather ephemeral and its influence upon the choice of representation of the depicted figures is greater than the effect upon reproduction of their spatial relationship. If this observation is correct then it follows that with the demonstrated difficulties of reproduction accounted for there would be a difference between the correctness of responses made to three-dimensional models and those made to pictures, the latter being more grossly erroneous. Unfortunately the published data do not allow us to comment on this.

Of the four techniques of assessing perception of pictorial depth hitherto described (i) elicitation of verbal responses, (ii) construction of a depicted array or a model, (iii) measurement of perceived pictorial depth by means of Pandora's Box and (iv) measurement of the difficulties with ambiguous figures (such as the two-pronged trident), the first has been by far the most frequent. It was generally the intent of researchers to replicate or to extend Hudson's observations.

A thorough and incisive critique of various studies purporting to replicate Hudson's study is provided by Jahoda and McGurk (1974c). They rightly contend that many of the studies which may be thought to have used Hudson's test did not in fact do so, but have used either a selection of stimuli derived from the test, or even of stimuli based on the test; but so different from the test stimuli that it cannot be claimed that they measured precisely the same effects. In some cases such deviations from the original were deliberately introduced for heuristic purposes and as such are, of course, admissible, but on some occasions the deviations present appear to be entirely accidental. The case of Hagen and Johnson's (1977) stimuli and the resulting dubiousness of the claim that they were testing subjects on Hudson's test has already been discussed. Some of the other investigations analysed by Jahoda and McGurk have just as little claim to be considered replications of Hudson's original findings because, as has been said, they employed test materials which diverged from Hudson's test or because they used different methods of scoring. Indeed the review mentions but one experiment as having used Hudson's entire set of stimuli. Such heterogeneity of data does not mean that the results obtained are valueless, indeed some of the results merit very careful consideration, but it implies that the data obtained cannot be related directly to Hudson's original findings.

Curiously, while relevant data have not been obtained speculative criticism of Hudson's work has, nevertheless, flourished. This generally refers to (i) the "poor quality" of Hudson's drawings and (ii) the ambiguity of the question "Which animal is nearer to the hunter?", which can be interpreted either "Which animal is nearer to the hunter in the plane of the paper?" or "Which animal would be nearer if this were not a picture but a real scene?"

The first of the criticisms need not concern us much. It is quite certain that had the pictures used by Hudson been more realistic the significant differences between samples drawn from different cultures would have been less and, indeed, that making the drawings progressively more and more realistic and presenting them in special settings, allowing only monocular views from carefully chosen positions would *in fine* have led to the disappearance of such differences; unless, of course, there were inter-cultural differences in perception of the "real" world. There is, however, no suggestion or evidence in Hudson's work that the cultures differ in their perception of the real world, but merely in interpretation of portrayals of the world. (The validity of the notion that no perceptual differences relevant to the "real" world exist can, however, be questioned in view of the evidence obtained by Leibowitz *et al.* (1969), and Brislin and Keating (1976) about the differences of susceptibility to the three-dimensional Ponzo illusion in various cultures (see p. 36).)

The variation of the extent to which various figures may diverge from the three-dimensional reality and the effect this may have on perception have already been discussed, but it needs to be stressed again, as does the danger of gradually and imperceptibly drifting towards "reality" in order to explain abstraction, and thus following the footsteps of Mein Herr, who said:

> That's another thing we've learned . . . map-making. But we've carried it much further than you. What do you consider the largest map that would be useful?" "About six inches to the mile." "Only six inches!" exclaimed Mein Herr. "We very soon got to six yards to the mile. Then we tried a hundred yards to the mile. And then came the grandest idea of all! We actually made a map of the country, on the scale of a mile to the mile!" "Have you used it much?" I enquired. "It has never been spread out, yet," said Mein Herr, "the farmers objected: they said it would cover the whole country, and shut out the sunlight! So we now use the country itself, as its own map, and I assure you it does nearly as well (Lewis Carroll).

The primary importance of Hudson's finding clearly lies in his demonstration of a cultural difference on a previously uninvestigated task. This finding would be just as significant had it been obtained with even more rudimentary drawings.

The second objection depends on the relative weights attached to each of the two questions in Hudson's test used for scoring, and on the frequency with which the responses given to them are contradictory.

Zambian data obtained using Hudson's test (Deręgowski 1968c) show the following frequencies of 2D and 3D responses to each of the two questions.

The figures in each cell represent the number of subjects making a particular response to each picture. The figures without brackets are

Table III.   *Responses obtained from Hudson's test on Zambian subjects (Deręgowski 1968c).*

Type of response	Hudson's figures No. (and letter in Fig. 4.9)						
	1, a	2, b	3, c	4, d	5, e	6, f	7
Both responses 3D	6(0)	17(5)	13(2)	11(2)	14(1)	15(4)	8(0)
(i) Elephant nearer than the Duiker (2D) (ii) Duiker is hunted (3D)	6(1)	4(2)	3(3)	0(1)	2(1)	4(0)	1(1)
(i) Elephant further away than the Duiker (3D) (ii) Elephant is hunted (2D)	5(0)	6(1)	7(1)	13(3)	7(2)	5(2)	11(4)
Both responses 2D	31(47)	21(40)	25(42)	24(42)	25(44)	24(42)	28(43)
% inconsistent	12.5	13.5	14.5	17.7	12.5	11.5	17.7

those for the sample of 48 Zambian school children and those in brackets for 48 men with little or no formal education.

It is apparent that the majority of subjects were consistent responders, that is both their answers indicated that either the pictorial depth was seen or that it was not seen. The frequency of such consistent responders to the stimuli fluctuates between about 82 and 88%. There is therefore relatively little reason to claim that the large numbers of subjects were responding in the manner suggested by the critics. Further examination of the inconsistent responders supports this claim; with the sole exception of the first picture, the more frequent of the two sets of inconsistent responses was that in which subjects claimed that the elephant was further away from the hunter than the duiker and yet that the elephant was being hunted, a response therefore contrary to the suggestion that owing to a misunderstanding, distances in the plane of the paper were taken into account by the subjects. Indeed, the data show that when all the inconsistent responses which could possibly be attributed to this effect are taken into account, they amount only to at most 7% of the total, and are in general much lower. This percentage is considerably less than the difference between African and Western subjects obtained by Hudson. The critics, it appears, have been rather rash.

A conspicuously high frequency of the inconsistent responses, in which the elephant is said to be hunted in spite of the claim that it is further from the hunter than the duiker, was made to the fourth of

Hudson's figures. As Hudson's test presents figures in a sequence of increasing potency of depth cues one would not expect such a sudden increase of inconsistent responses.

Closer examination of the figure hints at the possible cause of this dramatic deviation from the normal pattern of scores. In Fig. 4.9d the overlap cue between the hunter's spear and the elephant, which could lead to perception of pictorial depth, does not do so. This is contrary to the expectations which one derives from the Pandora's Box study, which show that overlap cue affects perception of pictorial depth in a Western sample (p. 128). This effect could be entirely absent in the African samples; it could scarcely, however, be negative as such a dramatic increase in the number of "failures" suggests. The reason for these strange responses probably lies in the nature of the overlap. The tip of the spear overlaps with the elephant's eye. One need not be a hunter to realize that an eye might be a convenient spot to aim at when throwing a spear at the animal. Hence it seems that in the case of this particular drawing, owing to an unfortunate juxtaposition by the draughtsman, a configuration which was intended to provide an eidolic cue to depth has provided a highly symbolic epitomic cue, and the latter cue proved to be dominant for some of the subjects.

The plausibility of this explanation is sustained by the following experiment (Deręgowski 1968b), in which Zambian school children had to adjust a figure of a hunter aiming a shotgun so that it pointed in the same direction as in the photograph with which they were provided. The hunter occupied one corner of a large cardboard rectangle and could be rotated so as to face any direction. Two of the corners far away from the hunter were used to display the following combinations of figures of buffalo at a size appropriate to that of the hunter: in two conditions only a single buffalo was used and occupied either position A or position B (see Fig. 4.19); in the third condition two buffaloes were used and both

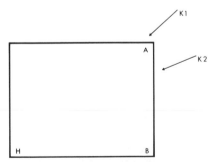

Fig. 4.19   Plan of the "hunting scene" used in an investigation of perception of depicted orientation (Deręgowski, 1968b).

F

positions occupied. In each of these arrangements the hunter's gun was pointed in the direction of B whether this position was occupied or not. All the arrangements were photographed with the camera in positions K1 and K2 and directed slightly downwards and towards the centre of the display. When photographs were presented to the children and they were told to set the figure of the hunter just as it was in the photograph their responses appeared to be swayed more by interpretation of the photograph than by its content. When there was an animal in front of the hunter's gun the errors made were rather small; when the animal was not there, there was a significant tendency to set the hunter so that it did not aim into the void by rotating him towards the only animal displayed. (This effect, however, was not present in the case of both sets of photographs. It may well be, therefore, that the angle from which the figures were photographed and the resulting relationship between the depicted figures also affected perception.)

Since the difficulties described arise from the paradoxical nature of pictures, from the fact that whilst flat, they perceptually convey three-dimensionality; they can be analysed by considering both elements of the paradox. One can attempt to investigate the efficaciousness of those pictorial cues which convey pictorial depth, such as depicted density gradients of perspective cues, and one can also investigate those cues which convey the flatness of the picture, such as those density gradients inherent to the surface on which the picture is made, or the cues opposing perspective and contained in the framework provided by the edges of the picture. Such division of the influences into positive and negative as far as perception of pictorial depth is concerned is not intended to suggest that the perceptual mechanism treats them separately but that such cues can conveniently be and indeed have been treated separately by some of the research workers.

Attempts at inter-cultural analysis of the cues which foster perception of depth are relatively few and do not generally attempt to manipulate the variables to any large extent. Most workers have been concerned–as our review shows–with enriching the cues in order to elicit perception of pictorial elevation and familiar size and other cues are added to these; the possibilities of interaction between cues have therefore to be borne in mind when considering the data obtained with their help. An identical restriction applies of course to all the figures inspired by Hudson's stimuli. Similarly all the Construction test stimuli (Fig. 4.14) share the cue of pictorial elevation. The other cues do not appear to affect the response, the typical frequencies of 3D responders to the A series of figures being A1: A2: A3–11 (12): 12 (13): 13 (13) and for B series B1: B2: B3–19 (17): 20 (17): 22 (14). The figures without brackets show the numbers of Zambian school boys, those within brackets, numbers of domestic men servants. In both cases the largest frequency possible was 24. The influence of the additional cues, such as overlap or perspective, seems in these cases to be negligible. In order to arrive at the proper evaluation of a particular cue's importance in perception of pictorial depth one would wish to observe its effect under a variety of conditions and in a variety of pictures, and to measure this effect by a variety of methods, just as it has been done in the case of perception of pictorial depth. Such procedures have, to our knowledge, not been carried out on any of these cues, with the exception of the "perspective" cues. These were investigated in a number of studies inspired by Leibowitz's work, which we have discussed, and were found to be responsible for a systematic variation in perception of depth extending from abstract figures to "real world" arrangements (Leibowitz and Pick 1972, Brislin 1974, Kilbride and Leibowitz 1975, Kilbride and Robbins 1968, 1969).

Before commenting briefly upon the largely neglected negative pictorial depth cues provided by the pictures surfaces, we shall pause to examine two further objections to Hudson's findings which implicitly postulate that such cues affect the operation of the perceptual mechanism.

Hudson's (1969) report contains a passage in which he says that in two of the eight samples the responses were noticeably slower, the subjects unlike those of the other groups not indicating immediately whether their percepts were 2D or 3D. This was especially so in the group of graduate teachers some of whom took as long as an hour to respond to a simple picture. This statement evoked comments claiming that this clearly shows the essential ambiguity of the task. This may be so and it may therefore be that the test is not suitable for use with highly sophisticated groups. Although the subjects visibly hesitated (and Hudson attributes this to the difficulties of perceptual organization), one cannot say with any certainty what was the nature of the difficulty. It is possible that the subjects saw both 2D and 3D possibilities and weighted them in order to decide which to choose, but it is also possible that they saw only one of them but thought that they should also see the other which they had encountered in other pictures, either richer (in the case of 3D perception) or poorer (in the case of 2D perception) in pictorial cues. They were then groping for the alternative which they knew should be available but which they could not find.

Without knowledge of which process occured it is impossible to make a cogent comment on the significance of the performance of these rather sophisticated subjects other than that already made, that the test was probably not suitable for them.

Unease has also occasionally been expressed about the possible effect of stress on Hudson's industrial subjects. There are no indications of such an influence in the original paper nor do the critics adduce any. There is on the other hand evidence obtained from a rural Zambian population by an anthropologist who has for a considerable time lived in a village in the area. These data, which were collected by Mrs Annette Jere (née Wong) show a predominance of 2D responders of about the same magnitude as that found in unsophisticated adults by Hudson. The Zambian subjects had at best some primary schooling and ranged in age from about ten to about 35 years of age. They were either Bisa or Lamba. The following summary table gives the distribution of responses made to the complete set of Hudson's pictures. It will be recalled that a total of fourteen responses is obtained in the test.

Table IV.   *Distribution of responses to Hudson's test made by Zambian villagers.*

Number of 3D responses	Number of responders.			
	Lamba		Bisa	
	Men and boys	Girls	Men and boys	Girls
0	24	9	37	8
1–4	3	1	5	2
5–9	4	1	1	1
10–13	2	0	0	0
14	0	0	0	0

If the top two categories in the above table are taken to contain 2D perceivers and the bottom two to contain 3D perceivers the proportions of these two groups in the combined sample are 89% and 2% respectively. If, puristically, only the extreme categories are taken into account then the corresponding figures are 78% and 0% respectively. This in spite of the fact that the testing was done by a worker familiar to the subjects and presumably free of suspicion of gathering information with some obscure but nefarious intent.

The reservations of Hudson's critics are it seems unfounded. They derive neither from the relevant field experience, nor from analysis of available data, but rather from speculation; the most free flowing, yet not the richest source in an area wherein data are scarce.

The notion that cues derived from a picture's surface may be an important influence for the difficulty is of course implicit in Gregory's Pandora's Box, an apparatus which has been used both in investigation of illusions and to a lesser extent in investigation of perception of pictorial depth (p. 128). The results obtained suggest that removal of the eidolically negative cues of the picture surface may indeed be a more efficient manner of inducing perception of pictorial depth. The same conclusion is implicit in Forge's observation of the Abelam, whose difficulties with epitomic pictorial perception have been described. The Abelam, it appears, shed those difficulties when examining slides in a hand viewer. It is also implicit in the behaviour of the audience which attended the Ugandan slide show (p. 109), and in the apparent effectiveness of stereoscopic figures as means for training of pictorial perception, an aspect which we shall consider more fully in our review of remedial methods.

The surface of the picture plays an especially important role in its perception under two circumstances; in the case of the ordinary pictures viewed obliquely and in the case of special anamorphic pictures which are so made that they have to be viewed obliguely in order to perceive the depicted pattern correctly. Some of the outstanding examples of anamorphic art have recently been discussed by Baltrusaitis (1977).

When an ordinary picture is viewed obliquely the information derived from its surface *qua* surface can be used to derive the notion of the correct viewpoint. An analogy with the implicit-shape constancy observations and the observations on density gradients is readily apparent. Just as in these cases so here the information (derived in this case from its surface *and* often from the pictorial pattern) can be used by the perceptual apparatus to correct for the perceived slant and in consequence to transform the retinal projections of the pictorial patterns so as to alter both epitomic and eidolic percepts. In the case of the anamorphic pictures viewed at an angle the effects are different. There the information derived from the surface *qua* surface has to be dismissed as irrelevant and any corrective implications resisted, the retinal projections of the picture being treated as the correct stimulus for the derivation of the relevant percepts.

The different role played by the surface cues in the two types of stimuli would lead one to expect a pronounced difference in their perception by the observers' differing in their proneness to surface cues. The anticipated effects would be as follows:

A. Ordinary picture
   1. Frontal view: surface cues hinder correct perception
   2. Oblique view: surface cues aid correct perception
B. Anamorphic picture
   1. Frontal view: correct perception impossible
   2. Oblique view: surface cues hinder correct perception

Accordingly observers prone to the influence of the surface cues would, one expects, be superior to their less prone counterparts in perceiving ordinary pictures presented at an angle and inferior to them under all other relevant conditions.

The effect of viewing a picture at a slant has not been tested inter-culturally and even within the Western world the effect has not been thoroughly explored. Gombrich (1972) argues that generally a viewer is likely not to compensate for such distortions of an ordinary picture as might occur when it is viewed obliquely because the resulting distortions are unlikely to be incompatible with the experience. A portrayal of a person when viewed obliquely would lead to such a person being perceived as slimmer. This percept is entirely acceptable for there are slimmer persons.

An experiment using simple line drawings was conducted by Perkins (1973). It was inspired by Gombrich's observations described above and the apparently contradictory observations of Pirenne (1970), who furnishes as evidence of distortion of exact central projection onto a plane two pinhole camera photographs of rows of vertical cylinders supporting spheres. The cylinders when photographed stood in a plane parallel to the plane of the film and the resulting picture shows a row of cylinders whose width increases away from the centre of the picture and a row of supported solids of which only that in the centre looks like a sphere. The others are ovoid and this characteristic shape becomes more pronounced as one moves away from the centre of the picture. These photographs do not however present an antithesis of Gombrich's observations since, unlike a picture seen at an angle, they are in the plane normal to the line of viewing.

An observer looking normally at Pirenne's photographs experience no contradictory cues from their surface and therefore sees the figures for what they are (not for what they depict). Gombrich's dictum need scarcely be altered to cope with this case; one can simply paraphrase it so as to say that: "well, there are cylinders of various widths and eggs aplenty". Notwithstanding this comment it is possible to put forward a hypothesis contrary to that of Gombrich, that when a surface of a picture is viewed at an angle this will be taken heed of by the perceptual mechanism and the percept arrived at will embody compensation for the slant.

This hypothesis and Gomrich's dictum provided the polar opposites for Perkins' study, in which observers judged whether the figures depicted rectangular or non-rectangular parallelepipeds. The figures were presented normally or slanted at two different angles so chosen that (i) the slant compensated for the distortion in the drawing, i.e. the figures which when viewed normally would yield non-rectangular percepts were so slanted that if the information about the slant were ignored they would yield rectangular percepts; and (ii) the slant was such as to distort the figures, i.e. such figures which would when normally viewed yield rectangular percepts were so slanted that if the slant were ignored they would yield non-rectangular percepts.

The results reported were that the responses were on the whole such as would have been obtained had most of the stimuli been viewed normally, although the effect of compensation seemed to be less for the more acute of the two angles of viewing. The surface cues (and such other non-pictorial cues as were embodied in the stimuli) were therefore clearly used by the observers.

Stereoscopy offers another method of breaking away from the surface of the paper. Usual stereoscopic pictures of solids do more than this and provide a three-dimensional percept which appears to float in the air above the surface of the paper. Such an image would not be suitable to our immediate purpose, although it has other important uses (p. 160). However, an image freed from the surface of the paper, yet seen as flat and floating above the surface, as is the case with some of Julesz's figures, would offer another hitherto inter-culturally unexplored way of investigating the importance of the surface cues. Julesz demonstrates that a Necker cube thus produced reverses in the usual way, but it is possible that such reversals would not be equally frequent with the two types of Necker cube: the stereo and the usual drawing. It may be that the coplanarity resulting from the stereoscopic presentation would be so strong as to override any gains resulting from freeing the figure from its background and therefore the effect would be the opposite of that expected to follow such freeing. Gregory (1970) observes that stereo-zero-perspective Necker cubes reverse rarely, which suggests that, indeed, such an outcome is likely. It may, however, be less probable in the case of figures having little or no overlap among various elements, such as some of the stimuli used in the Construction task.

SOME THEORETICAL
CONSIDERATIONS

If it is accepted, and it would be difficult to argue otherwise, that the eidolic elements in pictures are the same as those found in the studies of illusions, then obviously such theories as may be used to account for illusions can be invoked to explain the cognate aspects of pictures, and additional theories would need to be put forward to deal with epitomic aspects with the resulting combination of the two aspects. This particular approach has not, however, been generally followed by those who accepted that the difficulties observed by Hudson were real. Commonly the difficulties were not analysed and a single cause was proposed to account for them.

Any characteristic on which the two populations sampled by Hudson differ can be suggested as an explanation for the difference of scores on Hudson's test. Du Toit (1966) put forward the hypothesis that such differences arose from the difference in languages spoken by the two groups, an explanation derived from the earlier works of Sapir (1928, 1958) and Whorf (1958), and enshrined in the Sapir-Whorf hypothesis. This postulates a dominant role for language as a cognitive filter and as the provider of schemata for thought. In the words of Sapir: "we see and hear and otherwise experience very largely as we do because the language habits of our community predispose us to do so". The value of the hypothesis has been questioned by several workers and its claim in the sphere of perception somewhat eroded by Heider's work (1971) on colour vision and colour naming among the Dani of New Guinea.

The Dani it appears have only two terms for "colour" meaning approximately "light" and "dark", yet they are superior at remembering unambiguous focal colours such as green or red than at remembering nonfocal colours which occupy in the colour spectrum positions intermediate between the focal colours. This superiority parallels that found in American subjects who had a relatively elaborate colour vocabulary.

The inapplicability of the linguistic hypothesis to Hudson's data in particular is shown by demonstrations of similar perceptual difficulties in the populations which differ linguistically from those tested by Hudson. Hence either similarities between crucial and as yet undefined linguistic elements in samples drawn from such disparate populations as South African Whites (Mundy-Castle and Nelson 1962), South African Bantu (Hudson 1967), Ghanaian (Mundy-Castle 1966, Jahoda and McGurk 1974b), Indian (Sinha and Shukla 1974), Sierra-Leonese (Dawson 1967a,b), New Guinean (Waldron and Gallimore 1973) and others, exist in some as yet undefined sense, or the hypothesis does not apply to the present data. It appears far more parsimonious to set aside the linguistic hypothesis and search the explanation elsewhere.

An equally fundamental influence to that just discussed was put forward by Littlejohn (1963), who thought that the quality of the concept of space entertained by an observer may influence his pictorial perception. Since a thorough examination of the Temne concept of space as embodied in the language showed it to be different from that commonly held in Western cultures, and since similar differences are said to prevail in the case of other African peoples, this might explain Hudson's results. Littlejohn accepts that such peoples do not ordinarily perceive the world in two dimensions. They must inhabit, he contends, the "same objective space" which geometrical analysis has revealed to us; but for them "objective space" is not explicitly apprehended background to space in which they are conscious of living. The concept of geometric space and of "geometrical–technical perception" associated with it, and its polar opposite, "physiognomic" perception, are both related to Werner's (1948) treatise on comparative psychology of mental development. This distinguishes between the mode of perception in which "things are known according to their 'geometrical– technical' matter of fact qualities" and a process which is "dynamized" because its object is perceived predominantly through the "motor and affective attitude" of the observer. The latter kind of perception, which is especially powerfully evoked by the "faces and bodily movements of human beings and higher animals", Werner calls *physiognomic*. It is this type of perception which, according to Littlejohn, dominates the processes of the Temne and extends to such stimuli as Hudson's drawings. The difficulties with acceptance of this hypothesis are similar to those encountered in the discussion of the linguistic hypothesis. Werner's evidence is not strong, it is based to a large extent on unsystematic observations, which can serve as a source of hypotheses but cannot be thought of as convincing; in addition, some of the data considered by him are in the form of drawings, which, as we shall see later, are untrustworthy witnesses, since they embody both perceptual and motor skills of the draughtsmen and create special interpretative problems. Furthermore, and more importantly, there is evidence neither that "physiognomic" perception of drawings is common to all the samples concerned, nor that in some of them the difficulties are not of the very opposite origin, weak *dynamization* of the depicted scene leading to poor pictorial integration. It is probably justified, therefore, to adopt here the same stratagem as in the case of the linguistic hypothesis, regard the "conceptual" case as "not proven", and to seek an explanation elsewhere.

The obvious hypotheses, those of differences in genetic endowment and the effect of different cultural environments, especially lack of contact with pictures at an early age in those populations which experience difficulties, have all been suggested by various authors; generally without even an attempt being made to sustain the validity of such claims empirically. This is so for the very good reason that the separation of the genetic and environmental elements is in practice very difficult in view of selective migration, selective admission to schools, and other socio-economic factors. Sinha and Shukla's (1974) comparison on Indian pictorial perception tasks of children from orphanages and nurseries could only yield valid data if children from the same genetic pool could be found in orphanages and nurseries. A discussion of the tangled problems of genetic and environmental effects falls outwith the scope of this book. One ought, however, to note that attribution of the difficulties to differences in skill (Serpell 1976) although implying a specific approach, does not resolve the difficulty, since the genetic element which determines acquisition of a skill may be of prime importance.

REMEDIAL APPROACHES

There are two diametrically opposite ways in which a definition of a perceptual difficulty can be sought. One can observe the changes of such a difficulty whilst systematically varying the stimuli or one can investigate the nature of the remedial measures required for elimination of the difficulty. The former, direct, method has been employed in all the studies described above; the latter, indirect, method although less frequent has also been used with some success.

Unfortunately there are no known reports of systematic inter-cultural studies of teaching of epitomic perception of pictures. This aspect of pictorial perception has been largely ignored, perhaps understandably so because as our review of the literature shows it is likely to be readily observable only in very remote populations. However, as our review also shows, use of appropriate stimuli should make it possible to investigate it even in sophisticated populations and such investigations would generally benefit the psychological theories of vision.

The difficulties with perception of pictorial depth have, on the other hand, attracted attention of several workers. The resulting studies can be subdivided into two groups defined by the methods of instruction used, (a) an overtly explanatory group in which direct instruction was the most important vehicle by which training is attempted and (b) a smaller group of studies which try to alter the trainee's perceptual experience in such a manner as to *induce* him to perceive pictorial depth, without resorting to instruction.

The two categories, of course, overlap because studies of the former kind as a rule involve use of visual aids; it is, however, helpful to distinguish between them because of the implicit assumptions which they embody about the extent to which perception of the third dimension in pictures is a conscious process.

An interesting attempt to use drawing of objects at various distances as a means of instruction comes from Sierra Leone. The device used was essentially the same as that used by the sixteenth century artists to instruct and explain perspective. A woodcut by Durer (see Gombrich 1962, p. 259) shows such an apparatus in use. A woman reclines on a table and is separated from an artist, who sits at the table, by a vertical square grid. A similar grid is drawn on a piece of paper on which the artist is drawing the figure. He does so by constant transfer from the co-ordinates of the vertical grid to the grid on the paper. The artist's eye is kept in constant position by a fixed gnomon over the top of which he looks at his model. The very idea of this device was translated to Sierra Leone by Dawson, who replaced the frame with the windowpane of a classroom and the reclining woman with a mining company lorry and whatever else could be found in view. His subjects drew directly on the pane and had the essentials of perspective explained to them. This instruction was given to a sample of apprentices employed by a mine for eight weekly one hour sessions. It was found that it improved their three-dimensional perception of pictures significantly. The scores of the subjects on a test similar to Hudson's test used to measure their final achievement were also found to correlate with the Kohs' Block scores, which indicate the accuracy with which simple geometric patterns are reproduced (see p. 67) and can serve as a measure of field dependence. Dawson interpreted this correlation as showing that field dependence delimits achievements in perception of pictorial depth. This is a possible, but not the only, interpretation of the observations, for it is also possible that there was generalization or transfer of learning from pictorial perception to the skill called for in responding to Kohs' patterns.

Ferenczi's (1966) and Serpell and Deręgowski's (1972) projects relied about as heavily on verbal instruction and explanation of pictures as did Dawson. The final measure used by Ferenczi was interpretation of drawings as well as making of drawings. The latter is, as we shall see, a somewhat dubious device. Serpell and Deręgowski used the Construction test and the "two-pronged trident" copying test as their measures. Improvements were reported in both the African migrant workers and their families tested by Ferenczi and in Zambian children tested by Serpell and Deręgowski. Another method relying on elaborate verbal instruction and a simple auxiliary apparatus is that developed by Duncan *et al.* (1973), working in South Africa.

Of the attempts to improve perception by a more direct "perceptual"

means those involving stereoscopic stimuli are probably the most important and certainly the most numerous. Such devices were first tried by
Dawson (1967); the promising results obtained by him were later
confirmed by Davies's (1973) work on apprentices from various African
air forces sent to Britain for training. These young men were found to
have difficulties with interpretation of engineering drawings. Since
Davies's task was primarily didactic he was not concerned with precise
experimental procedures and merely introduced the stereoscopic task as
a device to facilitate learning, and reports a significant improvement in
his students' performance. His claim that the stereoscopic stimuli were
helpful seems to be justified, for it is supported by the finding
obtained later, that Kenyan school children benefit from instruction
using stereoscopic pictures (Derȩgowski 1974b). The procedure used in
that study was as follows. A sample of children wearing modified
motor-cycle goggles which enabled stereoscopic perception of special
stimulus figures was presented with the task of building bamboo and
Plasticine models of simple geometric lattices. Later the ability of these
children to build models from plain drawings was compared with that of
a control group. The results suggest that experience with the stereoscopic construction is indeed beneficial. How far this conclusion can be
extrapolated to form the narrow range of stimuli used, is however,
uncertain, especially so since apparently contradictory results have
been reported from Nigeria by Nicholson *et al.* (1977). Yoruba secondary
school pupils are reported as having gained significantly more from
instruction by means of stereoscopic pictures than by instruction involving either ordinary pictures or models, but no difference between these
three modes of instruction was observed in the case of Hausa pupils.
These findings led the experimenters to conclude that different teaching
methods may be effective in different cultural groups, a conclusion
which is of greater import to teachers than to students of perception.

Such indications of the effectiveness of the method, as the above
studies provide, hint that the difficulty of the perception of pictorial
depth may, in some subjects at least, reside in the unwillingness of their
perceptual mechanism to restructure two-dimensional stimuli, and that
enforced demonstrations of such restructuring provide the impetus
needed for further restructuring. Little however can be said at the
moment about the precise nature of the mechanisms involved.

PRACTICAL CONSIDERATIONS

Although not immediately relevant to the theoretical issues discussed the ability to interpret drawings has important implications, both didactic and practical, in such areas of knowledge as engineering or chemistry.

Anecdotal evidence that in some cultural groups achievement in those spheres is hindered by inadequate comprehension of drawings has been available for a considerable time and is augmented by observations carried out by teachers of those subjects. Thus Agbasiere and Chukwejekwu (1972) describe the difficulties of Zambian students of mechanical engineering and Davies (1973) those of Air Force apprentices. Bermingham's (1976) short note on the performance of students in a London college confirms these observations, as does a series of papers from the School of Chemical Education of the University of East Anglia, which describes chemists' search for a method which would facilitate comprehension of drawings of lattices by Nigerian students (Nicholson and Seddon 1977a, b, Nicholson *et al.* 1977.) Guthrie *et al.* (1971) noted similar difficulties in Vietnam.

A brief review of the problems experience by engineers and prospective engineers when interpreting drawings, as well as some data obtained from the students of engineering at the University of Rhodesia are presented by Deręgowski (1979). The data confirm the specificity of the problem. Black and white Rhodesians it appears did about as well in examinations in mathematics; however, in an examination in engineering drawing the two cultural groups diverged in the expected manner: the black students performing less well than the white students. Furthermore, whilst marks in mathematics did not correlate with the scores on simple tests calling for visualization of pictures, the marks in engineering drawing did do so (Fig. 4.20 a, b). Three tests involving visualization were used to obtain these measurements. In one of these (The South African National Institute for Personnel Research Blox Test) students were required to identify, in a set of figures, a figure portraying the same arrangement of cubes but from a different point of view than that depicted in the stimulus figure. In the second test (the Space Relations Test taken from the Differential Aptitude Test battery of the USA Psychological Corporation) students had to recognize a parallelepiped which would, if its surface were flattened out, yield the surface depicted in the stimulus figure; and in the third test a figure representing an assembly of identical bricks was presented and the students had to indicate which of the bricks would be in contact if such an assembly were built. All the tests thus involved perception of simple solids and perceptual transformation of such solids. Such drawings are not generally difficult to perceive. Even young and relatively inexperienced children did quite well, it will be recalled, on the Construction

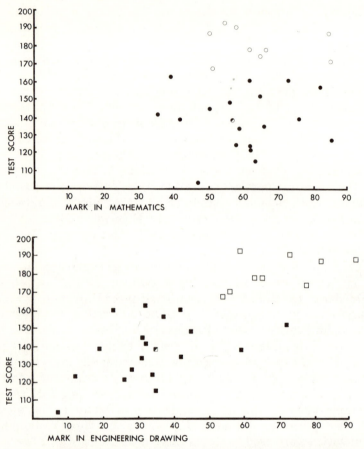

Fig. 4.20 Two graphs showing the relationships between examination marks and the scores on tests of spatial skills for a class of black (filled points) and white (open points) Rhodesian students. It is apparent that the marks in mathematics do not correlate with the test scores, and that the two cultural groups do not differ in their marks in this subject. On the other hand the marks in engineering drawing do correlate with the test scores and are higher in the white group than in the black group. (The single half-filled point on the graphs represents an Indian student.)

tasks which involved just such figures. The difficulty therefore probably lies in the required transformation rather than in more passive perception. The students who find these tests difficult would probably be able to reconstruct the depicted arrangement, given materials to do so, and then to answer the relevant questions. They find it difficult, however, to transform the percept without such physical reconstruction. Their percepts are not, it seems, sufficiently robust for that, just as on a much simpler level the percepts evoked by pictures in Aberdonian women were not sufficiently robust to match the percepts evoked by solid objects when their position in space had to be learned (p. 123).

Empirical studies of comprehension of posters, another important application, have been carried out by several workers. Among the earliest systematic investigations have been those undertaken in South Africa by Hector and Hudson (1962) and Winter (1963). Similar investigations were subsequently carried out in other parts of the world. In view of the general difficulties of pictorial perception already discussed the difficulties with posters ought not to surprise us. These studies do, however, bring to our attention certain aspects of pictorial display which have not been mentioned before and which have a profound influence on the comprehensibility of the messages conveyed pictorially. These are: (i) the portrayal of actions must accord with the social usage if it is to be readily understood. Portrayal say, of a man receiving money into an outstretched hand is not so seen in the cultures where two hands are normally stretched out to receive welcome goods, (ii) colour may have certain culturally determined symbolic meanings (e.g. red may stand for fire) which restricts its utility and (iii) certain conventions common in comic strip cartoons, such as representation of succession of events by a succession of pictures; use of "flashes" to convey impact and of "clouds" to convey thought are likely to be misunderstood in some cultures.

5. Drawings

Drawing, being the act of creation of patterns, can be thought of as an obvious counterpart of pattern perception.

The simplest form of drawing is probably that involving direct copying of patterns devoid of any eidolic or epitomic content such as, for example, copying of Kohs' patterns. More complex problems arise when subjects are asked to copy designs having such content or to draw from nature. It is the latter types of drawing which we will be primarily concerned with, although even the simple cases present interesting problems as Shapiro's (1960) data show.

In the Construction task which was used in assessing perception of pictures (p. 130) the subjects were required to make models of depicted figures out of Plasticine and bamboo. The model built was therefore a representation of the subject's internal representation of the depicted object, and was used to measure the subject's ability to deal with pictorial representations.

Schematically the process involved can therefore be described thus: P—R′—C, where P = pictorial stimulus, R′ = internal representation and C the constructed model. The building of a flat model in response to a picture defined an observer as a 2D-perceiver, thus defining in some measure the intervening variable R′.

Reversal of the sequence by presenting a subject with a model and asking him to draw it is not a symmetrical reflection of the above process. It could only be so if the perceptual skills involved in interpreting a picture were the same as those involved in perceiving an object, and those involved in building a model the same as those in drawing a picture. This is clearly not true. Perceptions of pictures and models do as we have shown differ, and drawing calls for special skill which is not as generally available as, say, the skills of pictorial perception.

In the case of drawing from a model the difficulties which the draughtsmen encounter may derive from the inability to extract the essential features of a model, or to portray these features. The difficulties of extraction may derive from an inability to decide which are the essential features. In the case of simple geometric figures these features,

as Attneave (1954) and others have shown, appear to be fairly unambiguous, and can be described as points and lines on the surface of a solid
object at which great changes occur, e.g. the edges (i.e. lines) at which
the surface of a solid changes direction, or vertices at which several
surfaces meet. The salience of these features is such that it seems
unlikely that they could be ignored in favour of other and more obscure
attributes. The drawings of children in which a solid is represented by
one of its surfaces, in which, for example, a cube is represented by a
square and a tetrahedron by a triangle, support this view. The essential
features may not, however, be as unambiguous in the case of more
complex models, such as animals or human beings. Such models, too,
may present a greater number of alternative characteristic features for
the draughtsman to select from. Indeed, as we shall show later, cultural
differences appear to affect selection of the features by which such
complex models are represented in drawings.

The distinction between the ability to abstract the essential features
and the ability to reproduce them on a drawing is clearly shown by
comparing Rhodesian pupils' ability to draw and to make models.

Thompson (1967) observed that black Rhodesian children are fond of
making wire models. At the time of that observation the models must
have been relatively less common than they are now. That this was so is
suggested by the absence of reference to such toys in Klepzig's (1972)
extensive review of African children's play, whereas nowadays they can
be fairly described as ubiquitous. This growth in popularity is due, we
suspect, in some part to the natural spread of such phenomena and in
some part to the fostering of model-building by inter-school competi-
tions and displays. A line tracing made from a photograph of a model
motor-car made by a Rhodesian boy is shown in Fig. 5.1. Models are
built by boys; girls neither build them nor play with them; but they do,
of course, see boys both making them and playing with them.

Building of a model, given a three-dimensional stimulus, presents a
subject with a task much in common with making a drawing in response
to such a stimulus. The tasks do, however, also differ significantly.
When building a model with thin strips of material, such as wire or
bamboo splints, the subject has to abstract the essential features of the
stimulus and reproduce them using the medium, which he can locate
freely in space. This is not so in the case of drawing, where the surface of
the paper imposes an additional constraint upon reproduction. Its
effects have been briefly commented upon by Deręgowski (1976c), who
observed that Bukusu school children from Kenya, on being given a
conventional drawing of a cube, which they recognized as such, and a
three-dimensional wire model of a cube and requested to draw them,

Fig. 5.1   A tracing from a photograph of a wire toy made by a Rhodesian (black) schoolboy.

responded differently to the two stimuli. It appeared that given the extra guidance provided by the drawing the subjects were able to recreate a drawing of a cube but that given a model and in the absence of such guidance they fumbled and produced drawings of an essentially different kind, incorporating many distortions commonly associated with drawings of a cube made by children. The same distortions were observed in drawings made in response to *drawings* of the cube when a short time interval was interposed between the end of the presentation of the stimulus and the beginning of reproduction. This confirms both that the subject saw the stimulus drawing as depicting a cube and that they were incapable of retaining both the nature of the depicted stimulus and the way in which it was depicted. They tended to retain the former and hence found creation of a correct drawing difficult. Although the stimuli used were not familiar to the subjects the degree of abstraction required was relatively low, since the "solids" used were wire models.

A sample of black Rhodesian urban school children was used in a further investigation comparing drawing and model building. Three groups of subjects were tested: urban schoolboys, urban schoolgirls and rural schoolboys. (The last group, it must be noted, although living in Rhodesia, consisted largely of relatively recent immigrants from Malawi and Mozambique.) The essential features of these samples were: both samples of boys had built wire models before, girls had not done so; rural schoolboys attended a poorer school and were from a poorer socio-economic background than the urban children.

Solid wooden models were used as stimuli. These had to be drawn and reproduced using thin wire.

The drawings obtained cover a wide spectrum of representation ranging from a simple depiction of one of the faces of a solid through various "distorted" representations to a perspective view. These drawings when judged by three independent judges were found to differ among the three experimental groups. The rural boys' drawings were judged to be considerably inferior. The three groups did not differ significantly in their ability to abstract the essential features necessary to build wire models. Little cross-cultural variation is, therefore, likely to be found on tasks involving abstraction of essential features of simple three-dimensional stimuli.

The contrast between the responses of the rural boys when asked to build models and their responses when asked to draw confirm our suspicions that the difficulties responsible for these subjects' relatively low scores on drawings repose not in their inability to abstract essential features, but in their inability to transform mentally such features once abstracted in such a manner as to arrive at a projection suitable for portrayal.

These observations suggest that changes which have been observed in childrens' drawings by several workers (e.g. Kerr 1937, Lewis 1963) are due to an increase in ability to draw rather than to the ability to abstract what should be drawn. Studies in non-Western cultures, such as those of Michelmore (1975) carried out in Jamaica, show similar trends. These trends cannot be attributed to maturation since the evidence gathered by anthropologists and presented by Werner (1948) shows that adults from cultures wherein drawings are scarce tend to have similar difficulties.

There is a stage in the process of learning to draw which is of particular interest because it appears to relate to an artistic convention practised in some cultures. During this stage, the artists depict a solid by reproducing approximately correctly the true shapes and relative sizes of its surfaces. These are drawn adjacent to each other so that the resulting figure gives an impression of being a collage of a series of views of the model obtained from various angles. Such drawings have been referred to as chain-type (Werner 1948), as split representations (Levi-Strauss 1963), or as development drawings (by borrowing a term from engineering).

Levi-Strauss notes that such figures can be found in the art of the peoples living on the northwest coast of America, in China, Siberia, New Zealand and perhaps even in India and Persia. What is more, such figures can be found in "entirely different periods: the eighteenth and nineteenth centuries for Alaska; the first and second millenia BC for China; the prehistoric era for the Amur region; and the period stretching from the fourteenth to the eighteenth century for New Zealand" (Levi-Strauss 1963, p. 246). This list is not exhaustive for isolated drawings in this style, as opposed to entire schools of art, are even more widespread. They have been found in the works of such cultures as the Saharan culture of the Bubale era (Lhote 1962), the central Indian culture of early centuries BC (Allchin 1958), and the European culture of the Halstad period (Kostrzewski *et al*. 1965). Furthermore in a recent study of sand drawings made by Kalahari Bushmen, Reuning and Wortley (1973) observed a large frequency (more than 50%) of drawings which they called "plan views" but which appeared to be similar to the "split-figures". White subjects and literate Bantu, whom they also tested, made no such drawings and only three such drawings were found in 53 drawings made by a group of illiterate Bantu subjects.

Reports of systematic preference for this type of figure make it seem unlikely that such drawings are simply a result of lack of drawing skills. Thus Hudson (1962) asked African adults and children to describe two drawings of an elephant, both showing the elephant as seen from above, (Fig. 5.2). "In one case legs were shown spread out as if the elephant had been flattened", in the other, a foreshortened view, the legs were not visible. The preference for the chain-type representation of an elephant was lower in the group of African school-goers than it was in the African illiterate sample. The entire latter group preferred this drawing. "They see the foreshortened elephant as dead, since it had no legs. The second (chain-type) drawing was seen as that of a live elephant, in spite of the fact that it was perceptually impossible" (Hudson 1967). But even the responses of the African school children were high in the preference for

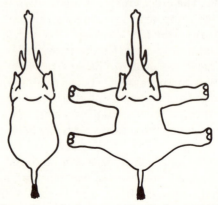

Fig. 5.2   Two drawings of an elephant used by Hudson (1962) to test preference.

chain-type drawings, when contrasted with the responses of school children of European descent. Hudson attributed these differences to the differences in experience with the pictorial material.

Deręgowski (1969a) asked subjects to choose between two of Hudson's drawings and extended the experiment by using geometrical figures as stimuli. His findings with Hudson's stimuli failed to indicate definite preference for either of the drawings, but merely showed that the Zambian population tested thought both drawings to be of about equal merit. This apparently unconvincing result can only be interpreted as showing a lack of definite preference within the Zambian sample and not as showing lack of difference between cultures, for these scores clearly differ from those of the European sample tested by Hudson. Use of geometric stimuli made it possible to extend the range of responses made by asking subjects to draw and not merely choose one of the stimuli presented. Two versions of the model shown in Fig. 4.14(A1) were made of thin black wire. One of these was flat and would correspond exactly with the pattern of lines constituting the figure if it were made to correct scale and placed upon it; the other was the three-dimensional interpretation of the figure which consisted of two squares connected by a length of wire normal to both of them. The subjects were presented with these objects

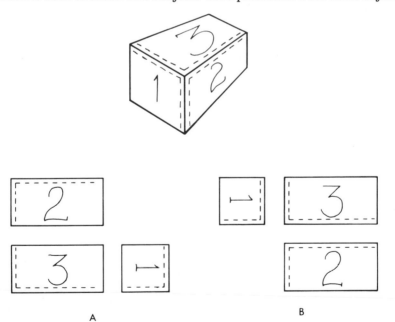

Fig. 5.3 **A perspective view and the (A)** *first angle* **and (B)** *third angle* **projections of the same object.**

and asked to draw them. The flat model was found generally drawn as such both by schoolboys and adult domestic servants, its shape corresponding to that shown in the figure from which it was derived. Not so the three-dimensional model. This frequently led to the creation of chain-type drawings consisting of two squares side by side and connected by short horizontal lines. Clearly then it is the third dimension in the model which leads to creation of this type of drawing. Furthermore choice of the development figure in preference to the conventional figure showed that the drawing in question is not simply a result of lack of the ability to draw but reflects a true preference. An extension of this work (Deręgowski 1969b) involving choice of a model given a drawing suggests that in dealing with geometric figures a paradox may be present in some cultures, namely figures which appear to be thought of as superior representations of models are in fact those which are less likely to lead to correct recognition of the model. No indication of such a paradox was found when dealing with meaningful figures. Both these findings need to be treated with a degree of caution both because the range of stimuli used was very narrow and because of the limitations of the techniques employed.

Such splitting of a figure is not the only transformation which can be used by an artist to show more of an object's surface than a viewer could possibly see or a photographer photograph from any particular stance. Purely rational considerations of engineering have led to establishment of two rival conventions serving this purpose. These are called the First Angle Projection and the Third Angle Projection. Both of them use three mutually orthogonal views to portray a solid, but although the views used are, in any particular case, identical their arrangements differ. The First Angle Projection arranges the three views as shown in Fig. 5.3a, the Third Angle Projection does so as shown in Fig. 5.3b. A comparison of these two figures reveals an essential difference between them. In the former those features of the depicted object, which are physically close but appear in different views, are not adjacent in the drawings, whereas in the latter figure this is so. Indeed by simply sliding any two of the views used in the Third Angle Projection so as to close the gaps between them and bring the common elements together one obtains split drawings.

Are both projections equally effective in conveying the intended information?

Spencer (1965) addressed himself to this query and in an extensive investigation found that indeed they are to experienced draughtsmen who have absorbed both conventions; for the laymen, however, the Third Angle Projection is significantly easier to understand. It would seem that the element of split representation which it contains renders it more "natural". Since however both experienced and inexperienced observers found these projections less effective than perspective drawings, the results of the study apart from showing the relatively greater intrinsic acceptability of the split representation, also show that in the Western culture adults do not respond as readily to such conventional portrayals as to more "natural" perspective drawings. They show above all that not all representational conventions are equally readily acceptable, and that those conventions which approximate more closely to retinal projections of the depicted objects seem to be superior in their ability to transmit information.

The split representations used by Hudson and by Deręgowski, as well as those made by the Bushmen, were drawn as seen from above. Indeed, this rather unusual aspect led Reuning and Wortley to speculate that the drawings made by the Bushmen reflected their experience of "reading" whatever happened to be written on the sand by viewing it from above as one would view foot prints of game, and their general familiarity with top or plan-views since they often saw things stretched on the ground. This observation is, however, difficult to apply to the preference for split drawings of an elephant observed by Hudson and even more so to the observations of Lewis (1963), who asked American children to choose the best drawing from a set of five drawings in the style of representation. The drawing represented a cubical house. Two of the drawings within the set can be said to be of the chain-type whilst of the remaining three, one represents a simple orthogonal view and the other two approximate to the conventional, Western, representations of a cube. The percentage of children who preferred the chain-type pictures was found to fall steeply with their age and grade from 52% ($N = 78$) in the kindergarten to about 13% ($N = 92$) in the uppermost grades of the primary school. This shows that the commonly observed chain-type drawings of children are probably at least in part the result of a definite preference (see Fig. 5.4.)

Such considerations led Deręgowski (1970) to speculate that the ambiguity of chain-type drawings and their development into artistic styles in some of the cultures may spring from the universal preference for this style of representation at certain ages. He argued as follows: in all societies there is, in children, an aesthetic preference for chain-type drawings and if this preference is not destroyed it persists into adulthood. In most societies this preference is suppressed; this is done because the preferred drawings are worse at conveying information about the depicted objects than are the non-preferred representative drawings. Thus aesthetic preference is sacrificed on the altar of com-

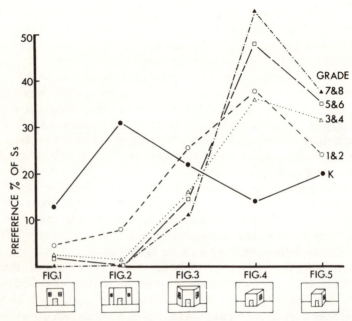

Fig. 5.4   Curves showing the percentage of preference amidst American children tested by Lewis. The patterns of preferences of the "unspoiled" kindergarten children (K) differs clearly from those of other groups (Lewis, 1963).

munication efficiency. However, some societies, notably northwestern American tribes, have developed the chain-type drawing to a considerable artistic level (Fig. 5.5). If the above remarks are correct, this could only occur if either the drawings were not regarded as means of communication *about* the depicted objects (such as is the case, for example, with purely ornamental patterns or armorial bearings or other identification marks), or if the drawings incorporated a system of cues which compensated for the loss of communication value due to stylization. It so happens that both these provisos are obeyed by this school of art. The paintings in question are not intended to convey to the viewer what a bear, a beaver or a sculpin looks like in order to enable him to identify the animal, but serve primarily as signs and ornaments. In order that this role may be well fulfilled they incorporate symbolic elements which enable the viewer to interpret the artist's intention. Thus, for example, "the large incisors, the tail with crosshatching, the stick and the form of the nose are symbols of the beaver and the first two of these are sufficient characteristics of the animal" (Boas 1927, p. 186). The introduction of complex symbolism made the creation of an intri-

Fig. 5.5 Two of the paintings collected by Boas. A Tsimshian bear and a Haida shark.

cate style of art possible, whilst still retaining some of the communication value.

Such introduction of a symbolic code carries, however, a penalty in that the facilitation thus achieved only extends to the persons familiar with the code. Highly stylized and arbitrary symbols are not likely to be understood outside a specific cultural milieu.

But even non-stylized figures have, it appears, certain "typical" orientations. In the case of animal models these appear to be the frontal view and the side view. The dominant role of these is shown by the following experiment. Rhodesian school children were presented with photographs of toy animals taken at a variety of angles so that in some of them the animal was shown *en face*, in some in profile and in some in an intermediate setting. After inspecting each of such photographs they were required to set the appropriate toy which was mounted on a turntable in the same orientation as that shown in photographs. The responses showed that the physical continuum of orientations extending from frontal setting (0°) to the profile setting (90°) was subdivided into two zones, a narrow zone extending from 0° to 15° and a wide zone covering the remaining 75° of the angle. The stimuli which fell within the former tended to evoke responses closer to the 0° than their true position and the stimuli which fell on the latter tended to evoke responses closer to 90° than their true position. This effect was not observed on the control subjects whose initial stimuli as well as response stimuli were toys. It appears therefore that the term "typical" can justifiably be used to label the extremes of the continuum towards which the subjects tended.

It may be noted that the stylized Indian figures described above combine symmetry of the figures with the presentation of two of the dominant typical views or even, on occasions, symmetry with three views, the frontal view being placed between the two profiles.

The most common of highly conventional representations are those used in the older armorial bearings. The constituent figures of these are generally drawn as flat, they are therefore epitomic, and often embody two of the characteristics which we have discussed at some length; typical orientation, *en face* or in profile, and symmetry. Typicality is clearly demonstrated by the figures of lions, eagles, griffins, unicorns and other specimens of the heraldic fauna as well as by the arrangements of other elements. Consider Fig. 5.6 showing the arms of the University of Aberdeen. When each of its quarterings is considered separately, as they should be since each of them represents a separate dominion, we have four different designs. In these the fish and the boars' heads are clearly seen as being in the *typical orientations* and the vase with its flowers and castle tower combine such typicality with median symmetry.

Fig. 5.6   Arms of the University of Aberdeen.

Whereas in the case of the tower it could be said that the symmetry is merely coincidental arising from the nature of the object portrayed, this could not be so in the case of the arrangement of the three flowers in the vase. A brief survey of armorial bearings confirms this impression, and shows that symmetry is to be found both in epitomic and purely geometrical designs. Furthermore it also reveals, as illustrated by Fig. 5.7 showing an ancient Polish stove, each tile of which shows a family arms, that when asymmetrical designs are used their enantiomorphs are not found. The pragmatic reason for this patently lies in the great con-

Fig. 5.7   Photograph of an old Polish stove covered with tiles decorated with a variety of armorial designs. (Courtesy of Arkady, Warsaw.)

fusibility which as studies of discrimination learning indicate would arise if such enantiomorphic designs were in fact used. In the days when family arms were commonly used as means of identification and when unlettered or scarcely literate men were probably more prone to confuse enantiomorphs than are the literate men of today such confusions, were they to occur, could have been highly embarassing and on occasions–fatal.

The use of medially symmetric chain patterns by the north western Indian artists and of symmetric arrangements by the European heraldic designers are but illustrations of a widespread propensity to use symmetry in the art forms which are essentially epitomic. These particular embodiments of the device are relatively culture-specific. There is however a symmetric design which is found in many separate cultures, and for this very reason constitutes a convenient arena for the confrontation of the diffusionist theories which some anthropologists favour and the spontaneous generation theories which are preferred by some psychologists. This design is known as the *heraldic woman*. Its distribution was investigated by Fraser (1966) who recognized the importance of the figure and named it.

The *heraldic woman* motif consists of a frontal view of a female figure, with her legs spread open exposing her genital zone. The figure is flanked by two other creatures, generally by two similar animals, so that the entire array is medially symmetrical. Fraser argues that the geographic distribution of the figure presents a clear case of diffusion of an artistic motif from the nuclear area to other parts of the globe. He admits that the evidence supporting the notion of diffusion is not conclusive but holds that it is stronger than that presented by anti-diffusionists. His case rests essentially on the belief that certain images can only be created in certain cultures where an appropriate social climate prevails. "A degree of social stratification", he maintains, "would appear to be a precondition for the advent of flanked images" (p. 79), but the forces of diffusion create a degree of artistic homogeneity in spite of the social differences between cultures. As an additional argument, to show that the widespread distribution is the result of such diffusion, Fraser postulated that the alternative process of independent engendering of such a form of art in a variety of otherwise culturally distinct groups throughout the world would be highly unlikely. "A fantastic degree of convergence tantamount to a repeal of the laws of chance", would according to him be needed to explain the observed distribution if the postulated diffusion were rejected.

To a student of perception these arguments may appear to overstress the impact of social values on artistic creation.

For a reason which seems to be so obvious as not to require elaboration images of women with their legs spread apart are commonly made in very many cultures. Such figures are of course symmetrical for such are the depicted models. The predilection which the perceptual mechanism seem to take in symmetry argues that any embellishment of such figures are likely to be symmetrically arranged, which, of course, is the case with the animal figures found in the *heraldic woman* assemblies. This argument does indeed repeal the laws of chance but does so because it rests on the justifiable tenet that the human perceptual mechanism is not ruled by the laws of chance.

The magnitude of influence of social climate upon artistic creation and hence on the perceptual processes of both the artists and the recipients of their work, which Fraser envisages, extends far beyond such mundane influences as the Ecological openness or Carpenteredness of the environment which have been put forward by the students of visual illusions. Those influences had no particular direct social significance. The influence suggested by Fraser does. In this it is at one with Levi-Strauss (1963) who in his study of chain-type drawings maintains that these are to be found in those mask cultures where individuals have to perform two different social roles, one whilst wearing a mask and one whilst not wearing a mask. The physical tension which this demand creates finds its reflection in art. The drawings portray figures which are torn asunder. Such an argument sounds so well, the phrases split-drawing and torn asunder match so well, that an experimental psychologist's suspicions are bound to be aroused by it. Leach (1974) detects in Levi-Strauss' writings a tendency to argue the case so characteristic of lawyers rather than to examine evidence. He also noted a poetic element in them. It might be that these two factors rather than the data influenced Levi-Strauss' hypothesis, which seems contrary to the observation that children in the Western cultures, which can scarcely be regarded as masked, draw such split-images.

An empirically demonstrated association between symmetry and the social structures of a society is obviously pertinent to the issue at hand. This demonstration was provided by Fisher's (1961) ingenious juxtaposition of the ranking of various cultural art styles reported by Barry (1957) in his paper concerned with the relationship between child training and pictorial arts and of judgements of social variables (published by Murdock (1957)). Fischer thought that symmetry, being a special case of repetition, should be found more often in the arts of the egalitarian than of the hierarchical societies. Symmetrical designs, he posited, reflect the social structure of the former, asymmetrical of the latter types of social organization. A comparison of the frequencies with which symmetrical art forms were found in societies of low and high stratificaion yielded a confirmation of the hypothesis. The finding can therefore be thought of as mildly contrary to the notion that symmetry is above all a purely artistic creation free of social taint; further, if the split representations are seen as embodiments of symmetry, the finding by putting forward a more general cause questions Levi-Strauss' postulate that the ritual wearing of masks is responsible for their existence of such representations. The very nature of Fischer's data, however, suggests that care must be taken in judging the validity of his conclusions. For symmetry is but an isolated aspect of the works which were judged. The posited social influences have also been found by Fischer to correlate with the simplicity of the artistic designs, with the extent to which they were thought to be crowded into space and the frequency of enclosure of figures. Examination of the data shows that there are correlations among these variables. For example, those of the 30 societies considered which produce art characterized by symmetry, also tend to produce simpler designs. Is symmetry therefore merely an epiphenomenon of simplicity?

Such a question is unanswerable if only the works of art spontaneously created in various cultures are considered, for symmetry may well form an ingredient of a more complex artistic style and thus never be seen in isolation either by the artists or by the laymen living in a society where this style prevails.

The Western psychological tradition postulates a development trend in children's drawings, which is enshrined in Goodenough's "Draw a Man" test. Recently detailed and ingenious analyses of the factors which affect responses of a child asked to make such a drawing have been made by Freeman (1972, 1977). Both Freeman's' analysis as well as the Goodenough test scores take it for granted that the essential features of the human body are portrayed by a closed loop or a series of closed loops. Young children tend to draw but one such loop which they embellish by drawing within it representations of the nose, the eyes and the mouth and by attaching to it both legs and arms. The "tadpole men", as such figures are known, have been investigated by Freeman (1975), who suggested a specific "grammar" which governs construction of these drawings.

Is this grammar universal? Studies from non-Western cultures suggest that it is not and that entirely different features of an object can be thought central in other cultures. A piece of relevant evidence has been provided by Fortes (1940). He gathered his data from a sample of the Tallensi of Northern Ghana. Both children and adults served as subjects. Two groups of the former were used, one drawn from the unschooled population having a minimal contact with cultures in which pictures are commonplace, and another drawn from a distant school which was attended by children from the same culture.

The subjects were tested individually; each subject was given a pencil and a sheet of paper of quarto size to draw on. In spite of the fact that "Tale culture (was) completely devoid of representational graphic art, so that there (were) no traditional models a child could follow", there was no difficulty in persuading subjects to draw. Fortes described their responses thus:

"A Tale child's first reaction to pencil and paper is an erratic scribble which eventually resolves itself into a rudimentary pattern of irregular wavy zigzag lines filling up the whole available space. This is reminiscent of the way women decorate house-walls and men leatherwork with simple patterns of irregular lines of chevrons, lozenges, etc. without design but calculated to fill maximum space." Such a response is shown in Fig. 5.8. Later the same subjects attempted to draw representational

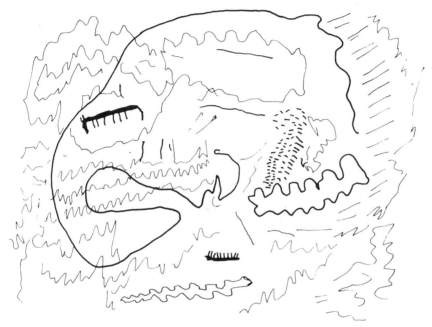

Fig. 5.8   Example of scribbles made by the Talensi who have never drawn before in response to request to draw.

figures. The resulting drawings were found to "consist of a set of lines making spatial, or better, functional diagrams stating in an abstract way the relation between the various defined volumes that constitute an object or body". These characteristics are clearly apparent in Fig. 5.9.

All the drawings, it will be noted, are of the pin kind. The essential bulkiness of human and animal figures passes unnoticed. The head and facial features which are thought to be so important by Goodenough are also left unrecorded. The linearity of the trunk and the limbs is stressed and so are the digits. Certain other features are also accentuated. Only a very naïve observer would find it difficult to decide the sex of the individuals represented in (a) and (b). This mode of representation of the human form was found by Fortes to be general in the unschooled subjects of all ages and children as well as adults.

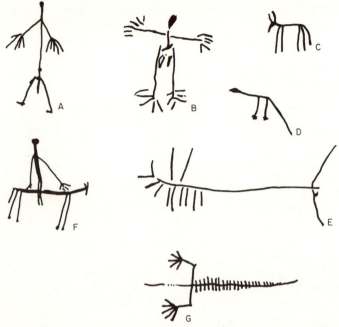

Fig. 5.9   Examples of recognizable drawings made by Fortes' subjects.

Other drawings obtained show that draughtsmen have selected and stressed certain features of objects which they drew. Thus a horse (Fig. 5.9e), drawn by an 11-year-old boy, has a distinctive mane, and the drawing of a cow (Fig. 5.9c) by another 11-year-old has unmistakable horns. There are occasional bizarre lapses; Fig. 5.9d, for example, shows a biped horse, but there is a general trend which is sufficiently consistent to suggest that, as Fortes says, the figures may be described as ideograms rather than as pictures. An adult's drawing of a crocodile makes this point forcibly. In it the crocodile's grooved trunk is shown by a series of short straight strokes (Fig. 5.9g).

The spontaneous use of ideographic representation noted is not unique to the Tallensi. Similar figures were obtained by Degallier (1904) from Pahouin subjects in the Congo; by Dennis (1960) from a sample of Syrian Bedouin, who were not as culturally isolated as the Tallensi but whose contact with cultures rich in pictures was merely marginal; by King (1925) in the Libyan Desert (see Fig. 5.10) and by Haddon (1904) from New Guineans.

A recent study of Kalahari Bushmen by Reuning and Wortley (1973) showed that similar abstraction of the linear elements of the features prevails in their drawings. The drawings in this case were ingeniously

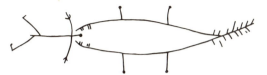

Fig. 5.10   A drawing of a crocodile swallowing a man(?) recorded by King (1925) in Libya.

obtained without the use of the culturally unfamiliar materials such as paper and pencil. Instead the subjects were provided with a tray of sand, and instructed to draw using their fingers. The drawings were categorized according to the technique used into three groups: outline drawings, match-stick drawings and mixed drawings, in the making of which both outline and match-stick techniques were present. Bushmen showed an overwhelming tendency to make match-stick drawings, i.e. drawings similar to those obtained from the Tallensi. This held for both drawings of a man and drawings of an animal which they were asked to do. The pure outline drawings were practically unknown in this group, there being only one such drawing in 332 drawings examined. All the drawings which were not of the match-stick kind belonged to the mixed category. Both the Whites and the literate Bantu gave responses which were diametrically opposite. In the white sample the outline drawings were by far the most common. There was but one match-stick drawing in 80 drawings obtained. The responses of the illiterate Bantu fell neatly between the two sets of responses just described.

The sand drawings of the Bushmen are simpler than those of the Tallensi. The toes and fingers, for example, which are so prominent in Tale drawings are not shown by the Bushmen. These simplifications may, however, be due to the medium used, a contention supported by the fact that pencil and paper drawings of Bushmen are much richer in detail.

A comparison of Fortes' data from the unschooled population with his data obtained contemporaneously from a sample of school children and with his data obtained from the following generation within the same population, shows that the ideogrammic style is easily superseded by a more "Western" style as a result of schooling and cultural exposure. This observation agrees with that of Schubert (1930). Her Orotchen school children came from a Siberian culture similar to that of Dennis' Bedouin, as far as pictorial art is concerned. Orotchen children, however, had some rudimentary schooling and in its course contact with some books. This contact was in all probability responsible for the fact that the drawings of the Orotchen children are similar to those of schooled Tallensi obtained by Fortes. Such influence need not, of course,

G

be external to the draughtsman's culture. Forge's (1970) observations show this clearly. Abelam children when drawing in the sand give their figures multiple outlines similar to those which encompass figures decorating the ceremonial houses of their tribe.

It follows that in the case of the making of drawings, just as in the case of their comprehension, cultural influences have to be considered when investigating perceptual processes. This is by now surely a familiar refrain.

In the review of Fortes' work Deręgowski (1978) remarks that the drawings obtained by Fortes from his sample of subjects entirely unfamiliar with the skill of drawing were on occasion oddly oriented relative to each other: an "upright" man could be found drawn next to an inverted animal. More systematic data pertinent to this phenomenon are reported by Reuning and Wortley. They categorized side-views of animals drawn by Bushmen in the sand into four groups: (1) upright, (i.e. those in which the legs of the animal were pointing towards the draughtsman), (2) upside down, (3) legs to the left and (4) legs to the right. Only six out of 157 drawings made by Bushmen were upright. The most common orientation was that with the legs to the left. It was almost as common as were the plan (chain-type) views. Comparison of the frequencies with which upright responses were made by Bushmen and other groups tested suggest a definite progression which, expressed in terms of percentages of drawings, runs:

Bushmen: illiterate black: literate black: white—4:40:83:100

The orientation differences described, while not confined to drawings of animals, are yet dependent upon the subject of the drawing. The percentages of "upright" drawings of a *man* obtained from the same populations were—86: 93: 100:100, and for a drawing of a bottle which was placed in front of the draughtsmen—72: 86: 100: 100. It is apparent that the extent of disorientation has in the last two cases been considerably lower. The drawings of the bottle from a model may not be directly comparable with the other drawings done from memory, but there is no *prima facie* reason for a different treatment of the drawings showing an animal and those showing a man. Why should Bushmen draw a man as upright in about 90% of cases and the animal as upright in only 4%?

It is of course impossible to attribute the disorientation effect to any specific root cause, because there are so many contenders for that role: literacy, familiarity with convention of drawing and possession of drawing skills; indeed, the entire issue of genetic and environmental determinants could be considered. The immediate cause of the errors can, however, be speculated upon, since additional and possibly clarifying data are available from the study of the Me'en interpretation of pictures carried out in Ethiopia to which we have already referred.

When the Me'en subjects were presented with a picture of an animal printed on cloth, which was spread on the ground, and asked what the animal was doing, they occasionally replied that the animal was lying down. When the same piece of cloth was lifted and held hanging in front of these subjects and the question repeated the answer changed to "Now it is standing up". These observations, which were made incidentally by Muldrow (Deręgowski *et al.* 1972) suggest, and this suggestion is also present in Reuning and Wortley's speculations, that the "disorientation" problem is that of regarding the plane in which the figure is placed as a valid cue to be considered when interpreting the pictures. Consequently, when Bushmen are requested to draw an animal figure on the ground it is thought of as lying on the ground; its orientation therefore becomes unimportant because an animal can be in any orientation. When no other cues (e.g. vegetation, background hills or the animal's posture) are present in the picture to convey the notion that a picture is to be regarded as showing an erect animal, such a picture is utterly ambiguous and the pictorially sophisticated viewer's interpretation is simply dictated by the assumption that the picture shows a vertical plane, an assumption which he incidentally would not make if he were looking at a map. An unsophisticated draughtsman, on the other hand, is free to lay out his figure however he wishes, and the choice which he makes is probably swayed largely by the ease with which he can execute his design.

This speculation appears to account well for both the orientation discrepancies and for the apparently unexplicable differences between categories of drawings of an animal and between the drawings of a man and an animal.

6. Some Implications About The Perceptual Mechanism

Our data do not present us with a comprehensive description of the perceptual mechanism, but by offering a hint here and a hint there they do provide information for tentative attempts at its reconstruction, just as exploratory drillings provide a geologist with information about the possible nature of the formations below. We shall therefore draw the data together and adduce some new data, and from combination of these try to distill the notion of the possible nature of some of the aspects of the mechanism concerned with perception of patterns.

In discussing the lawfulness of the orientation responses (p. 76), we have presented it as involving division of a perceptual continuum. The notions that the perceived stability of a pattern and the perceived shape of a pattern used in an implicit-shape constancy experiment are determined by the interaction of vectors "pulling" the percept, as it were, in opposite directions were combined with a hypothetical description of the manner in which the perceptual mechanism divides a continuum which is physically entirely uniform.

The essence of that description is the postulate that the position of the percept on the continuum is determined by two vectors, one of which can be called a "reality" vector. The latter combines all the factors tending to foster perception of a stimulus as it really physically is, and the other, the "ideal" vector, combines all the factors fostering perception of the stimulus in its transformed or "ideal" form. The transformation implied in the description of the latter vector is unconscious and involuntary. The resulting process, therefore, is akin to transformations evoked by the illusion stimuli and differs radically from the wilful transformations which occur when subjects actively seek to transform a stimulus to some purpose. Recent investigations involving such wilful transformations have been carried out by Shepard and Metzler (1971) but the problems involving them have long been familiar to psychologists and have led to incorporation of items involving such transformations in several tests concerned with the assessment of spatial ability, e.g. the

South African NIPR Blox test or the Psychological Corporations Space Relations test. In these tasks a subject is given a stimulus and *required* to visualize its specified transformation. In practice this is often achieved by presenting a subject with a stimulus drawing and a set of response drawings to choose from. The transformations involved are generally spatial rather than planar, although Jahoda's findings relating pattern difficulty to orientation errors suggest that tasks could be devised by which subjects' ability to respond to transformations within a plane could be investigated. In such an investigation one would expect to observe that wilful transformations consonant with the involuntary transformation would be easier than wilful transformations contrary to them.

A further distinction ought also to be drawn. This pertains to the type of involuntary transformations observed here and to the transformations described by Attneave (1974), as resulting from the instability of the perceptual system. Although the latter transformations are also arrived at without any conscious effort on the part of the observer, the observer is acutely aware of them once they have taken place. A Necker cube flipping over is probably the best known example of such a phenomenon. The perceptual mechanism is not here seduced into making an error as it is in the case of the implicit-shape constancy studies nor does it drift into it without subjects being aware of the fact. There is also no question of a perceptual compromise in the case of a Necker cube reversal; the issue is that of a choice of one of the three mutually exclusive available hypotheses. (These are the two alternative reversals commonly experienced and the perception of the entire figure as flat.)

Since there is a body of evidence showing that the ability to carry out wilful transformations when such are called for, as for example when reading engineering drawings, is relatively poor in those cultures in which the involuntary transformations due to implicit-shape constancy are relatively *less*; one can speculate that in those cultures the observed effects are largely due to the relative strength of the vectors fostering veridical perception of the stimuli, and a relative weakness of the vectors fostering perception of the stimuli not merely as pictures of objects but as object surrogates suitable for perceptual transformations. However an observer consistently treating a picture as an object would find drawing extremely difficult if not impossible, for the task of placing lines on a flat surface in such a manner as to create impression of depth requires a transition from two- to three-dimensions of which he is incapable. A good draughtsman, and a skilled perceiver, must therefore be able to see a drawing as a drawing and as the depicted object. In short, he must be able to change and to control his percepts.

The nature of the percept to which three-dimensional perception of pictures gives rise is ill defined. It could be that the percept is "as-it-stands", i.e. that it reflects directly the depicted orientation of the object drawn, or, alternatively that it does not do so but is an "idealized" transformation of the depicted object. Such a transformation need not be and generally is not the "ideal" form, but an intermediate form between the "ideal" form and "as-it-stands" form. This means that the mechanism may be thought of as needing to perceive the "ideal" form in order to arrive at the compromise transformation. Whatever the transformations, they are undertaken, therefore, not solely on the "as-it-stands" form but on a combination of this and the "ideal" form, the latter of which is derived from the former. This kind of rationale can be also applied to the involuntary transformations occurring on the orientation tasks. Under these circumstances, the tendencies towards stability and symmetry are relatively stronger in those cultures in which the tendencies toward three-dimensionality tend to be weak.

The notion of the discrepancy between the physical and the perceptual continuum above is of immediate relevance to the notion of similarity. Those stimuli which are placed close together on the perceptual (but not necessarily on the physical) continuum are *ipso facto* regarded as being similar. This can be re-stated as follows: those stimuli which engage the transformation mechanism to about the same extent are perceived as similar. The extent of engagement can only be assessed in terms of psychological, not in terms of physical units.

Consider Fig. 4.5 which shows the plot of the angular settings of responses against the trial number in the experiment concerned with the transformations of geometric figures in an implicit-shape constancy investigation. It is apparent from the curve that transformations in the early trials are more radical than transformations in the latter trials. The perceptual mechanism is taking bites of the physical continuum in those early stages and nibbling in a very genteel manner in the later stages. These disparate *physical* quantities presumably engage it equally. Hence the similarity between settings varies with the position of the physical continuum. The same physical distance between two stimuli near the 45° settings has lesser psychological impact than between two stimuli near to, say, the 20° setting. Given such two pairs of stimuli the stimuli in the former are likely to be seen as more similar to each other than those in the latter. Furthermore the results suggest that if additional stimuli were introduced exactly in the middle of the segments of the physical continua separating the stimuli forming each pair, these stimuli would be seen as more similar to those stimuli within corresponding pairs which lie closer to the "ideal" stimulus than to those lying further away. That is to say the similarity may not be perfectly reciprocal. The same argument can *mutatis mutandis* be applied to the data obtained in the studies of Kohs-type figures.

It must be noted that although monotonic curves have been obtained in both implicit-shape constancy studies and studies of Kohs-type patterns, such curves were purely artifactual and arose merely because the studies in question covered but a segment of the range of angular settings possible. Had the entire range been covered they would not have been monotonic, but approximately similar or enantiomorphic patterns would have probably been found in other sections of the compass. This is so because studies of symmetry show that the figures (such as Kohs' figures which we are presently discussing) apart from being similar to those within a certain zone wherein their characteristics are modified but slightly, are also similar to their own enantiomorphs. There is, therefore, a large part of the physical continuum separating the two kinds of similar items. Figures falling within this part are seen as differing from the stimulus figures.

Perceived similarity is important because it influences the manner in which stimuli can be grouped. Such grouping is the cornerstone of the theories concerned with the organization of percepts, most notably with such theories as that of Welford which deals with the economics which can be achieved in the course of organization. Welford proposes that changes in percepts occur when the perceptual system is so overloaded that it finds it more economical to recode the data in such a manner as to reduce the load. It may, for example, recode a series of lines of decreasing size as a portrayal of a number of equal lines but placed at different distances from the observer. A mere two or three bottom rows of such a stimulus (Fig. 6.1) may not, as Vickers (1971) has shown, involve the

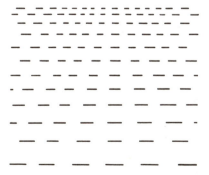

Fig. 6.1 A simple density gradient. No pictorial depth will be seen if only two bottom rows are exposed to the observer. Gradual exposure of further rows will however finally lead to a configuration evocative of depth.

recoding mechanism but a larger number is likely to do so. A reader can easily verify this statement by covering the entire figure with a piece of paper and then gradually sliding the paper so that rows are revealed in sequence. It must be noted that such recoding overrides the cues provided by the surface of the page which tell us that the stimulus is in fact flat. Thus one gains a new percept at the expense of overruling the perceptually contradictory aspects of the stimulus. This approach has much in common with the Gestalt notion of the "figural goodness" and the perceptual mechanism's tendency to transform the percepts in such a manner as to enhance this attribute. It is, however, more precise than this notion. It owes much to Hochberg and Brooks' (1960) classical and successful attempt to define the vague concept of "goodness" in quantitative terms by measuring various attributes of stimuli; in addition it implicitly extends the applicability of goodness to both the stimuli and the resulting percepts, since only by comparing the "goodness" of these two factors can the *gain* resulting from the transformation be assessed.

Such transformations can be found, as Newman (1969) has shown, even in perception of very young Western children. It would be tempting therefore to assume that they result from inherent and universal characteristics of the human perceptual system. Indeed there are no data which would enable one to seriously question such a thesis. There are data, however, which could be interpreted as suggesting that larger overloading may be needed in some observers than in others before transformation occurs, and that such observers may be more characteristic of some populations than of others.

In Attneave and Frost's (1969) investigation sophisticated adults were required to respond to simple pictures of parellelepipeds (solids contained by parallelograms), presented monocularly in a version of Gregory's Pandora's Box, by setting a movable rod collinearly with one of the lines (edges). The figures used were so drawn that they differed in the extent to which the equality of various characteristics would result from seeing them as three-dimensional rather than flat. At one extreme there was a figure which when seen as flat had equality and parallelism of lines but inequality of angles, but when seen as a rectangular parallelepiped lost the former two characteristics and gained the equality of angles. At the other extreme there was a figure which, when seen as flat, had none of the regularities of the three characteristics, but when seen as a rectangular parallelepiped became entirely regular (i.e. it was seen as a cube). Comparison of responses to such figures is, the authors conclude, consistent with a version of *Prägnantz* theory in which, as Koffka (1935) had postulated, simplicity of the percept determines the process of perception; a view compatible with that of the Economy Principle.

Since the gain in any transformation is dependent on the difference between the cost of sustaining a transformed and non-transformed pattern, one would expect that the ease with which a transformation is undertaken would depend on the perceptual complexity of the two percepts. Figure 2.10a for example can be perceived either as plane or as three-dimensional. Each of these percepts has a variety of characteristics which differ on a variety of criteria. All these characteristics are evaluated and their total effect is used in determining whether a transformation should take place. Hochberg's equation for determining complexity of patterns has the form: $C = a + d + 2c$, where "C" represents two-dimensional complexity; a = number of angles, d = average number of different angles and c = number of continuous lines. The variables are scored on a 1–10 scale, 10 indicating the highest score on the relevant variable within a given family of patterns. Since all patterns within a family are derived from the same solid figure, all of them being projections of such a figure the three-dimensional percept derived from them is the same and hence the discrepancy described above can be measured entirely in terms of C. However for the comparison figures which yield different three-dimensional percepts, i.e. for the figures belonging to different families, such a measure is not sufficient, and the relevant assessment of both simple percepts and percepts resulting from a transformation has to be made. Assuming that Hochberg's equation identifies correctly the elements involved in determining complexity, consider Fig. 4.3, a, b, and c. All three figures have the same number of *different* angles (three), all three figures have the same number of continuous lines (five), and A and B have the same number of angles, which is less than that of C. So apart from the number of angles the three figures are of equivalent complexity. Consider now three solid models which could be built using these figures as a guide. These would be as follows: Fig. 6.2a, two L-shapes facing in opposite directions with their longer legs resting upon a table and their shorter legs pointing upwards connected by a long rod resting on the table; Fig. 6.2b identical with Fig. 6.2a but with the two L-shapes in the same orientation; Fig. 6.2c, two inverted-T shapes with their legs pointing upwards resting on a table and connected by a long rod resting on the table. Their characteristics measured in Hochberg's terms are essentially the same but the variety of angles in all the figures is decreased to one, all angles now being right angles. Otherwise their ranking is unaffected. Since the differences between the percepts are about equal in all three figures and equal in the case of Fig. 6.2a and b, one would not expect much differ-

H

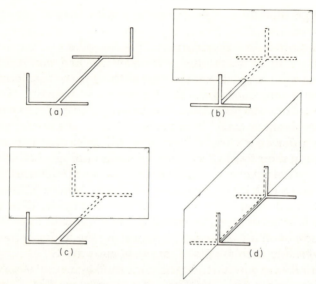

Fig. 6.2   The planes of symmetry of the simple three-dimensional models which can be built in response to stimuli shown in Fig. 4.3.

ence between the figures ability to evoke three-dimensional percepts. Certainly there should be no such difference between (a) and (b) which do not differ on the criteria used in respect either as two-dimensional or three-dimensional percepts. There is, however, considerable difference between the figures as shown by the data obtained by Deręgowski (1976) from a sample of Zambian school children. This is presented in an abbreviated form below.

	Number of responders responding	
Figure	*Two-dimensionally*	*Three-dimensionally*
a	15	3
b	6	12
c	4	13

The responses were obtained by asking the subjects to build Plasticine and bamboo models of the figures, a technique similar to that used by Deręgowski in testing of pictorial perception. A model was judged to be "two-dimensional" or "three-dimensional". There are important differences between these two types. The two-dimensional models have the same characteristics as the drawings described above. The "three-dimensional" models, on the other hand, vary in their symmetry. A model of (a) is skew-symmetrical. Its axis of symmetry bisects the member connecting two L-shapes and is parallel to the upright parts of the L-shaped members; that of (b) has a plane of symmetry which is normal to the connecting member as shown by dotted lines; whilst that of (c) has two planes of symmetry.

It therefore appears that as suggested by the principle of economy when the two-dimensional percepts are of about equal complexity, then the nature of the alternative three-dimensional percepts determines whether the transformation will take place. (The results, incidentally, agree with Reuning and Wittmann's (1963) observation that skew-symmetry is not readily perceived by unsophisticated subjects.)

A careful reader would have noticed that we have thought of only three three-dimensional percepts as if only one such percept could be derived from an infinity of lines oriented at various angles to the surface of the paper. What we have considered therefore are the simplest (i.e. most economical) percepts derivable from each figure. More complex percepts, although theoretically plausible, do not readily occur in practice. Indeed their occurrence would be contrary to the principle.

This experiment was extended to include a sample of Scottish school children from a third grade and aged between six and seven years and a sample of Buale children from the Ivory Coast. The latter came from the sixth grade of a primary school and were 12–16 years old. The experimental procedure was modified slightly; each child was required to respond to all of the three stimulus figures. The results obtained are notable for two reasons. They show that children tend to be self consistent either responding three-dimensionally to all three stimuli or to none, and that there is no significant difference between the two cultural groups, in both groups the largest subgroup being children who build flat models.

Because the ages of the children in the two samples differed markedly as did also their experience of formal schooling, it seems prudent to consider another similar experiment before comment can be made about the possible cultural effect.

In this (Deręgowski 1971b) the procedure used was similar to that described above. Scottish children were given drawings (Fig. 6.3, a, b), Plasticine and bamboo splints, and asked to build models. The figures as can be seen are geometrically congruent differing solely in orientation. This difference proved to be psychologically of great importance. Only four out of 19 pupils built a flat model in response to (a) whilst 15 out of 18 did so in response to (b). All the pupils who did not make flat models made a cuboidal cage. This result agrees with the intuitive impression created by the figures, and demonstrates clearly that here as in other experiments median symmetry evokes responses strikingly different from those evoked by non-median symmetry. An absence of median

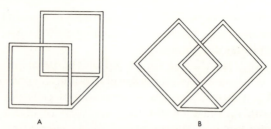

A   B

Fig. 6.3 Two orientation settings of the same figure which differ greatly in the strength with which they evoke perception of depth in Scots children.

symmetry appears to foster transformation of the stimulus in such a manner that perception of the third dimension is induced. The intuitively expected tendency to build more three-dimensional responses to the non-medially-symmetrical figure was present in both Scottish groups; it was not however so in the case of the Zambian children. In both cultural groups the proportion of three-dimensional models built increased with age or schooling but whilst in the Scottish sample such an increase in responses to (a) is accompanied by the decrease in responses to (b), in the case of the Zambian sample the increase occurs in responses to both figures. Since the differences in ages between the corresponding subsamples were relatively small as were the differences in schooling the data suggest that the perceptual mechanisms in the two groups do not work in the same manner, and notably that the effect of the difference in orientation (and hence of presence or otherwise of the median symmetry of the two figures) is not uniform across the cultures.

We shall return to the problem of orientation, meanwhile let us note that the Zambian responses are cccontrary to Hochberg and Brooks's observation that medially symmetrical figures are less likely to be seen as representing three-dimensional objects than are asymmetrical figures, an effect which can be interpreted in terms of overloading of the mechanism and a subsequent transformation. The present disagreement with this general principle is not unique. Variants of the Horizontal–Vertical stimulus yield results which question the generality of this proposition. Not only as Kunnapas and others have shown does the asymmetrical L version of the figure yield generally a lesser illusory effect than the symmetrical inverted-T version, but of the various versions of the inverted-T figure, that which has the stem in the middle of the horizontal bar evokes the strongest illusion. On the other hand, if instead of moving the stem along the bar we incline it (as Cormack and Cormack have done) we both destroy the symmetry of the figure and increase the illusion evoked. When such a modification is carried out on the L figure, which can be regarded as the extreme case of the inverted-T figure, the illusion is likewise enhanced provided that, as has been said before, the modification is such that the right angle of the L-figure is enlarged. The resulting illusion is however less than the illusion evoked by the corresponding central figure. Interpolation between these two results suggests, therefore, that the most asymmetrical variants of the inverted-T figure, those with the inclined sectioning member non-centrally placed, are not, contrary to expectations, those which are likely to evoke the greatest illusory effect.

The increase in the number of different angles has, it appears, the effect of increasing the illusion (an observation supportive of Hochberg's ideas) but destruction of symmetry of such a simple figure by moving the vertical line along the horizontal has no such effect.

These effects appear to be in agreement with the principle of economy as elucidated by the experiments which we have just discussed. It will be recalled that it is the difference in terms of the "pattern goodness" (which can be precisely defined) which determines whether a transformation will take place. Considered in these terms the various variants of the Horizontal–Vertical stimulus can be described as follows in terms of the characteristics which their two-dimensional (2D) and three-dimensional (3D) versions have.

(1) *Inverted-T with central orthogonal stem*
   2D characteristics: symmetrical, two right angles
   3D characteristics: symmetrical, two right angles
(2) *Inverted-T with central inclined stem*
   2D characteristics: asymmetrical, two different angles
   3D characteristics: symmetrical, two right angles
As expected the illusion is greater in the latter case. Consider now the figures with non-central stem.

(3) *Inverted-T with non-central, orthogonal stem*
   2D characteristics: asymmetrical, two right angles
   3D characteristics: asymmetrical, two right angles
(4) *Inverted-T with non-central inclined stem*
   2D characteristics: asymmetrical, two different angles
   3D characteristics: asymmetrical, two right angles
Again as expected the latter yields greater effect.

Comparing the two figures which yield greater illusion, (2) and (4) above, it is apparent that since asymmetry is eliminated in the case of (2) but not in the case of (4) the former type is more conductive to transformation and hence the illusion should be greater, as indeed suggested by the empirical observations.

The principle of economy can also be used to explain why one of the objections advanced against the postulate that the Ponzo illusion cannot be accounted for in terms of misplaced constancy scaling is not convincing. This particular objection derives from the effect of simple change of the traditional Ponzo stimulus; namely rotation of the two parallel lines through a right angle so that they are no longer parallel but collinear and lie on the bisector of the angle formed by the converging lines. Such a change eliminates the illusory effect, yet it is argued it should not do so if the constancy scaling processes are involved, for whatever the stimuli placed between the two converging lines the one placed nearer to the convergent end of the figure ought to be overestimated relative to the one placed nearer the divergent end. Thus the disappearance of the illusory effect, the argument continues, demonstrates that the constancy mechanism cannot be involved. The major fallacy in this argument lies in the assumption that the perceptual mechanism treats the stimuli in a similarly abstract manner as does the above description, distinguishing between the background or inducing lines and the stimulus figures and being concerned with the influence of the former upon the latter. This patently is not so. The mechanism treats the stimulus as a whole and tries to make sense of it as economically as it can; accordingly stimuli containing different elements are coded differently. This applies to all stimuli. In the case in question the modified figure is much simpler. The number and the variety of angles which lines make are less in the modified than in the standard figure. Furthermore, although both figures are medially symmetrical the two short lines are coincident with the axis of symmetry in the latter figure and thus stress it. This according to Deręgowski's and Bentley's observations should strengthen the impression of symmetry and thus make the figure appear simpler. Both these factors would therefore tend to decrease the tendency for perceptual transformation of the figure and so to decrease the illusory effect.

The difference between L and T figures should accordingly be the reverse of that commonly observed. The T figure should evoke lesser, not larger illusion. To explain contrary observations a notion of Dichosection has been invoked by Kunnapas, the dichosection effect is said to be so strong as to override symmetry of the figure. If this were so then a non-central placement of the vertical component of the T figure should lead to the enhancement of the illusion since the figure thus created is both asymmetrical and embodies the section effect. Kunnapas's results, however, strongly demonstrate a *decrease* of illusion under these circumstances. Hence it is probably better to think of the effect as reflecting the ease of comparison between the two lines in various settings relative to each other.

One of the important factors, which may affect perception and may on occasion affect it in such a manner as to diminish or perhaps even entirely obliterate the results of the application of the principle of economy, is familiarity. Subjects may through long process of exposure to particular stimuli become so familiar with them that they find it easier to process them than to process some other objectively less complex but also less familiar stimuli.

The term "familiarity" as used above means familiarity acquired through constant conscious interaction. A superficial kind of familiarity can have little effect, and the lack of its impact upon subjects' perceptual skills is well illustrated by the observation that Zambian domestic servants although familiar with pictures, which were to be found in their places of work, were less capable of perceiving pictorial depth than were young Zambian school children (Deręgowski 1968c). Similarly it cannot be seriously argued that American undergraduates are unfamiliar with rice, and yet they perform worse than do the Mano farmers from Liberia when required to sort rice (Irwin *et al.* 1974). The attributes of rice which may be of consequence to an American undergraduate are almost certainly different than those which are of consequence to a farmer from a community wherein rice is a major crop. The daily operation involving the relevant attributes, rather than the daily presence of the embodiments of such and other attributes seem to be of major consequence. In short, one has to learn what to look for and how to look. This is by no means an easy achievement especially when a new way of looking is in some manner contrary to an established habit, which suppress all alternative ways of perceiving. An industrial inspector, for example, may have to undergo lengthy and emotionally disturbing training at the end of which, and as the result of which, he may no longer be able to notice readily those differences between items which to a layman are startlingly obvious whilst distinguishing consistently between items on a characteristic of which a layman may be entirely unaware (Thomas 1962).

The notion of familiarity is the nexus of the concept underlying most of the "cultural" hypotheses in the realm of perception. It forms the foundation, of the Carpentered World and the Ecological theories of illusions advanced by Segall *et al.* The notion that the inability to perceive pictures is due to the culture put forward by Hudson, and the idea that perception of symmetrical patterns is determined by the presence of such patterns in the environment, has also been widely entertained.

This basic assumption, however, is not equally acceptable in all the cases in which it has been put forward. It is easier to advance it in illusion theories than in studies of symmetrical patterns: it is easier to make a plausible case that correct perception of distance or correct perception of rectangularity are important for survival in certain cultures, and thus to demonstrate that it is not only the familiarity with open spaces or rectangular solids but the ability to use information derived therefrom that influences perception; than it is to demonstrate that skew-symmetry which is undubitably more common in industrialized communities than in nomadic tribes is responsible for the superior manner in which South African trainee teachers handled skew-symmetrical Patco patterns when contrasted with Kalahari Bushmen.

Indeed even the readiness with which bilateral symmetry is perceived cannot be easily explained. True it is fairly common but certainly less common than asymmetry. An argument based on purely incidental familiarity is as we have said scarcely acceptable. The argument that in practically all the cases in which symmetry is encountered it is embodied in the single object, is a red herring of the purest breed because it could also be said that asymmetry (which is encountered more often) is encountered in single objects, because most objects yield one or two symmetrical projections but an infinity of asymmetrical ones.

It is of course possible to postulate (see Corballis and Beale 1976) that perception of symmetry is a result of the structure of the organism. This does not imply that the properties of the organism derived owing to such a structure are not subject to modification with experience. The crucial problem presented by the differential familiarity of the two types of symmetry put forward by Reuning and Wittmann (1963) is therefore that of postulating conditions under which perception of bilateral symmetry and perception of skew-symmetry constitute one of culture's demands.

7. Concluding Remarks

Our objective was to examine the contribution of cross-cultural studies of pattern perception to psychology in general. This we have briefly done and in so doing have repeatedly adduced data conveying implications which in all probability could not have been arrived at had psychologists confined their activities to the societies within which most of them live. The cross-cultural differences which we have encountered refine psychological concepts commonly held in two ways; (i) they show that the generally accepted "Western" norms are not universal and (ii) perhaps more importantly that responses obtained from different cultures differ considerably. Neither of these refinements is entirely unexpected because isolated observations from other cultures have long hinted that such differences may exist. Some of those early observations however lacked the measure of precision which is nowadays expected in descriptions of behaviour and which can be found in most of the recent studies which we have mentioned.

The importance of inter-cultural studies as the moderator of the conclusions drawn from observations obtained in a uniform cultural milieu was convincingly demonstrated by Jahoda (1970). The data considered by him came from a different branch of psychology than perception. They concern child development. We adduce his argument here to show convincingly that inter-cultural comparisons are important to the advancement of Psychology in general. The study considered by Jahoda is that of Sears and Wise (1950) who showed clearly that in Kansas babies the emotional unease increases with the age of weaning. The age range investigated by them extended from two weeks to 12 months and the relationship between the measure of amount of stress and age of weaning is quite unambiguous. Extension of this age range by adding the data obtained by Whiting (1968) from a number of cultures alters the picture entirely. The curve obtained could be extrapolated from the Kansas data only up to about the age of 18 months. At that point a dramatic change takes place. For infants over 18 months of age, it seems just the opposite of the relationship obtained in the younger groups relationship holds; the later the weaning the less the stress induced thereby. Thus not only do some social behaviours occur at different times in different cultures but the time at which some culturally sanctioned behaviours (such as weaning) occur may lead to behavioural repercussions (such as anxiety).

In considering pattern perception we have dealt with both these aspects; the cultural determinants and their consequences. Discussions of these factors can be found in all inter-cultural studies but they are not always equally stressed. Investigations of illusions are examples of studies wherein the impact of the hypothesized determinants is the chief concern. The information which they provide is therefore primarily about the factors which can influence perception of illusions and hence visual perception in general. On the other hand studies of perception of orientation, say, are not generally primarily concerned with the influences responsible for the errors made but with the analysis of the errors made.

The cultural variations, the examined data suggest, are not random but lawful. Subjects from different cultures do, generally speaking, display diversity of responses owing to a systematic tendency to respond in a particular manner. Such lawful influences do not appear to be singular to particular cultural groups but rather they tend to occur in each cultural group with a characteristic intensity. Therefore certain phenomena which could be thought trivial or even pass unnoticed in certain groups may be readily observable in others. Furthermore they may occur in different age-groups and such age differences may well extend the range of experimental techniques which may be used in their investigation. A phenomenon which occurs only in very young subjects in one culture may, for example, be investigated more fully in some other culture where it occurs in older children who can be subjected to much more elaborate and exhaustive investigations than their younger counterparts.

Many of the cross-cultural differences which we have discussed have previously been observed in the course of administration of standard tests. Thus Vernon (1969) noted that responses of subjects from certain cultures showed specific difficulties when tested with Kohs' Blocks. He suggested two aspects of these difficulties as particularly striking; the difficulty with reproduction of orientation of the pattern and the difficulty with reconstruction of a stimulus provided in a pattern using solid wooden cubes. Both these difficulties have subsequently been demonstrated by the data obtained in a course of experiments specially designed to investigate operation of the perceptual mechanism.

Such agreement suggests that a detailed examination of the responses obtained to various items of intelligence tests may prove to be a useful source of perceptual hypotheses. Indeed the very responses which are plainly a hindrance to the psychologists engaged in selection work may thus prove a blessing to a psychologist interested in the perceptual mechanisms. This bipolarity of the psychological approach is clearly shown by the modifications of the measures intended to eliminate such unexpected "noise" effects which are sometimes adopted by personnel psychologists. Thus the South African National Institute for Personnel Research has modified the Kohs' test in such a manner that tiles are used instead of cubes as a medium of reproduction, the subject thus being freed from some of the difficulties of "2D" to "3D" translation and from the need to find the appropriate face of each cube. Furthermore provision of a recessed tray ensures that only the required number of tiles is used and the orientation errors are eliminated. The number of errors which are particularly difficult to interpret is thus removed, to the psychometrician's satisfaction. Yet these very errors are the source of great interest to an experimental psychologist, who may therefore resort to procedures which educe such errors so that he may study them better as has been done by Jahoda (1976) and by myself (Deręgowski 1972, 1974) and which I have described.

In an apparent contradiction to the sentiments expressed above, Mandler and Stein (1977) make light of the usefulness of the tests of intelligence as indicators of perceptual differences although they admit that Block Design tests (of which Kohs' test is one) yield results which ought to be further examined. Their suspicion attempts to extrapolate from the differences in the intelligence test results to perceptual differences and rests mainly on the assertion that the intelligence tests have not been designed to measure differences in perception. This assertion is indubitably valid but it does not contradict the fact that those tests contain a perceptual element. They could not exist without it. Such an element may not be possible to isolate but its presence may be hinted at by specific aspects of subjects' performance. (It must be noted *passim* that factorial analysis of the results of a test cannot indicate the nature of such an element nor does finding of, say, three orthogonal factors show that the test is a complex function of several cognitive (rather than perceptual) operations, as Mandler and Stein suggest. The complex factorial analyses of responses to "simple" illusion figures which I have reviewed, clearly argue against such an interpretation.)

Although Mandler and Stein's remarks about the value of tests of intelligence as the indicators of perceptual functioning are in the gross acceptable, their conclusion implying that cross-cultural perceptual differences do not exist is not so. It is not so, because it lacks supportive evidence. Their data are derived largely from comparisons between

American Whites and American Negroes, and are practically confined to the results of intelligence tests ignoring, for example, very pertinent work of Sigel (1968) concerned with sorting tasks (also reviewed), which was carried out in the very same populations.

More diverse populations and a variety of perceptual tests yield results which incline us to argue, to the contrary, that cross-cultural differences in perception do exist.

Throughout our discussion we were more concerned with the nature of the perceptual mechanism which cross-cultural comparisons reveal than with identification of the factors which may be responsible for such differences, although such hypotheses as were put forward by various research workers were discussed.

There is one group of such hypotheses, however, which because of its appeal deserves a special mention. This is not intended to argue for their rejection, but to serve as a warning of the non-scientific allurements which they offer. These hypotheses which can be best described as "compensatory" derive, one suspects, from the egalitarian inclinations of their proponents rather than from the data. Such hypotheses are characterized by assumptions that populations which are relatively inferior on some tasks must be relatively superior on some others. Thus populations thought to be inferior on visual tasks are thought to be superior on auditory tasks, for example. This notion, common outside psychological literature, was introduced into the context of cross-cultural comparisons by Ombredane (1954, 1967) and Rollings (1961); and Wober (1966) suggested that the term "sensotype" could be used to describe such differences.

There is as I have stated no satisfactory data to support the notion.

A comparison of the dominance of vision and touch in Xhosa and white children from South Africa carried out by Page and Locke (1977) is inconclusive. The two groups were tested under a variety of conditions in which they had to match, for size, stimuli presented visually and/or tactually using vision only, touch only or a combination of both. In only one respect did the samples' results differ. When, after simultaneous visual and tactile exploration tactile matching was called for, the white children showed *greater* influence of the tactile experience than the Xhosas. There were no differences between the samples when only visual or only tactile exploration was followed by matching in the same modality.

A thorough investigation comparing the abilities of African and Western subjects to judge brightness and loudness and to discriminate between various intensities of sound and light also showed no differences, which the compensatory notions would lead us to expect. (Poortinga 1971, 1972).

It can however be argued that the experiment described above tests inappropriate aspects of performance. This is the view taken by Biesheuvel and quoted by Poortinga (1971). According to this view preference for a particular modality in perceiving the environment does not necessarily imply or lead to greater ability either to detect or differentially perceive stimuli in the preferred modality. Such a comment calls for careful consideration. Obviously if a preferred modality were generally less efficient it would be difficult to offer a reason for its persistent use other than that it may result from some form of physical disorders. The use of the term *preference* becomes under such circumstances rather strained, *propensity* would probably describe the phenomenon better. If the particular modality, on the other hand, is not consistently preferred but the same tasks in two cultures appear to involve different blends of modalities, or even different ways of using the same modality, then the issue may perhaps be better thought of in terms of skills.

This speculation, however, fails to answer the crucial question, namely "what is the source of the cross-cultural differences on tasks involving such as, for example, Kohs' Blocks?". It merely suggests that these differences reflect cross-cultural differences in skills.

Another implication of Biesheuvel's objection is that the differential preference for modalities may be undetectable when very simple tasks are involved but may come increasingly to the fore as the complexity of the tasks increases. Thus the involvement of the "preferred" modality is not automatic, as it would be had it been determined by either idiosyncratic factors, genetic endowment or skill, but is a result of an interaction between the subjects and the tasks which he has to hand. There are unfortunately no definitive experiments to support any of the possible interpretations.

"So what?"

This somewhat uncouth question is more often thought than asked. At the end of each learned seminar at the end of each presentation of elaborate research there are, one suspects, seven "so what's" strangulated rudely at birth to each glorious delivered and debonair "I wonder whether the author could expand upon . . .?", and yet it is apparent that is should be asked at the end of lengthy presentations of relatively little known data.

The answer has, in part, been given in the introduction. The purpose of the presentation was to show how cross-cultural studies relate to the mainstream of Psychology of Perception, to evaluate their contribution and to indicate briefly what impact they may have upon further work in the area. If in this I have been successful I am well satisfied.

Cross-cultural studies by their very nature touch upon so many more aspects of the populations studied than "traditional" studies, that it has been found necessary to make brief digressions into art, anthropology and other neighbouring disciplines. It was hoped that this would not only show the relevance of these disciplines to psychologists but also convince those anthropologists and students of art, into whose hands this volume may stray, of the, in my view, central role of experimental psychology of cognition in explaining visual phenomena.

References

Agbasiere, J. A. and Chukwujekwu, S. E. (1972). Teaching mechanical engineering design in Africa. *Chartered Mechanical Engineer* **19**, 62–64.

Ahluvalia, A. (1978). An intra-cultural investigation of susceptibility to 'perspective' and 'non-perspective' spatial illusions. *British Journal of Psychology* **69**, 237–241.

Allchin, B. (1958). "Morhana Parahi: a Rediscovery" *Man* **58**, 152–155.

Antonovsky, H. F. and Ghent, L. (1964). Cross-cultural consistency of children's preferences for orientation of figures. *American Journal of Psychology* **77**, 295–297.

Arnheim, R. A. (1966). "Towards a Psychology of Art." Faber and Faber, London.

Attneave, F. (1954). Some information aspects of visual perception. *Psychological Review* **61**, 183–193.

Attneave, F. (1955). Symmetry, information and memory for patterns. *American Journal of Psychology* **63**, 209–222.

Attneave, F. (1968). Triangles as ambiguous figures. *American Journal of Psychology* **81**, 447–453.

Attneave, F. (1974). Multistability in perception. *In* "Object Image and Illusion" (Ed. R. Held). Freeman, San Francisco.

Attneave, F. and Frost, R. (1969). The determination of perceived three dimensional orientation by minimum criteria. *Perception and Psychophysics* **6**, 391–396.

Avery, G. C. and Day, R. H. (1969). Basis of the horizontal–vertical illusion. *Journal of Experimental Psychology* **81**, 376–380.

Baltrusaitis, J. (1977). "Anamorphic Art" Chadwyck-Healey, Cambridge.

Barroso, F. and Braine, L. G. (1974). "Mirror image" errors without mirror image stimuli. *Journal of Experimental Child Psychology* **18**, 213–225.

Barry, H. (1957). Relationship between child training and the pictorial arts. *Journal of Abnormal and Social Psychology* **54**, 380–383.

Beach, H. P. (1901). "Geography and Atlas of Protestant Missions." Student Volunteer Movement for Foreign Missions, New York.

Berry, J. W. (1966). Temne and Eskimo perceptual skills. *International Journal of Psychology* **1**, 207–229.

Berry, J. W. (1968). Ecology, perceptual development and Muller-Lyer illusion. *British Journal of Psychology* **59**, 205–210.

Bentley, A. M. (1975). Cross-cultural Studies of Pattern Reproduction with Special Reference to Symmetry. M.Sc. Thesis, University of Aberdeen.

Bentley, A. M. (1977). Symmetry in pattern reproduction by Scottish and Kenyan children. *Journal of Cross-cultural Psychology* **8**, 415–425.

Bentley, A. M. (1980). Pattern reproduction in two cultures. *International Journal of Psychology* **15**, 1–9.

Bermingham, P. J. (1976). Racial variation in Aptitudes. The Times Higher Education Supplement, November 19.

Biesheuvel, S. (1952a). The study of African ability, Part 1. The intellectual potentialities of Africans. *African Studies* **11**, 45–48.

Biesheuvel, S. (1952b). The study of African ability, Part 2. A survey of some research problems. *African Studies* **11**, 105–117.

Binet, A. (1890). Perception d'enfant. *Revue Philosophique* **30**, 512–514.

Boas, F. (1927). "Primitive art." Instituttet for Sammenlignende Kulturforskning, Oslo.

Bonte, L. (1960). Contribution a l'etude des illusions optico-geometriques: Essais de measure de L'Illusion de Muller-Lyer chez les Bashi et Les Bambuti (Pygmées) de Congo Belge. Thesis, Université Catholique de Louvain.

Braine, L. (1973). Perceiving and copying orientation of geometric shapes. *Journal of Research and Development in Education* **6**, 44–55.

Brislin, R. (1974). The Ponzo illusion: additional cues, age, orientation and culture. *Journal of Cross-cultural Psychology* **5**, 139–161.

Brislin, R. W. and Keating, C. F. (1976). Cultural differences in perception of the three-dimensional Ponzo illusion. *Journal of Cross-cultural Psychology* **7**, 397–411.

Brown, L. B. (1969). The 3D reconstruction of a 2D visual display. *Journal of Genetic Psychology* **115**, 257–262.

Brunswik, E. (1956). "Perception and the Representation Design of Psychological Experiments." University of California Press, Berkeley.

Cameron, N. (1938). Functional immaturity of the symbolization of scientifically trained adults. *Journal of Psychology* **6**, 161–175.

Cole, M., Gay, J., and Glick, J. (1968). Some studies in Kpelle quantitative behaviour. *Psychonomic Monographs* **2**, 173–190.

Cole, M., Gay, J., Glick, J. A. and Sharp, D. W. (1971). "The cultural context of learning and thinking." Methuen, London.

Cole, M. and Scribner, S. (1974). "Culture and thought, a psychological introduction." John Wiley, New York.

Corballis, M. C. and Beale, I. L. (1976). "The Psychology of Left and Right" Lawrence Earlbaum, New Jersey.

Corballis, M. C. and Rodlan, C. E. (1975). Detection of symmetry as a function of angular orientation. *Journal of Experimental Psychology: Human Perception and Performance* **1**, 221–230.

Corballis, M. C. and Rodlan, C. E. (1974). On the perception of symmetrical and repeated patterns. *Perception and Psychophysics* **16**, 136–142.

Coren, S. and Miller, J. (1974). Size contrast as a function of figural similarity. *Perception and Psychophysics* **16**, 355–357.

Coren, S. and Porac, C. (1979). Heritability in visual-geometric illusions; a family study. *Perception* **8**, 303–309.

Coren, S., Girus, J. S., Erlichman, H. and Hakstian, A. R. (1976). An empirical taxonomy of visual illusions. *Perception and Psychophysics* **20**, 129–137.

Cormack, E. O. and Cormack, R. H. (1974). Stimulus configuration and line orientation in the horizontal–vertical illusion. *Perception and Psychophysics* **16**, 208–212.

Crawford-Nutt, D. H. (1974). Symmetry completion test (SYMCO): Development of a scaling method. *Psychologia Africana* 15, 191–202.

Davies, T. N. (1973). Visual perception of engineering drawings. *Engineering Designer* 4, 22–31.

Davis, C. M. and Carlson, J. A. (1970). A cross-cultural study of the strength of the Muller-Lyer illusion as a function of attentional factors. *Journal of Personality and Social Psychology* 16, 403–410.

Davis, C. M. (1970). Education and susceptibility of the Muller-Lyer illusion among the Banyakole. *Journal of Social Psychology* 82, 25–34.

Dawson, J. L. M. (1967a) Cultural and physiological influences upon spatial-perceptual processes in West Africa, Part I. *International Journal of Psychology* 2, 115–128.

Dawson, J. L. M. (1967b). Cultural and physiological influences upon spatial perceptual processes in West Africa, Part II. *International Journal of Psychology* 2, 171–185.

Day, R. H. (1972). Visual spatial illusions: A general explanation. *Science* 175, 1335–1340.

Degallier, A. (1904). Notes psychologiques sur les Negres pahouins. *Archives de Psychologie* 4, 362–368.

De Loache, J., Strauss, M. S. and Maynard, J. (1979). Picture perception in infancy. *Infant Behaviour and Development* 2, 77–89.

Deręgowski, J. B. (1967). The horizontal–vertical illusion and the ecological hypothesis. *International Journal of Psychology* 2, 269–273.

Deręgowski, J. B. (1968a). Pictorial recognition in subjects from a relatively picture-less environment. *African Social Research* 5, 356–364.

Deręgowski, J. B. (1968b). On perception of depicted orientation. *International Journal of Psychology* 3, 149–156.

Deręgowski, J. B. (1968c). Difficulties in pictorial depth perception in Africa. *British Journal of Psychology* 59, 195–204.

Deręgowski, J. B. (1969a). Perception of the two-pronged trident by two and three-dimensional perceivers. *Journal of Experimental Psychology* 82, 9–13.

Deręgowski, J. B. (1969b). Preference for chain type drawings in Zambian domestic servants and primary school children. *Psychologia Africana* 12, 172–180.

Deręgowski, J. B. (1969c). A pictorial perception paradox. *Acta Psychologica* 31, 365–374.

Deręgowski, J. B. (1970). Note on the possible determinants of "split-representation" as an artistic style. *International Journal of Psychology* 5, 21–26.

Deręgowski, J. B. (1971a). Symmetry, Gestalt and Information theory. *Quarterly Journal of Experimental Psychology* 23, 381–385.

Deręgowski, J. B. (1971b). Orientation and perception of pictorial depth. *International Journal of Psychology* 6, 111–114.

Deręgowski, J. B. (1971c). Responses mediating pictorial recognition. *Journal of Social Psychology* 84, 27–33.

Deręgowski, J. B. (1972a). Reproduction of orientation of Kohs' type figures; a cross-cultural study. *British Journal of Psychology* 63, 283–296.

Deręgowski, J. B. (1972b). The role of symmetry in pattern reproduction by Zambian children. *Journal of Cross-cultural Psychology* 3, 303–307.

Deręgowski, J. B. (1974a). Effect of symmetry upon reproduction of Kohs' type figures: an African study. *British Journal of Psychology* **65**, 93–102.

Deręgowski, J. B. (1974b). Teaching African children pictorial depth perception: in search of a method. *Perception* **3**, 309–312.

Deręgowski, J. B. (1976a). Implicit-shape constancy as a factor in pictorial perception. *British Journal of Psychology* **67**, 23–29.

Deręgowski, J. B. (1976b). Principle of Economy and perception of pictorial depth: a cross-cultural comparison. *International Journal of Psychology* **11**, 15–22.

Deręgowski, J. B. (1976c). Coding and drawing of simple geometric stimuli by Bukusu school children in Kenya. *Journal of Cross-cultural Psychology* **7**, 195–208.

Deręgowski, J. B. (1977). A study of orientation errors in response to Kohs' type figures. *International Journal of Psychology* **12**, 183–191.

Deręgowski, J. B. (1978). On re-examining Fortes' data: some implications of drawings made by children who have never drawn before. *Perception* **7**, 479–484.

Deręgowski, J. B. (1979). Lack of applied perceptual theory; the case of engineering drawings. *In* "Cross-cultural Contributions to Psychology" (Eds L. H. Eckensberger, W. J. Lonner and T. H. Poortinga). Swets and Zeitlinger, Lisse.

Deręgowski, J. B. and Byth, W. (1970). Hudson's pictures in Pandora's box. *Journal of Cross-cultural Psychology* **1**, 315–323.

Deręgowski, J. B. and Ellis, D. (1974). Symmetry and discrimination learning. *Acta Psychologica* **38**, 81–91.

Deręgowski, J. B. and Jahoda, G. (1975). Efficacy of objects, pictures and words in a simple learning task. *International Journal of Psychology* **10**, 19–25.

Deręgowski, J. B. and Serpell, R. (1971). Performance on a sorting task: a cross-cultural experiment. *International Journal of Psychology* **6**, 273–281.

Deręgowski, J. B., Muldrow, E. S. and Muldrow, W. F. (1972). Pictorial recognition in a remote Ethiopian population. *Perception* **1**, 417–425.

Dennis, W. (1960). The human figure drawing of the Beduins. *Journal of Social Psychology* **52**, 209–219.

Doob, L. W. (1961). "Communication in Africa: A search for boundaries." Yale University Press, New Haven.

Doob, L. W. (1966). Eidetic imagery: a cross-cultural will-o'-the-wisp? *Journal of Psychology* **63**, 13–34.

Duncan, H. F., Gourlay, N. and Hudson, W. (1973). "A study of pictorial perception among Bantu and White primary school children in South Africa." Witwatersrand University Press, Johannesburg.

Du Toit, B. M. (1966). Pictorial depth perception and linguistic relativity. *Psychologia Africana* **11**, 51–63.

Ekman, G. and Junge, K. (1961). Psychophysical relationships in visual perception of length, area and volume. *Scandinavian Journal of Psychology* **2**, 1–10.

Elkind, D. (1969). Development studies of figurative perception. *In* "Advances in Child Development and Behaviour" (Eds L. P. Lipsitt and H. W. Reese). Academic Press, New York.

Elkind, D. and Scott, L. (1962). Studies in perceptual development: I, The decentering of perception. *Child Development* **33**, 619–630.

Farquhar, M. and Leibowitz, H. (1971). The magnitude of the Ponzo illusion as a function of age for large and for small stimulus configurations. *Psychonomic Science* **25**, 97–99.

Ferenczi, V. (1966). "La perception de l'espace projectif." Didier, Paris.

Finger, F. W. and Spelt (1947). The illustration of Horizontal–Vertical illusion. *Journal of Experimental Psychology* **37**, 243–250.

Fischer, J. L. (1961). Art styles as cognitive maps. *American Anthropologist* **63**, 79–93.

Fisher, G. (1968). An experimental and theoretical appraisal of the inappropriate size-depth theories of illusions. *British Journal of Psychology* **59**, 373–383.

Fisher, G. M. and Lucas, A. (1969). Illusions in concrete situations: I, Introduction and Demonstrations. *Ergonomics* **12**, 11–24.

Forge, A. (1970). Learning to see in New Guinea. *In* "Socialization." (Ed. P. Mayer) Tavistock, London.

Forsman, R. (1967). Age differences in the effects of stimulus complexity and symmetrical form on choice reaction and visual search performance. *Journal of Experimental Child Psychology* **5**, 406–429.

Fortes, M. (1940). Children's drawings among the Tallensi. *Africa* **13**, 239–245.

Fraser, A. K. (1923). "Teaching healthcraft to African women." Longmans, London.

Fraser, D. (1966). The Heraldic woman: A study of Diffusion. *In* "The Many Faces of Primitive Art" (Ed. D. Fraser). Prentice-Hall, New York.

Fridjhon, S. H. (1961). The Patco test, symmetry and intelligence. *Journal of the National Institute for Personnel Research* **8**, 180–188.

Freeman, N. H. (1975). Do children draw men with arms coming out of the head? *Nature* **254**, 416–417.

Freeman, N. H. (1972). Process and product in children's drawing. *Perception* **1**, 123–140.

Freeman, N. H. (1977). Children's planning problems in representional drawing. *In* "The Child's Representation of the World" (Ed. G. E. Butterworth). Plenum Press, New York.

Gay, J. and Cole, M. (1967). "The New Mathematics in an Old Culture." Holt, Rinehart and Winston, New York.

Ghent, L. (1961). Form and its orientation, a child's eye view. *American Journal of Psychology* **74**, 177–190.

Gibson, E. J. (1969). "Principles of Perceptual Learning and Development." Appleton-Century-Crofts, New York.

Gillam, B. (1979). Even possible figures can look impossible. *Perception* **8**, 229–232.

Gollin, E. S. (1969). Development studies of visual recognition of incomplete objects. *Perceptual and Motor Skills* **11**, 289–298.

Gollin, E. S. (1961). Further studies of visual recognition of incomplete objects. *Perceptual and Motor Skills* **13**, 307–314.

Gombrich, E. H. (1962). "Art and illusion." Phaidon Press, London.

Gombrich, E. H. (1972). Perspective in the representation and the phenomenal world. *In* "Logic and art: Essays in honor of Nelson Goodman" (Eds R. Rudner and I. Scheffler). Bobbs-Merrill, Indianapolis.

Greenfield, P. M., Reich, L. C. and Olver, R. R. (1966). On culture and equivalence, II. *In* "Studies in Cognitive Growth." (Eds J. S. Bruner, R. R. Olver and R. M. Greenfield). John Wiley, New York.

Gregor, A. J. and McPherson, D. A. (1965). A study of susceptibility to geometric illusion among cultural sub-groups of Australian aborigines. *Psychologia Africana* **11**, 1–13.

Gregory, R. L. (1968). "Eye and brain." World University Library, London.

Gregory, R. L. (1970). "The intelligent eye." Weidenfeld and Nicolson, London.

Gregory, R. L. (1973). The confounded eye. *In* "Illusion in nature and art." (Eds R. L. Gregory and E. H. Gombrich). Duckworth, London.

Gregory, R. L. (1974). "Concepts and Mechanisms of Perception." Duckworth, London.

Guthrie, G. M., Sinaiko, H. W. and Brislin, R. (1971). Non-verbal abilities of Americans and Vietnamese. *Journal of Social Psychology* **84**, 183–190.

Haddon, A. C. (1904). Drawings by natives of New Guinea. *Man* **4**, 33–36.

Hagen, M. A. and Johnson, M. M. (1977). Hudson pictorial depth perception test: cultural content and content with western sample. *Journal of Social Psychology* **101**, 3–11.

Hector, H. (1958). A new pattern completion test. *Journal of the National Institute for Personnel Research* **1**, 132–134.

Hector, H. (1959). A coloured version of the Pattern Completion test. *Journal of the National Institute for Personnel Research* **7**, 204–205.

Hector, H. and Hudson, W. (1962). "An investigation into the usefulness of safety posters designed for Bantu industrial workers by the National Occupational Association." National Institute for Personnel Research, Johannesburg.

Heider, E. R. (1971). Focal colour areas and the development of colour names *Developmental Psychology* **4**, 447–455.

Herskovits, M. J. (1948). "Man and his works." Knopf, New York.

Herskovits, M. J. (1959). A cross-cultural view of bias and values. Lecture delivered under the auspices of the Danforth College, Greenville, North Carolina.

Heuse, G. A. (1957). Études psychologiques sur les noirs Soudanais et Guinéens. *Revenue de Psychologie des Peuples* **12**, 35–68.

Hochberg, J. and Brooks, V. (1960). The psychophysics of form: reversible perspective drawings of spatial objects. *American Journal of Psychology* **73**, 337–354.

Hochberg, J. and Brooks, V. (1962). Pictorial recognition as an unlearned ability: a study of one child's performance. *American Journal of Psychology* **75**, 624–628.

Hudson, W. (1960). Pictorial depth perception in sub-cultural groups in Africa. *Journal of Social Psychology* **52**, 183–208.

Hudson, W. (1962). Pictorial perception and educational adaptation in Africa. *Psychologia Africana* **9**, 226–239.

Hudson, W. (1967). The study of the problem of pictorial perception among unacculturated groups. *International Journal of Psychology* **2**, 89–107.

Hutton, M. A. and Ellison, A. (1970). "Some aspect of pictorial perception amongst Niuginians." Psychological Services Section, Department of the Public Services Board, Territory of Papau and New Guinea, Konedobu.

Irwin, M. H., Schafer, G. N. and Feiden, C. P. (1974). Emic and unfamiliar category sorting of Mano farmers and U.S. undergraduates. *Journal of Cross-cultural Psychology* **5**, 407–423.

Itteson, W. H. (1952). "The Ames demonstrations in Perception." Princeton University Press.

Jahoda, G. (1956). Assessment of abstract behaviour in a non-western culture. *Journal of Abnormal and Social Psychology* **53**, 237–243.

Jahoda, G. (1966). Geometric illusions and environment: a study in Ghana. *British Journal of Psychology* **57**, 193–199.

Jahoda, G. (1970). A cross-cultural perspective in psychology. *The Advancement of Science* **27**, 57–70.

Jahoda, G. (1976). Reproduction of Kohs-type drawings by Ghanaian children: orientation error revisited. *British Journal of Psychology* **67**, 203–211.

Jahoda, G. (1978). Cross-cultural study of factors influencing orientation errors in reproduction of Kohs-type figures. *British Journal of Psychology* **69**, 45–47.

Jahoda, G. and McGurk, H. (1974a). Pictorial depth perception, a developmental study. *British Journal of Psychology* **65**, 141–149.

Jahoda, G. and McGurk, H. (1974b). Development of pictorial depth perception in cross-cultural replications. *Child Development* **45**, 1042–1047.

Jahoda, G. and McGurk, H. (1974c). Pictorial depth perception in Scottish and Ghanaian children: a critique of some findings with Hudson's test. *International Journal of Psychology* **9**, 255–267.

Jahoda, G. and Stacey, B. (1970). Susceptibility to geometrical illusions according to culture and professional training. *Perception and Psychophysics* **7**, 179–184.

Jahoda, G., Cheyne, W. B. Deręgowski, J. B., Sinha, D. and Collingbourne, R. (1976). Utilisation of Pictorial Information in Classroom learning: A cross-cultural study. *AV Communication Review* **24**, 295–315.

Jahoda, G., Deręgowski, J. B., Ampene, E. and Williams, N. (1976). Pictorial recognition as an unlearned ability: a replication with children from pictorially deprived environments. *In* "The Child's Representation of the World" (Ed. G. E. Butterworth). Plenum Press, New York.

Julesz, B. (1971). "Foundations of Cyclopean Perception." University of Chicago Press.

Kerr, M. (1937). Children's drawings of houses. *British Journal of Medical Psychology* **16**, 206–218.

Kennedy, J. M. and Ross, A. S. (1975). Outline picture perception by the Songe of Papua. *Perception* **4**, 391–406.

Kilbride, P. L. and Leibowitz, H. (1975). Factors affecting the magnitude of the Ponzo illusion among the Baganda. *Perception and Psychophysics* **17**, 543–548.

Kilbride, P. L., Robbins, M. C. and Freeman, R. B. (1968). Pictorial depth perception and education among Baganda school children. *Perceptual and Motor Skills* **26**, 1116–1118.

Kilbride, P. L. and Robbins, M. C. (1968). Linear perspective, pictorial depth perception and education among the Baganda. *Perceptual and Motor Skills* **27**, 601–602.

Kilbride, P. L. and Robbins, M. C. (1969). Pictorial depth perception and pictorial depth perception and acculturation among the Baganda. *American Anthropologist* **71**, 293–301.

King, W. J. H. (1925). "Mysteries of the Libyan Desert." Seeley, Service, London.

Klapper, Z. S. and Birch, H. G. (1969). Perceptual and action equivalence of photographs in children. *Perceptual and Motor Skills* **29**, 763–771.

Koffka, K. (1935). "Principles of Gestalt Psychology." Harcourt Brace, New York.

Kostrzewski, J., Chmielewski, W. and Jażdżewski, K. (1965). "Pradzieje Polski." Ossolineum, Wroclaw.

Klepzig, F. (1972). "Kinderspiele der Bantu." Verlag Anton Hain, Meisenheim am Glan.

Kluckhohn, C. and Leighton, D. (1946). "The Navaho." Harvard University Press, Cambridge, Mass.

Kunnapas, T. M. (1955). An analysis of the vertical-horizontal illusion. *Journal of Experimental Psychology* **49**, 134–140.

Kunnapas, T. M. (1957). Horizontal-vertical illusion and the surrounding field. *Acta Psychologica* **13**, 35–42.

Larken, P. M. (1927). Impressions of the Azande. *Sudan Notes and Records* **10**, 87–134.

Laws, R. (1886). "Women's work in heathen lands." Parlane, Paisley.

Leach, E. (1974). "Levi-Strauss." Fontana, London.

Leach, M. L. (1975). The effect of training on the pictorial perception of Shona children. *Journal of Cross-cultural Psychology* **6**, 457–470.

Leibowitz, H. W. and Judisch, J. A. (1967). The relation between age and the Ponzo illusion. *American Journal of Psychology* **80**, 105–109.

Leibowitz, H., Brislin, R., Perlmutter, L. and Hennessy, R. (1969). Ponzo perspective as a manifestation of space perception. *Science* **166**, 1174–1176.

Leibowitz, H. and Pick, H. A. (1972). Cross-cultural and educational aspects of the Ponzo perspective illusion. *Perception and Psychophysics* **12**, 430–432.

Levi-Strauss, C. (1963). "Structural anthropology." Basic Books, New York.

Lewis, H. P. (1963). Spatial representation as a correlate of development and a basis for picture preference. *Journal of Genetic Psychology* **102**, 95–107.

Lhote, H. (1962). L'art prehistorique Saharien. *Objects et Mondes: la Revue du Musee de L'Homme* **2**, 201–214.

Littlejohn, J. (1963). Temne Space. *Anthropological Quarterly* **63**, 1–17.

Lloyd, A. B. (1904). Acholi country, Part II. *Uganda Notes* **5**, 18–22.

Lloyd, B. (1972). "Perception and cognition." Penguin, Harmondsworth.

Lucas, A. and Fisher, G. H. (1969). Illusions in concrete situations: experimental studies of the Poggendorf illusion. *Ergonomics* **12**, 395–402.

Makanju, O. O. A. (1976). Comparative Study of comprehension of Pictures in two Nigerian Schools. Magisterial Thesis. University of Aberdeen.

McFie, J. (1961). The effect of education of African performance on a group of intellectual tests. *British Journal of Educational Psychology* **31**, 232–240.

McGurk, H. and Jahoda, G. (1975). Pictorial depth perception by children in Scotland and Ghana. *Journal of Cross-cultural Psychology* **6**, 279–296.

Mach, E. (1897). "Contributions to the Analysis of the Sensations." Open Court, Chicago.

Maistriaux, R. (1955/1956). La revolution des noirs d'Afrique. Sa nature, ses causes, ses remedes. *Revue de Psychologie des Peuples* (1955) **10**, 167–189; and (1956) **11**, 397–456

Maistriaux, R. (n.d.). "L'Intelligence noire et son destin." Les Editions de Problemes d'Afrique Central, Bruxelles.

Mandler, J. M. and Stein, N. L. (1977). The myth of perceptual defect: sources and evidence. *Psychological Bulletin* **84**, 173–192.

Marton, M. L., Szirtes, J. and Urban, J. (1971). "Proceedings of the 3rd International Congress of Primatology." Kraegs, Basel.

Maturana, H. R., Vareln, F. G. and Frank, S. G. (1972). Size constancy and the problem of perceptual space. *Cognition* 1, 97–104.

Michael, D. N. (1953). A cross-cultural investigation of closure. *Journal of Abnormal and Social Psychology* 48, 225–230.

Mitchelmore, M. C. (1975). Development and validation of the solid representation test in a cross-sectional sample of Jamaican students. *In* "Applied Cross-cultural Psychology" (Eds J. W. Berry and W. Lonner). Swets and Zeitlinger, Amsterdam.

Morgan, P. (1959). A study of perceptual differences among cultural groups in Southern Africa, using tests of geometric illusions. *Journal of the National Institute of Personnel Research* 8, 39–43.

Morinaga, S., Noguchi, K. and Ohishi, A. (1962). The horizontal-vertical illusion and the relation of the spatial and retinal orientations. *Japanese Psychological Research* 1, 25–29.

Mundy-Castle, A. C. (1966). Pictorial depth perception in Ghanaian children. *International Journal of Psychology* 1, 290–300.

Mundy-Castle, A. C. and Nelson, G. K. (1962). A neuropsychological study of the Knysna forest workers. *Psychologia Africana* 9, 240–272.

Murdock, G. P. (1957). World ethnographic sample. *American Anthropologist* 59, 664–687.

Nadel, S. F. (1939). An application of intelligence tests in the anthropological field. *In* "The Study of Society" (Eds F. C. Bartlett, M. Ginsberg, E. J. Lindgren and R. H. Thouless). Kegan Paul, London.

Newman, C. V. (1969). Children's size judgements in a picture with suggested depth. *Nature* 223, 418–420.

Newman, C. V. and Newman, B. M. (1974). The Ponzo illusion in pictures with and without depth. *American Journal of Psychology* 87, 511–516.

Nicholson, J. R., Seddon, G. M. and Worsnop, J. G. (1977). Teaching understanding of pictorial spatial relationships to Nigerian secondary school students. *Journal of Cross-cultural Psychology* 8, 401–414.

Nicholson, J. R., and Seddon, G. M. (1977). The understanding of pictorial spatial relationships by Nigerian secondary school students. *Journal of Cross-cultural Psychology* 8, 381–400.

Nissen, H. W., Machover, S. and Kinder, E. F. (1935). A study of performance tests given to a group of native African Negro children. *British Journal of Psychology* 25, 308–355.

Olson, D. R. (1970). "Cognitive development: the child's acquisition of diagonality." Academic Press, New York.

Olson, D. R., Yonas, A. and Cooper, R. (1980). Development of pictorial perception. *In* "The Perception of Pictures, Vol. II" (Ed. M. Hagen). Academic Press, New York.

Omari, I. M. and MacGintie, W. H. (1974). Some pictorial artifacts in studies of African children's pictorial depth perception. *Child Development* 45, 535–539.

Ombredane, A. (1954). "L' exploration de la mentalite des Noirs au moyen d'une épreuve projective: Le Congo T.A.T." Institut Royal Colonial Belge, Brussels.

Ombredane, A. (1967). Points of view for psychologists working with Africans. *In* "Readings in African Psychology from French Language Sources" (Ed. R. Wickert). Michigan State University, East Lansing.

Ord, I. G. (1971). "Mental tests for pre-literates." Ginn, London.
Page, H. W. (1970). Pictorial depth perception: a note. *South African Journal of Psychology* **1**, 45–48.
Page, H. W. and Locke, H. W. (1977). Relative dominance of vision and touch in Black and White children. *South African Journal of Psychology* **7**, 50–56.
Paraskevopoulos, I. (1968). Symmetry recall and preference in relation to chronological age. *Journal of Experimental Child Psychology* **6**, 254–264.
Parker, D. M. (1974). Evidence for the inhibition hypothesis in expanded angle illusion. *Nature* **250**, 265–266.
Perkins, D. N. (1972). Visual discrimination between rectangular and non-rectangular parallelepipeds. *Perception and Psychophysics* **12**, 396–400.
Perkins, D. N. (1973). Compensation for distortion in viewing pictures obliquely. *Perception and Psychophysics* **14**, 13–18.
Piaget, J. (1969). "The mechanisms of perception." Routledge and Kegan Paul, London.
Pirenne, M. H. (1970). "Optics, painting and photography." Cambridge University Press.
Poortinga, Y. H. (1971). Cross-cultural comparison of maximum performance tests; some methodological aspects and some experiments with simple auditory and visual stimuli. *Psychologia Africana* Monograph Supplement No. 6.
Poortinga, Y. H. (1972). A comparison of African and European students in simple auditory and visual tasks. *In* "Mental tests and cultural adaptation" (Eds M. C. Cronbach and P. J. D. Drenth). Mouton, The Hague.
Potter, M. C. (1966). On perceptual recognition. *In* "Studies of Cognitive Growth" (Eds J. S. Brunner, R. R. Olver and P. M. Greenfield). John Wiley, New York.
Reuning, H. and Wittmann, G. (1963). Relative difficulty in two kinds of symmetry in the Patco test. *Psychologia Africana* **10**, 89–107.
Reuning, H. and Wortley, W. (1973). Psychological studies of the Bushmen. *Psychologia Africana* Monograph Supplement No. 7.
Rivers, W. H. R. (1901). Vision. *In* "Reports of the Cambridge Anthropological Expedition to Torres Straits" (Ed. W. H. R. Rivers). Cambridge University Press.
Rivers, W. H. R. (1905). Observations on the senses of the Todas. *British Journal of Psychology* **1**, 321–396.
Rivers, W. H. R. and Darwin, H. (1902). A method of measuring a visual illusion. *Journal of Physiology* **38**; *Proc. Physiol. Soc.* p. xi–xii.
Robinson, J. O. (1972). "The Psychology of Visual Illusion." Hutchinson University Press, London.
Rock, I. and Leaman, R. (1963). An experimental analysis of visual symmetry. *Acta Psychologica* **21**, 171–183.
Rock, I. (1973). "Orientation and Form." Academic Press, New York.
Rollings, P. J. (1961). A note on the cultural direction of perceptual selectivity. *Acta Psychologica* **19**, 669–700.
Rosch, E. (1975). Universals and cultural specifics in human categorisation. *In* "Cross-cultural perspectives on learning" (Eds R. W. Brislin, S. Bochner and W. J. Lonner). Halsted Press, New York.
Rudel, R. G. and Teuber, H. L. (1963). Discrimination of direction of line of children. *Journal of Comparative and Physiological Psychology* **56**, 892.

Salzen, E. A., Marriott, B. M., Corbett, J. M. and Trotter, C. (1980). Picture perception and learning in the Squirrel Monkey, Saimiri sciureus. (In press).

Sapir, E. (1928). The Unconscious patterning of behaviour in society. *In* "The Unconscious: A Symposium" (Ed. E. S. Drummer). Knopf, New York. Also (1958). *In* "Selected Writings of Edward Sapir in Language, Culture and Personality" (Ed. D. G. Mandelbaum). Heath, Boston.

Schiffman, H. R. and Thompson, J. G. (1975). The role of figure orientation and apparent depth in the perception of the horizontal–vertical illusion. *Perception* 4, 79–83.

Schubert, A. (1930). Drawings of Orotchen children and young people. *Journal of Genetic Psychology* 37, 232–244.

Sears, R. R. and Wise, G. W. (1950). Relation of cup feeding in infancy to sucking and the oral drive. *American Journal of Orthopsychiatry* 20, 123–138.

Segall, M. H., Campbell, D. T. and Herskovits, M. J. (1966). "Influence of culture on visual perception." Bobbs-Merrill, Indianapolis.

Segers, J. E. (1926). Recherches sur la perception visuelle chez des enfants ages de 3 a 12 ans et leur application à l'education, I. Perceptions simples. *Journal de Psychologie* 23,608–636.

Serpell, R. (1971a). Preference for specific orientation of abstract shapes among Zambian children. *Journal of Cross-cultural Psychology* 2, 225–239.

Serpell, R. (1971b). Discrimination of orientation by Zambian children. *Journal of Comparative and Physiological Psychology* 75, 312–316.

Serpell, R. (1976). "Culture's Influence on Behaviour." Methuen, London.Serpell, R. and Deręgowski, J. B. (1972). "Teaching pictorial depth perception—a classroom experience." University of Zambia, H.D.R.U. Report.

Shapiro, M. B. (1960). Rotation of drawings by illiterate Africans. *Journal of Social Psychology* 52, 17–30.

Shaw, B. (1969). Visual symbols survey. Centre for Educational Development Overseas, London.

Shepard, R. N. and Metzler, J. (1971). Mental rotation of three-dimensional objects. *Science New York* 171, 701–703.

Sigel, I. E. (1968).The distancing hypothesis: a causal hypothesis for the acquisition of representational thought. Paper delivered at University of Miami symposium on the effects of early experience.

Sigel, I. E. (1978). The development of pictorial comprehemsion. *In* "Visual Learning, Thinking and Communication" (Eds B. S. Randhawa and W. E. Coffman). Academic Press, New York.

Sinha, D. and Misra, P. (1975). Use of pictorial depth cues in children's paintings: a developmental study. *Indian Journal of Psychology* 50, 222–231.

Sinha, D. and Shukla, P. (1974). Deprivation and development of skill for pictorial depth perception. *Journal of Cross-cultural Psychology* 5, 434–451.

Smith, T. (1973). The susceptibility of Xhosa groups to a perspective illusion. *Journal of Social Psychology* 90, 331–332.

Snelbecker, G. E., Fullard, W. and Gallaher, G. M. (1971). Age-related changes in pattern prediction: a cross-cultural comparison. *Journal of Social Psychology* 84, 191–196.

Spencer, J. (1965). Experiments on engineering drawing comprehension. *Ergonomics* 8, 93–110.

214   *References*

Spitz, H. H. and Borland, M. D. (1971). Redundance in line drawings of familiar objects: Effect of age and intelligence. *Cognitive Psychology* **2**, 196–205.

Stacey, B. (1969). Explanations of the H-V illusion and the foreshortening of receding line. *Life Science* **8**, 1237–1246.

Taylor, T. R. (1974). A factor analysis of 21 illusions: the implications for theory. *Psychologia Africana* **15**, 137–148.

Taylor, T. R. (1976). The factor structure of geometric illusions: a second study. *Psychologia Africana* **16**, 177–200.

Tekane, I. (1961). An error analysis of responses to PATCO test by Bantu industrial workers. *Journal of the National Institute for Personnel Research* **8**, 189–194.

Tekane, I. (1963). Symmetrical pattern completion by illiterate and literate Bantu. *Psychologia Africana* **10**, 63–68.

Thomas, L. T. (1962). Perceptual organisation of industrial inspectors. *Ergonomics* **5**, 429–434.

Thomson, A. P. D. (1967). African ingenuity. *Native Administration Development Annual* **9**, 10–14.

Thomson, J. (1885). "Through Masailand: a journey of exploration." Sampson Low, Marston, Searle and Rivington, London.

Thompson, J. G. and Schiffman, H. R. (1974). The influence of figure size and orientation on the magnitude of the horizontal–vertical illusion. *Acta Psychologica* **38**, 413–420.

Thouless, R. H. (1932). Individual differences in phenomenal regression. *British Journel of Psychology* **22**, 217–241.

Thouless, R. H. (1933). A racial difference in perception. *Journal of Social Psychology* **4**, 330–339.

Travers, R. M. W. (1973). Age and levels of picture interpretation. *Perceptual and Motor Skills* **36**, 210.

Turnbull, C. M. (1961). Some observations regarding the experiences and behaviour of the Bambuti Pygmies. *American Journal of Psychology* **74**, 304–308.

Unesco, (1963). "Simple reading materials for adults: Its preparation and use." Unesco, Paris.

Valentine, C. W. (1912). Psychological theories of the Horizontal–Vertical Illusion. *British Journal of Psychology* **5**, 8–35.

Vickers, D. (1971). Perceptual economy and the impression of visual depth. *Perception and Psychophysics* **10**, 23–27.

Vickers, D. (1972). A cyclic decision model of perceptual alternation. *Perception* **1**, 31–48.

Vernon, P. E. (1969). "Intelligence and cultural environment." Methuen, London.

Wagner, D. A. (1977). Ontogeny of the Ponzo illusion: Effects of age, schooling and environment. *International Journal of Psychology* **12**, 161–176.

Ward, L. M., Porac, C., Coren, S. and Girgus, J. S. (1977). The case for misplaced constancy scaling: depth associations elicited by illusion configurations. *American Journal of Psychology* **90**, 609–620.

Watson, J. S. (1966). Perception of object orientation in infants. *Merrill-Palmer Quarterly* **12**, 73–94.

Waldron, L. A. and Gallimore, A. J. (1973). Pictorial depth perception in Papua,

New Guinea, Torres Strait and Australia. *Australian Journal of Psychology* **25**, 89–92.

Walters, A. (1942). A genetic study of geometrical-optical illusions. *Genetic Psychology Monographs* **25**, 101–155.

Wapner, S. and Werner, H. (1957). "Perceptual development." Clark University Press, Worcester, Mass.

Warburton, F. W. (1951). The ability of Gurka recruits. *British Journal of Psychology* **42**, 123–133.

Werner, H. (1948). "Comparative Psychology of Mental Development." International Universities Press, New York.

Whiting, J. W. M. (1968). Methods and problems in cross-cultural research. *In* "Handbook of Social Psychology" (Eds G. Lindzey and E. Avonson). Addison-Wesley, Reading. Mass.

Whorf, B. L. (1940). Science and Linguistics. *Technology Review* **54**, 229–231, 247, 248. Also (1958). *In* "Readings in Social Psychology" (Eds E. E. Maccoby, T. L. Newcomb and E. L. Hartley). Holt, New York.

Winter, W. (1963). The perception of safety posters by Bantu industrial workers. *Psychologia Africana* **10**, 127–135.

Winter, W. (1967).Size constancy, relative size estimation and background: a cross-cultural study. *Psychologia Africana* **12**, 42–48.

Witkin, H. A. (1967). A cognitive-style approach to cross-cultural research. *International Journal of Psychology* **2**, 233–250.

Witkin, H. A., Dyk, R. B., Fattuson, H. F., Goodenough, D. R. and Karp, S. A. (1962). "Psychological Differentiation: studies of development." Wiley, New York.

Witkin, H. A. and Berry, J. W. (1975. Psychological differentiation in cross-cultural perspective. *Journal of Cross-cultural Psychology* **6**, 4–87.

Wober, M. (1966). Sensotypes. *Journal of Social Psychology* **70**, 181–189.

Wober, M. (1972). Horizons, horizontals and illusions about the vertical.*Perceptual and Motor Skills* **34**, 960.

Wohlwill, J. F. (1960). Developmental studies of perception.*Psychological Bulletin* **57**, 249–288.

Yonas, A. and Hagen, M. A. (1973). Effects of static and kinetic depth information on the perception of size in children and adults. *Journal of Experimental Child Psychology* **15**, 254–265.

Zanflorin, M. (1967). Some observations on Gregory's theory of perceptual illusions. *Quarterly Journal of Experimental Psychology* **19**, 193–197.

Zimmerman, R. and Hochberg, J. (1963). Pictorial recognition in infant monkeys. *Proceedings of the Psychonomic Society* **46**.

Subject Index